MH00778915

"*Gopi Krishna—A Biography* is such an accomp[lishment.] ...is packed with information, and it presents the best review of Gopi Krishna's life there is. It portrays the importance of his life so well."

— Joan Shivapita Harrigan, PhD, author of *Kundalini Vidya* and *Stories of Spiritual Transformation*

"*Gopi Krishna—A Biography* is an inspiration. It offers us a vivid story of one human journey even as it reveals the heart and purpose of an extraordinary spiritual teacher. With meticulous care, Teri Degler puts this story in the context of the always changing local and global cultures, politics, and movements, and in this way offers us insight into how we are shaped by and are, at the same time, able to contribute to the collective dream. This book is an invitation to us all to dream awake for the sake of the planet."

— Oriah Mountain Dreamer, author of *The Invitation, the Dance, and the Call*

"I highly recommend this book! Degler's work is both scholarly in its meticulous research on Gopi Krishna's life and devotional in her respect for his accomplishments and teachings. Relying on his own best efforts to understand the directives of the innate power of the divine, known as kundalini in Tantra and yoga, he lived his life dedicated to making the world more aware of how this power radically transforms an individual, from their biology to their state of consciousness, as it hastens their evolution to enlightenment. Degler brings the reader's attention to Gopi Krishna's extraordinary poetry, writings, and lectures and to how he saw Kundalini as the evolutionary power we must draw on to literally save humanity from the dire circumstances we find ourselves in. Through this biography one can be inspired by the depth of his dedication to following this path and by the sacrifices he made to remain true to the Infinite while he lived fully engaged in the world."

— Lawrence Edwards, PhD, author of *The Soul's Journey: Guidance from the Divine Within*, founder and director of Anam Cara Meditation

"I was captivated by the simple yet lucid manner in which this book has been written... Degler can breathe easy in the knowledge that she has written Gopi Krishna's biography exactly as it should be."

— John Warren White, author of *Kundalini, Evolution, and Enlightenment*

Gopi Krishna

A BIOGRAPHY

KUNDALINI, CONSCIOUSNESS, AND OUR EVOLUTION TO ENLIGHTENMENT

TERI DEGLER

INSTITUTE FOR CONSCIOUSNESS RESEARCH

Gopi Krishna—A Biography:
Kundalini, Consciousness, and Our Evolution to Enlightenment
Copyright © 2023
by Teri Degler

Institute for Consciousness Research
The Institute for Consciousness Research is a federally registered
Canadian charitable organization. Registration # 87680 0673 RR0001
www.icrcanada.org

Library and Archives Canada Cataloguing in Publication

Title: Gopi Krishna–a biography : Kundalini, consciousness, and our evolution to enlightenment / Teri Degler.
Names: Degler, Teri, author.
Description: Includes bibliographical references and index.
Identifiers: Canadiana 20230177255 | ISBN 9781989793053 (softcover)
Subjects: LCSH: Gopi Krishna, 1903-1984. | LCSH: Hindus—India—Biography. | LCSH: Kuṇḍalinī. | LCSH: Consciousness. | LCGFT: Biographies.
Classification: LCC BL1175.G62 D44 2023 | DDC 294.5092—dc23

Permissions:
The author would like to thank the Institute for Consciousness Research and the Kundalini Research Foundation, Ltd. for material from Gopi Krishna's books and his other writings. Every effort was made to locate the copyright holders of copyrighted material contained herein. In case of inadvertent omission, please contact the publisher. See also the Bibliography section.

Cover Photo Credit: Tom Kieffer

Cover and text design by Kristy Twellmann Hill
Art direction by fleck Creative

To Kaz Kobielski,
without whose love, support, and patience this biography
could not have been written

Contents

Acknowledgments

Gopi Krishna's family deserves tremendous thanks for their exceptionally generous hospitality, encouragement, and willingness to be interviewed, including his daughter, Ragya Kaul; his sons, Jagdish and Nirmal Shivpuri; their wives, Mohini and Chuni; and his grandchildren, Rakesh Kaul, Jyotima Kaul, and Sunita Kehr. I am inexpressibly thankful that I was able to meet with Ragya and Jagdish before their passing.

Gratitude is also owed to the Institute for Consciousness Research and its volunteers, including Paul and Dale Pond, Ted Wood, Alf Walker, Sabine Bruestle, and especially Michael Bradford. Gopi Krishna once called Michael a karma yogi, and he was certainly one when it came to this book—his efforts were monumental.

Volunteer transcribers of the innumerable interviews done for this book include Myrna Filman, who spent countless hours transcribing the interviews done in India, and Helga Schroeder, Lyn Mytroen, Patrick Hayne, Ed Woynillowicz, and Sue Hodgson.

ICR made these interviews possible by helping with research trips to India, Switzerland, Boston, New York, and California. In addition to Gopi Krishna's family and several of the above mentioned people, the many individuals who gave their time to be interviewed include Gene Kieffer, J. Norman Reed, Chuck

Murenbeeld, and, now sadly deceased, Margaret Kobelt, Tontyn Hopman, George Tompkins, and Dr. Karan Singh. Correspondence with people who had met Gopi Krishna, such as researcher Dr. Edward Kelly, Jungian author Robin van Löben Sels, German author Rainer Kakuska, and artist Rhea Quien was very helpful, and author John White's comments and suggestions were invaluable. Subhash Chander also deserves thanks for his original work on creating and preserving the archive of Gopi Krishna material. I would also like to thank the Thad McIlroy of The Future of Publishing, and Sarah Brohman and Marian Hebb. More gratitude than I can possibly express goes to my husband, Kaz Kobielski. In memoriam, heartfelt appreciation goes to Thomas G. Howe.

Without all this generous, unstinting help this biography could not have been done.

Introduction

Well-done biographies of truly important people of the past are always relevant. But only in rare cases are they relevant to the here and now, to the way we live our lives today; to what we mean to others; to how much inner peace we know.

The life story of Gopi Krishna is, however, relevant in exactly this way. That his story can have such profound spiritual implications is somewhat ironic. For Gopi Krishna was not a spiritual teacher. Time and again he made the statement: "I am not a guru." He did not take disciples; he did not take followers, and he certainly did not seek them.

And yet, in some ways, he could hardly help but be a spiritual teacher: He was a simple, ordinary human being who had attained enlightenment. He lived in a state of perennial cosmic consciousness—a state that made it possible for him to see through the eyes of the great saints and mystics; a state that made it possible for him to communicate the astounding news that each and every one of us is on an evolutionary path that is leading to this radiant, light-filled state.

Because he was from Kashmir, steeped in the traditions of yoga and Tantra, he wrote about this evolution and transformation of consciousness in terms of the awakening kundalini. In this context, it is important to note that Gopi Krishna never used the terms "full awakening" of kundalini or the "highest" state of consciousness, preferring instead to refer to kundalini as being simply awakened or active and to states of consciousness that were simply "higher," making the point that humanity's ongoing evolution would lead to currently incomprehensible, ever-expanded levels of divine awareness. Although much of Gopi Krishna's writing is from this very Indian perspective, he was emphatic that kundalini is a universal force, known by various names in the world's spiritual traditions.

His writings also make it evident that research into this evolutionary energy could solve the cataclysmic problems facing Mother Earth today. Beyond this, he indicated that the time is ripe for an increasingly widespread awakening of kundalini. Traditionally in yoga, this awakening is seen as one that needs to be carefully nurtured. Gopi Krishna makes it clear that unless science, particularly the medical community, accepted the reality of kundalini awakening and understood the biological basis of this spiritual process, people experiencing this awakening might not receive the care they needed or be misdiagnosed or given erroneous treatments.

Most people who are part of this widespread awakening are having a partial activation of kundalini—in other words, undergoing a process of awakening. Confirmation that all these experiences are being triggered by the same universal force is evidenced by the fact that virtually everyone having them is experiencing, in varying degrees, the classic signs of kundalini awakening reported by the ancient yogis. As the gradual awakening progresses, so do these experiences.

Perhaps the most prominent sign is mystical experience—characterized, as it is in all the world's religions, by the perception of radiant light, love, bliss, and/or union with the Divine or all of creation. Another is the development of the extrasensory phenomena known as siddhis in yoga and charisms, or spiritual gifts, in Christianity. Yet another is the onset of inspired creativity and genius. While these signs —including the physical sensations noted by the ancient yogis such as fiery heat in the lower back, energy rushing up the spine, or inexplicable vibrations in the genital region—manifest dramatically in some people, others experience them so gradually that they are virtually imperceptible.

As the following chapters show, Gopi Krishna revealed even more about these partial awakenings in his talks and correspondence than he did in his books.

One way of understanding this partial, ongoing transformation is to think of the truly enlightened ones, such as a Buddha or a Christ, as living perennially in a state of radiant light, while an experiencer of a partial awakening might have only occasional glimpses of the light. In this same way, a Rumi might write reams of deathless poetry, while most of us today might be gifted with an occasional perfect poem. A further example would be the Old Testament prophets who had prophetic visions, while we might simply have an auspicious dream now and then.

Regardless, Gopi Krishna wanted us to understand that the light in which a Buddha dwells and the light we glimpse is the same light. Gopi Krishna lived in this light, and he wanted us to be able to do the same. Reading between the lines of his two autobiographies, *Kundalini: The Evolutionary Energy in Man* and *Living with Kundalini*, we can see that the way he lived his life was a key to attaining this state. Still, he never once praises himself or his actions in these books.

A biography, however, can do this and more; it can reveal him to be not only an enlightened sage, but an extraordinarily honest, courageous, and compassionate human being. It can also tell the story of a fascinating life—one filled with drama, defeat, and, sometimes, sweet victory.

The introduction to a biography, on the other hand, has to include the mundane, for example, explaining how I, as the author, arbitrarily chose to spell familiar Sanskrit words, such as Shiva, Shakti, kundalini, and chakra, as they are commonly seen in English, but to include diacritics—the little marks on letters—on less common words, such as sahasrāra. However, in quotes, book titles, etc. the spelling of these words appears as it does in the original. The same is true for all other spellings or grammar usages; in other words, quotes have not been edited for spelling.

Another technical issue concerns how people are identified. In general, after giving a person's full name, I refer to those who were very familiar with Gopi Krishna by their first names only. One exception is his daughter Ragya's husband, Radha Krishan Kaul. Although he played a huge role in his father-in-law's life, he carried such an air of quiet authority he was generally called Mr. Kaul, and I have done the same.

Citations also need to be addressed: While most quotes and references are cited as chapter endnotes in the usual manner, those that come from Gopi Krishna's correspondence or unpublished works are not cited. When you come across this unreferenced material, you can be sure it comes from restricted archival material that cannot currently be accessed. The same is true for quotes and references to Margaret Kobelt; these come from nearly thirty hours of interviews I did with her before her death. In hopes that a future scholar or biographer might have access to this material, I have provided a fully cited version of the manuscript for the archives. However, citations do not appear in this edition as I did not see the point of burdening the reader with well over a hundred additional endnotes on material that could not be accessed.

The choices an author makes on these types of details pale in comparison with the choices a biographer makes in choosing what is included and what is not out of all the research and information that has been amassed. For this biography, I read thousands of pages of Gopi Krishna's correspondence, interviewed family, friends, and supporters in four countries, and immersed myself in his written work and in the life stories of his most ardent supporters. I was also privileged to attend two conferences he spoke at, to meet with him in a small group three times, and to have an in-depth personal meeting with him once before his death. Out of all this, I have picked and chosen what would go into this book and what would not. With that, I offer it up to you, the reader, in hopes that you find his life not only fascinating and enriching, but enlightening.

— Teri Degler

Photographs for *Gopi Krishna—A Biography*

Unfortunately, this biography does not include photographs. Few were located that had survived in good enough condition to be included in a printed book. However, a collection of photos has been made available online for the interested reader at www.icrcanada.org/GopiKrishnaPhotos.

Chapter One

The Roots of Rebirth

Biographies often start with the where, what, and when of the birth of the subject and, then, if the biography is about a saint, mystic, or enlightened person, a marvelous tale is told that foreshadows the infant's illustrious future and extraordinary nature. The story of Gopi Krishna Shivpuri is no different.

Born in late May or early June in 1903 in Gairoo, a tiny village not far from the city of Srinagar in the Himalayan foothills of Kashmir, he fell ill several months later. His throat became swollen and inflamed, and he was not able to take milk from his frantically worried mother, CongMaal Shivpuri. Eventually she fell into an exhausted sleep and dreamed of a holy man of whose miraculous powers she had often heard. In the dream, the holy man gently opens the baby boy's mouth, places a finger on his inflamed throat, and tells her that he will now be able to drink. Awakening from the dream, she took the baby to her breast and found that he could indeed swallow the milk. Able to take nourishment, the baby soon regained his health. CongMaal, convinced of the miraculous nature of this occurrence, pledged that she would one day go on pilgrimage to the holy man and thank him in person for saving her son's life.

When Gopi Krishna was somewhere around six or seven—or at least old enough to remember the journey—CongMaal went on the long-promised pilgrimage. She was accompanied by her brother, who walked along as she and her son rode on a donkey. After being on the road for a day or two, they found the hermitage. The moment they entered the hut, the holy man looked up as if he knew exactly who she was and said, "Did it not succeed? Was he not able to drink?" Upon hearing this evidence of his miraculous powers, she prostrated herself before the holy man and asked for his blessings on her son. The man took the boy on his lap and stroked his hair. When Gopi Krishna began to fuss, his mother scolded him. In turn, the holy man chastised her, saying, "You must not scold him! He is a Vyasa!" Vyasa, as Gopi Krishna's mother well knew, was one of the most revered saints and sages of India, and she was convinced the holy man had gifted her with yet another miraculous portent regarding her son's future.[1]

But what is important about this tale is not whether it is miraculous or true or accurate, it is how Gopi Krishna later handled it. His mother was not reticent about telling the story; it became part of the lore of the village and was eventually passed down to his children and grandchildren. In spite of the story becoming known in this way, he refused to have it told in his first autobiography, *Kundalini: The Evolutionary Energy in Man*. According to his longtime secretary, Margaret Kobelt, he explained that he made this decision because he did not want to have "a fairy tale" in his book. Still, he did include the episode in his second autobiography, *Living with Kundalini*. There he stated carefully that he could not vouch in any way for the miraculous part of the story, adding only that he never knew his mother to be anything but meticulously honest. He went on to point out that for much of his life he discounted all stories of the miraculous powers of yogis and other Indian holy men as the vast majority of these tales had been, upon careful examination, shown to be false. In offering the story up, however, he revealed that he was eventually forced to come to the conclusion that there were indeed "more things in heaven and earth" than many of us, like Shakespeare's Horatio, could even begin to dream of. Still, he cautioned the reader, saying that "a real yogi in touch with the other world, capable of producing genuine physical phenomena at will, is one of the rarest beings on earth."

The way he handled this episode is an excellent example of the scrupulous honesty and painstaking care he took with everything he said and wrote. It is also significant for another reason: even though he recounts the story in some detail, he completely leaves out the yogi's pronouncement that the baby was "a Vyasa."

This omission is a telling clue to the man he was and what he spent his entire life trying to convey. He repeatedly said, "I am not a guru," "I do not take disciples," "I do not take followers." Instead, he urged those who would read his work and hear his words to follow their own hearts and use *viveka*—the yogic term often translated as *discernment* or, as he once defined it, "the power of discrimination between true and false or right and wrong."

In insisting that he was not a guru, he was also reminding us that he was nothing more than a very ordinary man—a midlevel clerk in an Indian government bureau—who came to have an extraordinary, profoundly transformative spiritual experience. In emphasizing this ordinariness, he was giving us a great gift. He was telling us that we, too, ordinary folks that we are, could experience this transformation. In fact—and this was at the core of his message—we, as a human race, *would* experience it. For what he had experienced was the result of an evolutionary process, and it had been triggered by an evolutionary energy that would eventually lead all of humanity to higher states of consciousness.

Although he used both *energy* and *force* to refer to this evolutionary agency in his writings, he cautioned that they were both inadequate words that could not begin to convey the magnitude and intelligence of this cosmic power. Being an individual whose culture was steeped in the tradition of yoga, he used the yogic terms *kundalini* and *kundalini-shakti* to refer to this force. He made it abundantly clear, however, that kundalini was just one name for a universal energy that had been given its own name in virtually every spiritual tradition in the world. By the same token, the expansion and transformation of consciousness he had experienced was what had been written about and experienced, in varying degrees of time and intensity, by Christian mystics, Sufi saints, Buddhist bodhisattvas, enlightened yogis, and the great spiritual masters of every religious tradition.

Gopi Krishna had his first astounding encounter with this transformative, evolutionary energy while meditating in a small room in a humble house in the city of Jammu during the Christmas season 1937. As strange as it may seem, he would not have been there, nor would he likely have had this experience at that time, if he had not at the age of seventeen failed his school exams. No one, and certainly not Gopi Krishna himself, had expected this failure. He had always been an exceptionally bright child and had always done well in school. In fact, two years earlier he had passed the usual school exams with distinction.

Although his family was far too poor to have books in their home, when he was about twelve years old he discovered an Urdu translation of *The Arabian Nights* in an aunt's library. Reading it triggered in him what he later called a "burning thirst" for fairy tales and romantic adventure stories. Once he had gone through the books in Urdu in his school's small library, he began reading simple tales in English. Eventually he also began to immerse himself in whatever books he could find on science and philosophy. By the time he was about sixteen years old, he had become completely obsessed with these books. For the next year, he spent virtually all his time reading them. He undoubtedly gained a great fund of knowledge from these books, but unfortunately, they were not his school textbooks.

With the cockiness typical of a teenager, Gopi Krishna was not at all worried about this. He expected to sail through these exams just as he had the earlier ones. Instead, he failed miserably. The effects of this fiasco were far-reaching, for the marks on these exams were the ones required for acceptance to a university. Although he was deeply ashamed and concerned about the future for himself, he was crushed by the realization of what this would do to his mother. Even though she might—or perhaps might not—have let go of the belief that her son would become "a Vyasa," she had still pinned all her hopes and expectations on her belief that her exceptionally bright son would go to university, enter a well-paid profession, and lift the family out of its poverty.

Gopi Krishna not only loved his mother, he adored her. He held her in the highest regard and understood both what she had sacrificed for him and what she had endured. She had been married at the age of sixteen to Ganga Ram Shivpuri, a man twenty-two years her senior. Such an age disparity was not particularly uncommon, and in many ways they were well matched. For several years, Ganga Ram's salary at his government post was enough to support the family. What was perhaps the most wonderful—and potentially disastrous—aspect of his character was that he had a deep mystical vein. He followed the teachings of the Vedas and other sacred texts to the utmost of his abilities and often sought out yogis and ascetics in order to learn from them.

Throughout his life, he also had flashes of paranormal abilities such as premonitory dreams and telepathy. The most famous family story passed down concerns a journey the family was once making from Srinagar to the city of Jammu by bus. At the foot of one of the mountainous passes, the bus needed to stop for repairs. Time passed until it was too dark and dangerous for the bus to start up the pass. Realizing that their journey would be delayed by hours and they would have to sleep overnight on the bus, the passengers became upset. Suddenly, Gopi Krishna's father, who had already been asleep, sat up and startled the other passengers by shouting out that it didn't matter. The bus, he said, would not be able to make it through the mountain pass in any case as there was a dead man on the road. He then went happily back to sleep. The next morning, the bus had not gone too far down the road before it had to stop at a blockade where police were still trying to determine how a man had come to die and be found lying in the middle of the road.

Although Gopi Krishna had a natural human curiosity about his father's paranormal abilities, which are called *siddhis* in the yogic tradition, he had an intuitive sense that he should not place too much importance on them. What was far more significant, he later came to realize, was his father's noble character and his scrupulous attention to the virtues such as honesty, compassion, and lack of greed that are taught in the eightfold path of yoga. One example of this comes from a time when the family thought that they had won a lottery so large that it would vastly improve their difficult lives. Before they learned that they had not actually won, Ganga Ram had already made it clear that, in spite of their straitened circumstances, they must give all the money to the poor the moment they received it, for it had not been honorably earned. These noble traits of his father's proved to be a double-edged sword. Even though his virtue was greatly admired, it often contributed to the family's hardship. His righteousness was so widely known that a line of the poor and destitute could be found along his pathway home on the first Monday of every month—payday at the government offices where he worked. Each of these poor people would have a tale to tell him about why they needed help, and by the time he reached home, most of the money CongMaal was anxiously waiting for would have been given away. Later, Gopi Krishna's mother confided to him that only about a quarter of her husband's pay was usually left by the time he got home. This was not enough. By the time she had been married ten years, CongMaal was the mother of two boys and two girls. With the little money she was given on payday, she had to feed the whole family and run the household. And she did have to run everything: by this point, every moment that Ganga Ram was not at work was spent absorbed in his spiritual pursuits, and he had turned over all the worldly responsibilities to her.

Soon, her situation was to become even more difficult. When Gopi Krishna was about two years old, his five-year-old brother became ill and died, and Ganga Ram became overwhelmed with grief. As Gopi Krishna later wrote, the tragedy disturbed the already-delicate balance of his father's mind. Before long he quit his government job and began to completely isolate himself, leaving his twenty-eight-year-old wife with not only complete responsibility for the survival of the family but no regular income to accomplish it with. The only money coming in was a small amount of rental income from a number of market stalls that Ganga Ram had once purchased.

Gopi Krishna's memories of the next fifteen years reveal that his mother doted on him. From the time he was very young, he was susceptible to any variations in his diet, and no matter how poor they were she made sure he got enough food and milk. He recounts that she would sometimes consume nothing more than the water the rice was cooked in so that the others could eat the grain. Even when the family was at its very poorest, she managed to send a container of milk with him to school each day. He was also aware that she made great sacrifices so that he would have the clothes he needed to wear to school and the books he had to have for his classes. Even though the clothes were of such poor quality that he was bullied and the books were dilapidated, at least he had them. He was able to get an education, and it was all due to her sacrifice.

Imagine, then, how he felt when he had to tell her he had failed his exams and it had all been for nothing.

This failure and his humiliation stunned him. The moment he realized the full impact of what he had done and how it had affected the person he loved most in the world, he determined to never let anything like this happen again. In *Living with Kundalini*, he wrote, "Realizing that by my lack of self-control I had betrayed the trust reposed in me, I determined to make up for the lost opportunity in other ways. At no other time in my life should I be guilty of the same offense again." He then sought to curb this "vagrant element" in his nature, regulate his conduct, and search out the best way to do this.[2] The ultimate result of this decision was that he took up meditation and did it with an unflinching resolve. For the next seventeen years, he rose virtually every morning to meditate, even in the freezing cold winter months. For many years these sessions lasted for as long as three hours. His dedication to this practice was so resolute, in fact, that he even left his bewildered bride in the predawn hours after their wedding night to sit on his rooftop and meditate.

References to Gopi Krishna's life and often his own words, like those above, make it seem as if a straightforward cause and effect was in play: his lack of self-discipline had caused him to let down those he loved most in the world, and so he had taken up the discipline of meditation to ensure that such a thing would never happen again. But this raises a very important question: Why, after crushing his mother's hopes for prosperity, didn't he take up one of the many other paths that could have led more directly to their financial security? He was, after all, known to be an exceptionally bright young man.

A number of factors from his earlier life provide a possible explanation for his taking the direction he did. During his childhood, his strictly religious mother took him to temples and made sure he participated in all the traditions associated with the branch of the Hindu faith most closely associated with the area he was raised in. A part of Kashmir known as the Kashmir Valley, or more poetically as the Vale of Kashmir, this area is a lush and fertile basin surrounded by the grandeur of the Himalayas. Today the Kashmir Valley, like all of Kashmir, is part of an official Indian state called "Jammu and Kashmir." In those days, however, the separate areas of Jammu and Kashmir formed an independent principality ruled by a maharaja. Like most Hindus in the Kashmir Valley, Gopi Krishna's people were Kashmiri Pandits, or Kashmiri Brahmins, a Hindu ethnicity whose history in Kashmir goes back for many centuries. As such they practiced Kashmiri Shaivism.[3] While this form of worship focuses on Shiva as the divine masculine, it holds tremendous reverence for and places great importance on his divine feminine counterpart, Shakti, keeping in mind that in this nondualistic tradition, Shakti and Shiva are seen as aspects of an all-pervasive Oneness. The early proponents of this faith, known as a form of Tantra, described detailed forms of meditation and practice that would awaken an embodied form of this divine feminine. Known in this form as kundalini-shakti, it was believed to reside in every individual, often depicted as coiled, resting in a dormant state, at the base of the spine.

How much of these specific teachings Gopi Krishna might have absorbed as a youngster is unknown, but it can be said without doubt that he was raised in a culture that was steeped in these beliefs. It is also clear that he had a religious inclination as a child. He listened raptly to a maternal uncle who would read to him from the great epic the *Bhāgavata Purāna* which tells how the god Krishna imparted the *Bhagavad Gītā* to Arjuna, the hero of the epic. Arjuna's feats of supernatural strength and valor in battle inspired the young Gopi Krishna so deeply that he longed to be just like Arjuna one day.[4] Another indication of this early spiritual inclination comes from a memory, which stayed with him his whole life, of walking down a muddy road on a spring day when he was only eight years old and being struck mute with wonder as the great cosmic questions of *What am I?* and *What does all this mean?* seemed to reverberate from every object in the world around him. A few nights later he had a dream of an alternate reality, filled with radiant beings, that was so glorious and luminescent he never forgot it either.[5]

This spiritual bent was challenged during his teen years by his foray into books on science. He emerged from this period as a hardheaded agnostic, full of doubts about the teachings he had so wholeheartedly embraced only a year or two before. Delving into the literature of other religions didn't allay any of his reservations. Even though he came across occasional passages from prophets and sages that would find an echo deep in his heart, nothing overcame his intellectual doubts. In spite of this, he wrote that he could remember thirsting "for rationality in religion, for the worship of truth."[6]

During the few months that passed between his exam failure and his decision to begin a rigorous, disciplined form of meditation, a number of other influences came into play. In searching out the best method to conquer his undisciplined nature, he read books on mind control and then on yoga. As part of this desire to overcome his lack of discipline, he became interested in self-mastery. Years later in a discourse he gave, he told how, when he had to take quinine against a malaria attack, he would force himself to hold the exceedingly foul, bitter substance in his mouth without grimacing or gagging.[7] For a brief time, he even became inflamed with a desire to become a renunciate—a longing that was fueled, at least in part, by a desire to escape the world in which he had become such a disappointment to himself and others. Even though he soon realized this was not the path for him, he found himself yearning for the peace, harmony, and deep fulfillment the path of a *sādhaka*—a dedicated spiritual seeker—could offer.

In a state of excruciating mental conflict, he began reading the *Bhagavad Gītā* for himself. It became a source of great solace to him, and as he read, he began to see that a "perennially peaceful life in tune with the Infinite Reality" was a possibility. He realized that this would mean sacrificing his worldly ambitions: this did not matter to him. In the space of a few short months, he turned from a young man who was looking forward to educating himself so that he could live a life of ease to someone who was committed to finding a perennially enduring happiness that, even more importantly, did not have to be bought at the cost of the happiness of others. Firmly convinced by the wisdom he had found in the *Bhagavad Gītā* that this was an attainable goal, he wrote, "I was soon exercising my will and practicing meditation, not for temporal ends, but with the sole object of gaining success in yoga...."[8]

But what was this success in yoga that he was seeking? The answer can perhaps be found in an exceptionally beautiful commentary on the *Bhagavad Gītā*: "At its highest level, yoga is a secret state of union within supreme love, bestowed by the divinity, who is also subsumed in this union."[9]

After seventeen years of meditating, Gopi Krishna had his first brief taste of this supreme union with the divine in that small room in Jammu at Christmas in 1937, a man in his early thirties with a wife, two young children, and a job as a simple government clerk.

The description of this awakening has been told and retold for decades. If you look up the definition of *kundalini-shakti* in the *Encyclopedic Dictionary of Yoga*, you even find it there.[10] One of the most interesting things about this wide retelling is that it is virtually never paraphrased; it is told in Gopi Krishna's own words.

> Suddenly, with a roar like that of a waterfall, I felt a stream of liquid light entering my brain through the spinal cord.
>
> Entirely unprepared for such a development, I was completely taken by surprise, but regaining self-control instantaneously, I remained sitting in the same posture, keeping my mind on the point of concentration. The illumination grew brighter and brighter, the roaring louder. I experienced a rocking sensation and then felt myself slipping out of my body, entirely enveloped in a halo of light.
>
> It is impossible to describe the experience accurately. I felt the point of consciousness that was myself growing wider, surrounded by waves of light. It grew wider and wider, spreading outward while the body, normally the immediate object of its perception, appeared to have receded into the distance until I became entirely unconscious of it. I was now all consciousness, without any outline, without any idea of a corporeal appendage, without any feeling or sensation coming from the senses, immersed in a sea of light simultaneously conscious and aware of every point, spread out, as it were, in all directions without any barrier or material obstruction.
>
> I was no longer myself, or to be more accurate, no longer as I knew myself to be, a small point of awareness confined in a body, but instead was a vast circle of consciousness in which the body was but a point, bathed in light and in a state of exaltation and happiness impossible to describe.

Chapter Two

From Suffering to Finding Solace

Just as Gopi Krishna's description of his initial experience has become widely known, so has the story of the difficulties he encountered between his first experience and an extraordinary occurrence twelve years later. In 1949, once again in Jammu, the transformative process he had been undergoing stabilized, and he reached a state of perennial higher consciousness where both his inner and outer worlds were bathed in radiant, luminescent light. In yoga, the yogi who reaches this perennial state is known as a *jīvan mukta*, one who is able to live and function in the everyday world and yet at the same time lives in a world of union with cosmic consciousness. For the rest of his life, Gopi Krishna would seek to find ways to describe this essentially indescribable state of being, always making it clear that the sum total of suffering he endured prior to this stabilization was nothing more than a drop in what would become an ocean of bliss.

Of course, he did not know this in 1937, nor did he know that the next nine weeks would be some of the most difficult in his life. Even directly after the experience during the Christmas season, he began to feel a vague depression and uneasiness. The next day he meditated again as usual, hoping to get another glimpse of the luminescent, cosmic radiance. He did, but the experience was shorter and less profound, and it was unfortunately followed by an even deeper malaise and more pervasive anxiety. Over the next while, these negative sensations increased until he reached a point of extreme distress. He was not only unable to meditate, he could not concentrate at all. His nights, prior to the experience characterized by peaceful dreams, were now riddled by nightmares when he could sleep at all. Food began to taste like ash. Unable to eat or sleep, he became paler and weaker.

Increasingly agitated and distraught, he was confounded by what was happening. The more he thought about it, the more he was convinced that his initial experience conformed in every detail to the experiences of spiritual illumination written about the great mystics and yogis of the ages. If so, why then was he experiencing this horror? This was especially true at night. Phantasmagorical images plagued his mind as he tossed and turned, and when he did manage to sleep, the distressing images were even worse.

A few of the books on yoga he had read long ago had had a little information about kundalini. It had been described as a cosmic force that lay dormant in the human body coiled at the base of the spine near the sexual organs. Through the intense, difficult practice of kundalini yoga, this force could be awakened. Often alluded to as the Serpent Power, this force would rise when roused through a *nāḍī*—sometimes translated as a "nerve channel"—in the spinal cord known as the *sushumṇā*. Rising sinuously upward like an awakened serpent, it would then pass through whirling centers known as *chakras*, until it reached the seventh, or crown, chakra. On reaching this goal, known as *sahasrāra* or the *thousand-petaled lotus*, kundalini was said to trigger the ecstatic, transcendental state of *samādhi* in which the yogi became one with the all-pervading Supreme Consciousness. In the symbolic renderings of this transformative process, kundalini was often represented as Shakti, the cosmic divine feminine, who lay resting in the lowest chakra at the base of the spine. Once awakened and rushing upward, her goal was to reach and attain Union with the cosmic divine masculine, her beloved Shiva, who waited for her just above the thousand-petaled lotus crowning the head.

In these descriptions, the rising kundalini, or kundalini-shakti, was often depicted as being like lightning or other forms of radiant light, and Gopi Krishna began to suspect that this awakening was what he had experienced—and was continuing to experience. From the initial event onward, he had been aware of the sensation of a stream of light that was continually rising from the base of his spine and filling his head with a strange radiance. After the first occurrence and on the following day, however, this light was no longer so transcendental or blissful. It was eerie and disquieting, making him recall occasional references in the books he had read on kundalini to the possible dangers associated with its premature awakening in one who was not prepared or who did not have proper guidance. Unfortunately, there had been no explanation of exactly what these dangers were or, more significantly, how to overcome them. In desperation, he sought guidance from a learned Kashmiri ascetic who was wintering in Jammu. After Gopi Krishna described his experiences, the ascetic replied that it could not be related to kundalini, for the awakening of this force could only have blissful, positive results.[11]

The confusion from these conflicting views was exacerbated by a discussion with his brother-in-law, the only person with whom he shared his concerns. This relative, who had practiced yoga and studied kundalini yoga, told Gopi Krishna that his own teacher had once said that grave difficulties could result if kundalini, instead of rising through the sushumṇā—in other words, the central channel—arose through one of the nāḍīs on the left or on the right, known as the *iḍā* and *piṅgalā*. According to this teacher, this misaligned rising of the energy could lead to complete madness or even death. The worst scenario ensued if the energy had arisen through piṅgalā for, while iḍā was said to symbolize the moon, piṅgalā represented the sun, and the fiery heat of a piṅgalā rising could become literally unbearable.

It is easy to imagine how horrifying this description must have sounded to Gopi Krishna when he was already confused and fearful about what was happening to him. This bit of information, however, was soon to become a saving grace. In the meantime, he tried to read texts on kundalini yoga but he found he could not concentrate. The one bit of information he did glean was that the yogi who awakened kundalini should never allow his stomach to become completely empty. Regrettably, this did not help as he was still so repelled by food that he was having difficulty eating even enough to keep alive. Although it is not known what he did manage to eat during this time, a brief reference in one of his autobiographies suggests it was nothing more than sips of milk and a few sections of orange at a time.

One of the most horrifying experiences for him during this period was that he felt as if his love and affection for his family had dried up. The night terrors also continued, and as his sleep became increasingly disturbed, he had become more agitated during the day, taking long, fretful walks. Although he struggled to keep what was happening from his family, they realized something was drastically wrong and urged him to see a physician. Intuitively, though, he knew this was not the answer. An inner guidance—which would come to rescue him again and again—told him that, in their complete ignorance of what was going on with him, a medical doctor or other healer might prescribe a medication that would prove harmful in his extraordinarily uncommon condition or, even more frightening, declare him to be mad.

This divine inner guidance came to his rescue on the night of the great annual Shivratri festival,[12] an extremely important celebration dedicated to Shiva. Just over nine weeks had passed since that extraordinary day in December, for Shivratri was celebrated in 1938 on February 28. That he had suffered intensely during those nine weeks there could be no doubt. That night was one of the worst. He forced himself to eat a few bites of the celebratory meal his wife had painstakingly prepared for the evening, but he quickly gave up. A fiery stream had rushed up to his head, and by the time he went to bed he felt as if he were on fire inside. As flaming currents darted around and through his body, the heat increased until he thought he could no longer bear it. Desperately, his mind dashed here and there trying to think of a way to save himself. He remembered what his brother-in-law had said about kundalini rising through piṅgalā and, consumed now by heat, he thought he was surely doomed. However, in a moment of divine inspiration it occurred to him to that if he could somehow activate the iḍā —the nāḍī traditionally associated with the coolness of the moon—it might somehow mitigate or balance out the horrific heat he was feeling. He later wrote that in his exhaustion and agony, he "distinctly felt the location of the nerve and strained hard mentally to divert its flow into the central channel." Then, as if waiting for the destined moment, a miracle happened.

There was a sound like a nerve thread snapping and instantaneously a silvery streak passed zigzag through the spinal cord, exactly like the sinuous movement of a white serpent in rapid flight, pouring an effulgent, cascading shower of brilliant vital energy into my brain, filling my head with a blissful luster in place of the flame that had been tormenting me for the last three hours.

Hardly able to believe that the torment was over, he fell into the first truly restful sleep he had had in weeks, his brain bathed in this silvery light.[13] In the morning, a second saving grace came to him: he remembered the stricture that the yogi who awakens kundalini must never let his stomach be completely empty, and he began to eat small amounts of food every two hours.

Throughout his later life Gopi Krishna alluded to the idea that such a thing as coincidence—at least in the way we understand it—does not exist. If this is so, it seems to be a particularly *apropos* bit of history that such momentous events in Gopi Krishna's life occurred at Christmas and Shivratri. For Christians, Christmas is seen as a time of new light coming into the world and is often symbolized in carols and imagery as light that overcomes darkness. In Shaivism, Shivratri is the night when Shiva, the Lord of the Dance, does his dance of creation, preservation, and destruction. It is a festival characterized not by revelry but by deep thought and reflection that focuses on overcoming ignorance and darkness, both in oneself and in the world. Those who knew Gopi Krishna would be adamant that he would never under any circumstances have seen himself or put himself forward as any kind of light to the world, but he did dedicate his life to the belief that the light he experienced on that Christmas and for the rest of his life would, when scientifically researched and widely understood, indeed provide a key to overcoming ignorance and darkness in the world.

Regardless, from that Shivratri onward he was able to live a good deal, but not all, of his life fairly normally over the next twelve years. During this period there were at least two episodes that were as dire as the one he endured on that night of Shivratri and many other very difficult periods. However, he came to understand that in order to avoid these arduous times as much as possible, he had to be extremely disciplined in many ways, particularly in regards to his eating habits, and that his life had to be one of regularity and moderation in absolutely every way.

Looking back at the period in his life between 1923 and his Christmas experience in 1937, he described those years as an exceedingly important time of preparation. Without the level of discipline he imposed on himself during those years, he later wrote, "it might not have been possible for me to withstand the rigor of the years subsequent to 1937. My practice of meditation paved the way for the awakening, but it was the attempt I had made at self-mastery which enabled me to brave the hazard."[14]

The year 1923 was so significant because this is the time he found a position in the government Department of Public Works. During the period between his school failure in 1920 and his finally getting this position, Gopi Krishna had had to consider options: dedicated to his meditation practice he might well have been, but if he wasn't going to be a renunciate, he had to find a way to earn a living. One particularly likely prospect seemed to be joining the forest service, an occupation that would provide him the time, peace, and solitude he would need for meditating. He applied for the position and the training it would require. It seemed certain he would be placed in the program, but at the last minute, corruption in the system allowed for a far less qualified candidate to be accepted. One after another, other opportunities arose, but each time the door would close. These disappointments were increasingly hard on his mother, and when the rather low-level position in Public Works was offered to him, it seemed in some ways ideal. It would not be a terribly demanding job and would thus allow him to focus on his practice. That it was not demanding also meant that it was not highly paid. This was of no concern to him as his earlier decision to begin meditating had gone hand in hand with a determination to live a simple life. After so many disappointments, his mother was relieved that he had finally settled on a career. Unexalted though the position was, it would at least provide enough for her son to help her and improve their circumstances. They needed less now because his two sisters were by then married, and his mother hoped the steady income, even a low one, would allow her son to marry and start a family of his own.

When Gopi Krishna finally took on his job at the Public Works Department, he had been committed to his practice of meditation for over two years. He had also continued to read, and take great solace from, the *Bhagavad Gītā*. In it, he had found a particularly powerful verse that he would quote many times in his life:

> Nonviolence, truthfulness, absence of anger, renunciation of the idea of doer in action, tranquility, restraint from malicious gossip, kindness to all creatures, detachment, mildness, sense of shame in doing things not sanctioned by the scriptures, abstaining from idle pursuits, sublimity, forgiveness, fortitude, purity, absence of self-importance—these are the marks of one who is naturally endowed with divine virtues, O descendant of Bharata.[15]

Such virtues also form the first two steps of the eightfold path of yoga. Known as *yama* and *niyama*, translations include such characteristics as nonharming, truthfulness, nonstealing, chastity, compassion, austerity, lack of greed, and devotion to God. Throughout his life Gopi Krishna would speak about the yamas and niyamas. Referring to their critical importance, he pointed out how similar virtues were included in the codes of conduct of all the great spiritual traditions and how one only had to look at the lives of the great saints and mystics from every religion to see examples of human beings who had mastered these spiritual virtues in their everyday lives.

With this teaching held so firmly in his heart, Gopi Krishna began his career in the Public Works Department and ran head-on into an implacable wall of graft, deceit, and corruption. While some level of corruption was not uncommon in many of the government service bureaus, because it was the department that assigned contracts for public projects to specific contractors, the system in this department was particularly susceptible to abuse. Contractors routinely offered kickbacks to clerks and other officials in order to win contracts, and once contracts were awarded, they colluded with the government workers in the procurement of shoddy materials and other illicit cost-cutting measures so that more money could be funneled into their pockets. In fact, jobs in this department were much sought after because of the opportunity they afforded for graft.

It is easy to imagine how Gopi Krishna, dedicated as he was to the teachings of that passage of the *Bhagavad Gītā*, was viewed by his corrupt coworkers and to realize how much pressure they must have put on him. In spite of how difficult this must have been, he continually stood up for the truth. An innate passion for justice and a corresponding abhorrence for injustice had been with him since childhood, and he objected to the unfairness he saw as much as the dishonesty. He was particularly unbending, for instance, when he discovered that inferior supplies were being considered, for not only would the final project be flawed, but these types of serious flaws could often result in people being killed or critically injured. Indeed, his truth-telling made him so unpopular in his early years that he certainly would have been fired if it had not been for one superior who respected and supported him.

Difficult as his relationship with his corrupt colleagues often was, his dealings with members of the public could be even more challenging. Whenever an individual brought a proposal to his attention that had absolutely no hope of being approved according to the rules, Gopi Krishna would bluntly tell them so. He felt by doing so he was not only being truthful, he was saving them the effort and expense of trying to carry the project further. Graft was so common, however, that it was often assumed he either wanted a very high bribe or was planning to give a similar project to someone who could pay him more or with whom he was somehow connected. After repeatedly increasing the amount of money they were offering, some became threateningly angry; others became outright enemies.

Of course, when he first started the job, he had no idea how difficult it would be or how, as he would later often comment, the years he spent there were a kind of exercise in the discipline and self-mastery that would stand him in such good stead in the future. In 1923 he was only aware that he was beginning a career. He was also soon made aware that his mother was determined to find him a wife. She set about this task with great enthusiasm. Her son's job might not have been much, but it was secure, and she no doubt still believed there was something special about this young man. It did not hurt that he was widely known to be exceptionally handsome. With this in mind she set off to find the best possible match for her son. Gopi Krishna had no objection to this arrangement. It was expected of him to marry, and it was customary for parents to arrange marriages. He told his mother he had complete faith in her and would leave the matter entirely in her hands. Only indicating that, in spite of dedication to meditation and self-discipline, he was still a very typical young man by adding that he would very much like to have a pretty wife.

Although this girl's appearance was in some ways only a small detail in the complex process of marriage negotiation, Gopi Krishna's mother took this to heart and made it an important factor in her search. Finally, a bride named Roopwanti Kuchroo from the Kashmiri village of Baramulla was settled upon. Roopwanti, who was known by those who loved her as Bhabi, had three brothers and was from a well-off family. She was around sixteen years old—a not uncustomary age—on her wedding day. She had not seen her future husband before that day, nor had anyone in his family ever met with her.

Later when he wrote about this event in his autobiography, Gopi Krishna recalled sitting in his groom's finery waiting to meet his wife for the first time and hearing his mother begin to make a loud, angry commotion in an adjacent room. This behavior was so unprecedented on her part that he broke custom, left the room where he was to be waiting, and went to find her. In the book, he carefully and kindly glossed over what had upset his mother so, making only a vague reference to his mother's possible opinion of the bride's "comeliness." In fact, others who later told the tale have said that Gopi Krishna's mother's extreme agitation and dismay were due to the fact that the pictures of the beautiful young woman she had been shown during the negotiations had definitely not been images of the one who stood before her.

The young Gopi Krishna immediately took in the situation. He instantly saw how his mother's tempest must have been affecting the girl and indeed her whole family as they looked on. In the marriage culture in that time and place, the family of the groom held all the cards. The bride would be coming into their home, where, in the very best of circumstances, she would be expected to obey her mother-in-law's every whim and wish; in the worst, she could be treated as a virtual slave or be abused. In either case, she would have no grounds for complaint. The groom's raging mother did not bode well for their daughter's happiness, and they must have been extremely upset and concerned. Gopi Krishna realized the girl herself must have been terrified.

Taking his mother aside, he calmed her and then returned to the girl's family, assuring them that the wedding would go forth and that their daughter would be loved and cared for. He refused to humiliate the girl by breaking the marriage contract, which in fact he would have had every right to do.

This story is a good example of the natural compassion that members of Gopi Krishna's family have said he had from childhood on. Beyond that, it illustrates an aspect of the yamas and niyamas that he had been practicing, and it is certainly mentioned as "kindness to all creatures" in Krishna's prescription for success in yoga.[16] Both his behavior and his attitude were also a perfect example of the practice of the niyama "contentment." In the West, contentment is not often thought of as something to be practiced, but in the sense of the word in the niyamas, it is the practice of not simply accepting but actually being satisfied with what you have or what, in essence, you have been given. That Gopi Krishna could practice this at a moment that had such momentous and far-reaching implications for his life says something important about either his character or the progress he was making in his efforts to be one who might one day have success in yoga.

When Gopi Krishna later spoke publicly about the development in himself of the desired traits described in the *Bhagavad Gītā*, he frequently pointed out that it was not so much he himself who was making this progress on these efforts as it was an inner force that was guiding him, urging him on. In other words, although he was telling us we needed to take a firm hold of ourselves and practice discipline, he was stressing that we had been led to do this in the first place by a divine, guiding force deep within our own being. What's more, he stressed, this divine force would help us along the way in our struggles to develop these lofty traits.

It was no coincidence that the Ten Commandments of Judaism and Old Testament Christianity can be found in the yamas and niyamas or that the Buddha's teachings are reflected in the code of conduct that Krishna sets out for Arjuna or that these strictures are found in virtually every world religion.

These guidelines, Gopi Krishna maintained, are very specifically the ones that are necessary for the evolution to a higher state of consciousness. An evolution that he, like the great Jesuit priest Teilhard de Chardin, believed was leading the entire human race to a point of God Consciousness and that he believed was taking place in each and every one of us today.

Chapter Three

Trial and Error —Learning to Live with Awakening

The story of Gopi Krishna's wedding is important not only because it is such a poignant example of how he was striving to live his vows to be compassionate and contented with his lot in life but also because he would look back on it as another example of divine guidance. Given how aggrieved his mother was, a halt could certainly have been called to the wedding. Although he had no way of knowing it at the time, he would later say that Bhabi was heaven-sent. Throughout his life, he would write and speak about her as the saving grace in his life. She never failed to love or take the utmost care of him. Even in circumstances described in the next chapter when they lived in near poverty or when her neighbors must have thought him mad, she didn't falter in her dedication to him. The gold jewelry she brought with her to the wedding as her dowry would one day save the family from absolute destitution. Her brothers would come to their aid in times of need, and one of her brothers would become one of Gopi Krishna's most loyal supporters. Even though Bhabi was a simple woman who might not have ever totally grasped what her husband wrote about—indeed, she had never learned to read—she was filled with love, tenderness, and dedication for her husband and her family. From the night of his wedding in 1925 onward, Gopi Krishna would not be entirely alone in his struggle.[17]

By that year Gopi Krishna was fairly well settled in his work, even though his specific division within the broader Department of Public Works was occasionally changing. For the first year or so, his placement had been in Srinagar, and for some time after that he was placed back in the city of Jammu. With this steady work, by 1925 Gopi Krishna's life had taken up a rhythm in which he continued to meditate for three hours each morning and to strive throughout the workday to follow the principles and disciplines he had set out for himself.

Always sensitive to heat and cold, Gopi Krishna found the extremely hot summers in Jammu difficult, and it benefited his health greatly when his department began to alternate twice a year between Srinagar and Jammu. The city of Jammu was the main city in a wider region of the same name. The two regions that made up a princely state known as Jammu and Kashmir were ruled at that time by the Maharaja, Hari Singh.[18] As the two regions functioned essentially as a single province, it was possible for the departmental offices to move back and forth, taking advantage of the cooler Kashmiri summers and the more moderate Jammu winters.

In the years following the wedding other important events occurred in his personal life. The first of these was during one of the yearly periods in Kashmir: on November 28, 1929, his only daughter, Ragya Shivpuri, came into the world. She was born in the village of Gairoo, where Bhabi was staying with family while Gopi Krishna worked in Srinagar, remaining near his office and bicycling two or three times a week to see her. The second major family event was in April of 1934 with the birth of their first son, Jagdish Chander Shivpuri. A major sadness occurred in the family's life when Gopi Krishna's beloved mother died in 1935.

With these and other normal events in the cycle of life, Gopi Krishna's existence proceeded rather normally until the extraordinary event that occurred in Jammu at Christmas in 1937. Although there is no specific reference in Gopi Krishna's autobiographies about what happened in terms of his work directly after the disturbances caused by his initial awakening, it seems very unlikely that he could have been going into his office many, or even any, days during the nine weeks leading up to Shivratri. Even after the dramatic improvement that occurred that night, it took time for him to regain his strength, and later references to a leave of absence make it evident he must have taken a lengthy one.

By about the second week of March, the nourishment he was finally able to take and the sleep he was getting were beginning to have an effect, and he was soon able to walk around his room, and he continued to gain strength. He found his dreams seemed to have a particularly restorative quality that aided his recuperation. In them he was transported to a fairyland where the images were imbued with a strange phosphorescence streamed against a luminous backdrop. During his waking hours the degree of inner radiance that had been with him since December remained undiminished, but instead of being jangly and fiery, it was soft and soothing. Over the next several weeks he continued to improve, and the road to recovery began in earnest when he was able to leave Jammu and return to Kashmir. There is a reference in his autobiographies to the fact that "being on leave" allowed him to leave Jammu in April, rather than having to wait until the office transfer that occurred annually in May. It seems that the heat of Jammu had already been affecting his weakened body, and he was very happy to leave. On reaching the Himalayan foothills of his home, he found the cooler weather and the lush greenery and budding flowers a balm. For the most part his dreams continued to be restorative: his appetite began to improve, and most thankfully, his love and affection for his family had returned. The loss of these feelings of warmth and caring had been one of the, if not the most, distressing aspects of the dark period he had endured. That these emotions had returned was not just a great source of comfort, joy, and relief, it was yet another sign of hope.

The weeks of his continued leave passed, and by the time the rest of the office staff had transferred to Kashmir and opened the summer office, he was able to return to work. He was still unable to read or concentrate to any extent, but this was easy enough to deal with as he could easily take breaks to chat with his colleagues, and he found it particularly helpful to rest his mind and eyes by looking out his window.

Bringing all the self-discipline that he had gained in his earlier years to bear, he continued to make a concerted effort to appear as usual and follow his normal routine, allowing only Bhabi to know that he was still struggling. Although the inner light that now washed through his whole being was peaceful, its presence still represented an utterly incomprehensible alteration in his entire being: a constant stream of radiance flowed from the seat of kundalini upward along his spine into his brain; a halo of light encircled his brain and radiated outward, waxing and waning and although his vision remained acute, his visual perception had altered so that colors had a crystalline brilliance, and the world appeared to be painted with the glitter of fresh snow.[19] Slowly he became aware of the radiance moving along his entire nervous system and through his internal organs. His hearing had also been affected during this ongoing process. Outwardly, it became more fine-tuned and acute, while there was a buzzing in his inner ear.

In spite of the mysterious and incomprehensible transformation that was going on in his inner world, outwardly he had a home and work life that was as normal and unremarkable as possible. As his health gradually improved throughout the summer months of 1938, another joy was added to his life when Bhabi became pregnant again. By November, when his office was ready to transfer back to Jammu for the winter months, he felt quite restored. Confident that he could function on his own, he left Bhabi, who was now five months pregnant, behind so that she could remain in Kashmir and be cared for by her family. When he returned from Jammu to Srinagar in the spring of 1939, he found Bhabi, Ragya, and Jagdish were all doing well and that his second son, Nirmal Chander Shivpuri, who had been born on March 2, was a fine, healthy baby.

Life had regained its rhythm for the family and continued along with the annual summer and winter transfers from Jammu to Srinagar for close to five years without any major upsets. The one major outward difference in his life was that he no longer meditated, and his once-burning desire to contemplate the spiritual had vanished.

Even though his life was proceeding outwardly in a seemingly normal manner and without any major crises, it is worthwhile to imagine what this ostensibly average life, especially his work life, must have been like for this naturally kind, sensitive man during these years: he had become increasingly sensitive concerning food and rest and needed to have rigid control of his eating and sleeping habits; a completely incomprehensible and unfathomable light and radiance was coursing through his body night and day; an unearthly buzzing was a constant in his inner ear; his consciousness was expanding and contracting in ways he could not even begin to explain to anyone; and his entire nervous system was in an extraordinarily heightened and sensitive state. Yet every day, in this condition, he went to work in an office that was a hotbed of graft, corruption, and discord. It is no wonder he says he would not have survived without his earlier years of practicing not only self-control but also the yamas and niyama and the *Bhagavad Gītā*'s directives on developing love, compassion, and understanding while conquering anger and hatred.

Transfers and changes within the Department of Public Works continued during these years, sometimes landing him unexpectedly in positions he had not been prepared for and where there were more and different types of graft involved and where his determination to fight the corruption and deal with everyone honestly must have taken a great toll. The battles he participated in were often not inconsequential: they sometimes involved fighting to prevent the use of shoddy materials in a bridge that might eventually collapse or a building where people would use their life savings to buy an apartment only to have it fall into disrepair.

Years later during a talk to a group of young people in New York, he would make a brief but telling remark about his days working in those government offices. At the audience's request, he was offering his thoughts on "how to win to cosmic consciousness." In describing the moderate and disciplined life they should live, he gave the example of the seemingly straightforward determination to never speak a falsehood. "It is a most difficult task," he said. "I know what it means. You make enemies everywhere, sometimes. Just this one thing, that 'I will speak the truth always.' It is not a simple matter...."[20]

Remaining truthful and following his other principles was undoubtedly especially challenging while working in the government during those early years following 1937. As Gopi Krishna observed the energy moving in his physical body and consciousness during these years, he became increasingly aware of how intelligent and alive it appeared to be. With these observations he became increasingly convinced that he had awakened kundalini. The dictum that he had once come across about the significance of food for the awakened yogi became his watchword. Through a painful process of trial and error, he discovered that both the timing and quantity of his food intake were critically important. Even the slightest deviation would cause agonizing digestive upsets and, even worse, disturbances in the flow of the radiance through his brain and his internal organs. This could, in turn, bring on temporary gloom and anxiety. These issues remained with him to some extent for the next twelve years.[21]

One of the greatest challenges was that, because he was undergoing a process of transformation, he was constantly having to adapt to the changes. He was also never totally free of the deep-down concern for his sanity. He could not completely forget the dire warnings of his brother-in-law's guru about the madness that could result from a misaligned kundalini awakening or the other vague caveats he found in writings on kundalini. In spite of being convinced that he had indeed awakened kundalini, he did not understand exactly what was happening to him. His critical, analytical mind and his self-searching nature demanded that he question himself and what he was experiencing with every rational faculty at his disposal. Even though he couldn't help but remain somewhat anxious about his future sanity, especially considering the unpredictability and changeability of what he was experiencing, his continued rational analysis and examination of himself assured him that he was not insane. Still, he knew that if he tried to tell anyone else what he was experiencing, they would certainly think him so.

Another issue adding to his uncertainty was that his experiences seemed to be totally of the physical realm. Earlier in his life he had been drawn to the stories of the great saints and mystics and had read about them voraciously. From this, he knew that his initial experience of cosmic Oneness and his ongoing experience of unearthly, radiant light corresponded "in every particular" with their descriptions of mystical experience. In contrast to this, there did not seem to be anything mystical or spiritual about his experience at all. Moreover, in the Tantric tradition of Kashmiri Shaivism of his own culture, the texts were clear that an awakening of kundalini would be accompanied by the onset of the extraordinary abilities known as *siddhis*. For example, a line in the Kashmiri Tantric text known as *Panchastavi*, says the awakened yogi "acquires the gift of limitless flow of words, rich with the ambrosia of sweetness and beauty of expression," and another verse tells of how kundalini grants "the talents of a poet."[22] Other siddhis, such as the paranormal abilities displayed by his father, were also described in many of these Tantric texts, but he was not experiencing siddhis of this nature to any great extent either.

Both the possibility that his condition might be mistaken for—or, worse, even become—a form of mental illness and the obvious lack of the mystical and transformative elements described by the saints and yogis contributed to Gopi Krishna never ceasing to examine and question his state. This tendency toward rational inquiry and investigation was, however, also just part of his basic nature. Although he never trained as a scientist, even a cursory look at his published works shows that he had the critical, analytical mind of a scientist. Nowhere is his reasoned, rational mind more obvious than in the way he examined himself and what was happening in his life. He observed keenly what was occurring in his physical body and in his consciousness, and at no point did he ever stop questioning his observations.

This intensive observation played a particularly important role in the process of trial and error involved in regulating his diet. As he became increasingly able to observe the changes in the ways the energy behaved and moved throughout his body, he was able to see the connections with how his dietary needs were changing. However, because these alterations often occurred without warning, he was often—especially in the early years—one step behind. Errors on his part could result physically in excruciating digestive upsets and mentally in a contraction in the halo of his expanded consciousness and a diminishment in the quality of the radiance that streamed through his body. This went hand in hand with the depressed moods mentioned earlier.

To comprehend this, it is essential to realize that Gopi Krishna felt he could see and feel the radiations that were moving in his body. Because he realized this would be difficult to imagine for those who had never had such a visual and tangible experience, he took care to describe in vivid detail the way this luminescent force raced along his neural pathways and darted in and out of his internal organs. He also made it clear that the physical sensations at the seat of kundalini—in other words, near the reproductive organs—were undeniable and unmistakable. Although imagery and information on these aspects of kundalini awakening were not widely available here in the West when Gopi Krishna first started making his experiences public, it is now easy to find reproductions of age-old Tantric drawings that show a complex of countless nāḍīs, or nerve pathways, in the human body that are lit up like a Christmas tree. Translations and interpretations of Tantric texts that elucidate the intricate relationship between the sexual organs and the awakening of kundalini are also available to us today. So available, in fact, that it is difficult for us to imagine that Gopi Krishna would have had difficulty finding information on kundalini awakening living as he did not just in India but in the homeland of the Tantric tradition of Kashmiri Shaivism. One explanation for this is that the teachings about kundalini have always been shrouded in mystery. It is widely accepted that the reason for this secrecy is that the Tantric adepts were aware of the potential difficulties and dangers that could be inherent in premature kundalini awakening and did not want anyone, especially not the uninitiated and unprepared, to attempt this awakening without the guidance of an already-awakened guru. As mentioned earlier, Gopi Krishna had seen and heard vague references to these dangers, but the information was not specific enough to help him understand exactly what was going on in his body or avoid the sometimes dire effects of his missteps. While life might well have been easier for him if he'd had more of this information, through his process of trial and error—and of course with Bhabi's help—he was able to proceed with an appearance of at least outward normalcy much of the time.

This pattern continued in general for about five years after the initial awakening. Then, in December of 1943, he made a grievous misstep. Earlier that year, when his department was still in its Kashmir summer offices, Gopi Krishna had noticed a powerful "urge for a more nourishing and substantial diet"[23] than he had become accustomed to. Because the effects of World War II in other parts of the world had inflated the price of food in Kashmir so badly, he tried to resist this impulse. That he ignored what his body was trying to tell him may well have contributed to the crisis he would soon face. In the meantime, however, it seemed to him that his diet in Kashmir had been more than adequate. By the annual November return to Jammu he felt he was in extremely good physical health. His mental state was also good as the halo of expanded consciousness and the radiant, luminescent energy seemed to have become a normal, if extraordinary, part of his existence. Once again, he felt so good that he was sure he would be fine on his own and left Bhabi and the children in their home in Srinagar.

Not having the family with him, he stayed on the outskirts of Jammu in the home of one of Bhabi's brothers, who was at the time the municipal engineer of the area. Shortly after becoming settled, he felt so healthy and energetic that he started a vigorous early-morning exercise regime that gave him a feeling of glowing good health and increased his energetic feeling. Slowly and imperceptibly over the next few weeks, this feeling of strength and energy began to transform into an urge to meditate—a desire he had not had in years. An internal debate ensued in which the longing to reenter those states of cosmic bliss and awareness he had once tasted battled with his fear of reigniting the terrible suffering that he had undergone in the early days of 1938. Eventually he convinced himself that the fact that the halo of expanded consciousness, the radiance streaming along his nerves, and the changes to his perception had become so much a part of his daily life meant that his body was now acclimatized to the phenomenon. Confident that this indicated that he could meditate safely again, he resumed the practice during the first week of December. After only a few attempts, he says that he was being carried away by an incandescent tide each morning and becoming lost in an "unbounded, glowing, conscious void." At the same time, he was experiencing an incomparable bliss that flowed from his fingers and toes to his spine, where it intensified and rose in a "rapturous and exhilarating stream" to the upper regions of his brain. Later, he referred to this as a "nerve secretion" and identified it as what the ancient yogis had called "nectar."[24]

Given this description, it is easy to see why—in spite of his niggling doubts about the wisdom of what he was doing—he not only continued to meditate, he spent longer and longer periods each morning lost in this world of splendor. Caught up not only in the glory of the experience itself but also in the realization that he might actually be attaining the cosmic state that was the ultimate goal of yoga—and that so many yogis had failed to attain—he became so eager to meditate each morning that his sleep became disrupted. Over the next few weeks, he became increasingly excited, and in this feverish state he failed utterly to keep in mind the lessons he had learned about what the lack of sleep or a strain on his nervous system could do to him. On the night of December 23, he failed to sleep at all and meditated as usual the next morning. Busy preparing for a trip he was planning to take over the Christmas period to visit a cousin he hadn't seen for years, he hurried about all day and neglected to eat. That night, the moment he lay down on his bed, he realized his mistake. His head reeled, the inner buzzing sound became harsh and discordant, and a column of flame had replaced the radiant light in his spine.

The trip he had been anticipating was canceled, and he began once again to pay strict attention to the regularity of his diet. Although this helped somewhat, he could not force himself to eat more than a mouthful at a time. His insomnia worsened, and lacking sleep, his condition deteriorated. The new year of 1944 dawned, and by the middle of January his brother-in-law determined that they should telegram Bhabi to come. Thinking of her traveling over the treacherous winter mountain passes, Gopi Krishna resisted the idea until his condition became dire. Accompanied by her father, in spite of his age, she arrived with the boys as soon as possible, while Ragya, now fourteen and considered a young lady, remained at home.[25] Once Bhabi arrived in Jammu, she began to care for her husband day and night with no concern for herself. In spite of her diligence, he did not improve. He remained repulsed by food and able to sleep only sporadically and fitfully. In desperation, gurus and the holy men and women known as *sadhus* were consulted. After one caused frightening spasms of pain by trying to force Gopi Krishna to eat a large plate of food, even the hope that a sage could help was abandoned.

Some days later, the now four-year-old Nirmal entered his father's room with his own little dinner bowl in his hand. Settling down, he began to eat, smacking his lips with delight. Watching him, Gopi Krishna looked at the food, if only briefly, without revulsion and felt the stirrings of hunger. This unexpected sensation caused Gopi Krishna to reflect on food again. His scattered thoughts roamed until it occurred to him that perhaps he was waiting too long between attempts to eat. Paying rigorous attention the next day, he took a swallow of milk every three hours. Although no noticeable improvement occurred, there was also no extreme negative reaction to the intake of nourishment. Over the next few days, he continued this regime. Unfortunately, he was still not receiving enough nutrition, and he deteriorated physically and mentally further.

One night, losing all hope and even the will to live, he called his sons and Bhabi to him and said what was, in his own mind, good-bye. Giving one last thought to the image of his beloved daughter Ragya, who was not with him, he consigned himself to the fate of taking his own life before it could end in complete delirium. The question, however, of how he could actually accomplish this when he was so debilitated that he could hardly stand seemed to have escaped him. Tossing, turning, and trying to find an answer to his dilemma, he somehow fell asleep near dawn and, in the first peaceful sleep he had had in weeks, dreamed of eating from a plate that held rice and a simple Kashmiri meat dish.[26]

Upon awaking, the peaceful glow from the dream remained in his consciousness for a short while, and he asked Bhabi to bring him milk every two hours now and with it a bit of the well-cooked and easy-to-digest meat. By the end of the day, he was feeling some relief, and he fell asleep that night once again wrapped in a peaceful light. The next day, he ate every hour, and then after about a week, stretched the intervals back to an hour and a half. In the meantime, Bhabi was spending her entire day in the kitchen preparing tempting food and making sure it was given to her husband precisely on time. Within two weeks Gopi Krishna was able to walk around his room again. A new, more powerful, more radiant energy was now flowing through his being.

All the while, a source of inner guidance seemed to be counseling him on exactly when and what to eat. Paying strict attention to these inner urgings, he soon moved the intervals between eating back to every two hours. Astonishingly, over the next while his appetite, which had been nonexistent, became voracious. Drawn to some foods and rejecting others, he began to meticulously select the ingredients for each meal. The amount of food he was consuming increased to four and sometimes even six times what he had been eating during the more normal and uneventful period of the previous five years. It seemed to him that this intake was necessary in some way to support the new level of radiance he was experiencing. He continued to gain strength, and by April he was able, with the help of Bhabi and his father-in-law, to make the arduous two-day trip from Jammu to Srinagar.

It is unclear how long his period of voracious eating lasted—or whether this was the first and only experience of it. Certainly, in interviews done decades later, family members recalled times when the vendors with carts equipped to make sugarcane juice would come by and crank kilos of sugarcane through their presses to create the quarts of juice he was able to consume in a day.

When Gopi Krishna was faced throughout his life with questions about the regularity and quantity of food consumption he needed to survive and about the extraordinary sensations and activity level he experienced in the genital region, he never failed to stress that the answers would ultimately be found in research. Certainly allusions to the importance of food and the relationship between the sexual energy and spiritual energy abound in Tantric texts. But, couched as they are in poetic and symbolic language, they do not provide the answers needed to assure safe passage for an individual on their journey of kundalini awakening today. As is seen in the following chapters, promoting the idea of serious scientific research into kundalini—regardless of the name it might be given—became his life goal.

Chapter Four

Fighting for Women's Rights in the 1940s

Once back home in Kashmir and the beauty of the spring surroundings, the loving care Gopi Krishna received restored him even more, and it was not too long before he was able to return to work. Although he still had to eat with meticulous regularity, the quantity of food he needed to consume became more normal. He found that the level of radiance and expanded consciousness he was experiencing had increased yet again and that when he looked at the world around him it sometimes seemed as if he had been transported to a heavenly scene. His dream life, too, became even more lucid and luminous. His dreams continued to have what seemed to be a restorative effect, and soon they were also containing detailed descriptions of events that would take place in the near future. While he was intrigued with this phenomenon at first, it caused a vague uneasiness that might well have been due, at least in part, to the difficulties linked in his memories with his father's paranormal abilities. Whether by this time in his life he associated these premonitions with the development of the siddhis described in the Tantras is not known. Regardless, he intuitively turned away from them.

For the most part, the rest of 1944 proceeded fairly normally in terms of his mental and physical health. This was aided by the fact that he had received a transfer out of the Department of Public Works. While the date of this transfer remains uncertain, its cause does not: once again his refusal to be drawn into unethical behavior and his insistence on standing up for the truth had gotten him into trouble. This time the situation was so problematic to that it could not be ignored, and he was virtually kicked out of the department. Instead of being fired, though, he was transferred into the Department of Education. Since there were no massive public construction projects on the line in this department, much less opportunity for graft existed; consequently, a transfer to it was viewed as a punishment. But for Gopi Krishna, it presented a degree of relief. With payoffs being made for choice positions within the school and university system and illegitimate disputes needing to be settled, he still found a good deal of corruption to fight. Nonetheless, the graft was not as endemic, and the atmosphere was generally less fraught. The amount of stress he was under decreased tremendously, and it seemed to him that once again some sort of divine guidance was helping him along his way.

Thus, the next few years proceeded fairly calmly in terms of his overall well-being. This did not mean that his entire life was particularly tranquil. After the disastrous effects of his short-lived but obsessive return to the spiritual and supernal, he focused his mind firmly on the world around him. Even though he was not consciously focusing his thoughts on spiritual goals and disciplines, it is unimaginable that, after all his years of practice, his very being was not imbued with the principles of honesty and compassion. He also had an innately kind, caring, and sympathetic nature, and he had been since childhood deeply affronted by injustice. Given that he was motivated by compassion and a desire for justice by both his principles and his character, it is not surprising that he eventually became involved in matters of social reform and what we would today call social justice. This was especially unsurprising as the Kashmir of the 1940s was a world troubled by tremendous cultural, political, and religious strife.

Although his social-justice work is not referred to extensively in his autobiographies, this work was central to his life for years, and it remains one of the most revealing indicators of just what an extraordinary human being he was. Exactly when Gopi Krishna's more formalized focus on social justice began is difficult to pin down. What is known, however, is that by 1946 he had founded an organization dedicated to the cause of serving society called Samaj

Sudhar Samiti, or social reform committee. The early roots of the organization arose out of his work in the Department of Education. Through this work he came in contact with many teachers and professors throughout the consolidated Jammu and Kashmir region. Spurred on no doubt by his long-held abhorrence of injustice, he frequently found himself fighting for the rights of educators who had been unfairly treated. Over time his reputation as a crusader spread, and although he undoubtedly made some enemies, he made many more friends. When the idea came to him to start an organization that would fight for social justice, he had a ready pool of potential supporters.

It is typical of Gopi Krishna's humility that in the autobiographies he plays down his own role both in the formation of Samiti and in its later accomplishments. However, according to friends and family, he was unquestionably the driving force behind both its founding and its continued existence. In fact, he was still informally heading the group at his death in 1984. In a way, the organization was a reflection of both his rational way of thinking and his deeply compassionate nature. When he turned from his deep introspection to look analytically at the society he lived in, he could see that a number of cultural traditions that he, like everyone else, simply accepted as a normal part of life were in actuality causing economic misery for families and in particular for the women in them. Three of these were the dowry system, the traditional wedding, and the way widows were treated.

Families with daughters, unless they were well-off, were forced to scrimp and save to amass enough money for each girl's dowry. Without a good dowry, a young woman was doomed to marry poorly or not marry at all. The amount of money demanded by an eligible groom's family could take most, if not all, of the girl's family's resources. If the family had only girls and no sons to bring a dowry back into the family, the marriage of their daughters could, and often did, leave them in poverty.

The likelihood of this was compounded by the cultural traditions around typical weddings. These customs required the family of the bride to provide food, drink, and entertainment for excessive numbers of guests not just on one day but for several days. As part of the pomp and show, scores of different dishes would be prepared. Sometimes, in addition to the invited guests, literally hundreds of people from the village would expect to be fed. Massive amounts of food had to be prepared, and more often than not, much of it was left uneaten and thrown away. If the bride's family did not provide this spectacle, they would be humiliated in the eyes of the community, and the young woman would go into the marriage in shame.

Once the young woman was married, she would move into her husband's family home, where she would be at the beck and call of her mother-in-law, who would train her in the ways of the household. Of course, many mothers-in-law treated their daughters-in-law kindly. But in families where this was not the case, the young woman could endure mental and physical abuse and be treated as a virtual slave, and she would have no recourse against this treatment.

The best way to make sure this didn't happen to a daughter was to arrange a marriage into a fine family and to send her off with a wedding that would increase her status and standing in her new home. Naturally, families who loved their girls wanted this for them above all else and were willing to run themselves into poverty to attain it. Unfortunately, their depleted financial situation now left them even less able to help a daughter who did get into a terrible situation. Once she was married, her dowry belonged to the husband's family, and if the husband died she could be—and, by a cruel family, would be—thrown out of the house. With her family now too poor to be able to take her back, the widow would have no option but to live on the streets, becoming either a beggar or a prostitute.

It is widely accepted today that these sorts of deeply engrained cultural traditions are some of the roots of how, in many cultures, sons have come to be desired over daughters and boys have come to be valued more than girls. In India, certainly, it was a central factor in horrific customs such as *sati*, where a young widow would throw herself on her husband's funeral pyre rather than face a dreaded future.

Sati was outlawed in British India in the 1800s, and feminist efforts have increased awareness of the harm caused by traditions such as the dowry system and of the terrible injustice of valuing boys over girls, and yet change still has a long way to go. Sadly, instances of daughters-in-law being brutalized, cast out, or burned to death in supposedly accidental cooking fires still make the news in India today. Imagine, then, the courage and commitment it must have taken and how incredibly outrageous it must have seemed for Gopi Krishna's band of reformers to take on deeply entrenched traditions of the dowry, the wedding, and the fate of widows in the remote, rural area of Kashmir in 1946. But that is just what Samaj Sudhar Samiti did. In organizing this group and setting out its goals, Gopi Krishna was leading a radical movement for what we today call *women's rights* literally decades before it would even begin in North America and far, far ahead of its time in less developed nations.[27]

When Gopi Krishna founded the group, its first act was to create a small brochure, and later handbills and flyers, that set out their goals of reducing the social ills that arose out of the traditions related to dowries, weddings, and widowhood. The enthusiastic members then took the information out into the community, where they met with more resistance than they expected. Although they had some success over time, few people wanted to give up the dowry system—especially, it can be somewhat cynically assumed, families with more sons than daughters—and the extravagant weddings that could increase the family's and the bride's social standing. In his writings Gopi Krishna admitted that the degree of resistance his group encountered took him by surprise. This is perhaps because he did not think of himself in those early days, or perhaps ever, as the revolutionary that he truly was. Ideas that seemed immanently sensible to him and fellow Samiti members represented radical trail-blazing.

It does not seem to be any coincidence that Gopi Krishna founded an organization dedicated primarily to the betterment of the lives of women. Throughout his autobiographical writings, he speaks not only of his love for his mother and his wife but of his deep admiration for their courage, strength, and commitment. Later in life, when he spoke widely about kundalini awakening, he made it clear that, although many age-old yogic traditions made it sound like reaching enlightenment was the purview of men, this was not the case. He even went so far as to state firmly that women were in some ways better adapted biologically for reaching higher states of consciousness than men.

As will be seen in the next few chapters, Samiti's size and influence grew, and although it was not the goal of their activities, some of their more radical actions became somewhat political. To understand this and to have a better sense of what Gopi Krishna's life was like in these later years of the 1940s, it is necessary to take a brief—and therefore oversimplified—look at what the overall political and cultural situation was in Kashmir in those days.

World War II had ended in 1945, but India, like much of the world, was still feeling the effects in 1946, and this was true in Kashmir, even though it was still a princely state and not technically a part of British-controlled India, which had entered the war in 1939 or, to put it more accurately, which had been entered into the war by Britain. Gandhi, whose campaign for India's independence from Britain had been gaining ground before the war, denounced Nazism but opposed India's involvement in the war on the grounds that people should not be fighting in the name of democracy when they were being denied democracy themselves. This was not one of Gandhi's most popular stands. Many Indians supported the Allies' efforts, and more than two and a half million Indians fought on Britain's behalf in the war. Another of Gandhi's less popular positions during this period was his stand on the question of the creation of a Muslim state, in other words a separate Muslim country. The number of Muslims in India had been growing, as had the tension and conflicts between Hindus and Muslims. Gandhi was firmly against the creation of a Muslim state, instead believing in an India free from Britain in which the two religions could coexist in harmony—as indeed the majority of Hindus and Muslims had done in everyday life for generations.

Using the excuse that such far-reaching decisions could not be made in the middle of the war, Britain put off addressing the issues both of independence and of partition. Gandhi, however, increased his cries for the British to "Quit India," and after a speech by this name in Bombay in 1942, he was imprisoned. On his release due to extremely poor health in 1944, he found that the Muslim position in the country had strengthened and that the conflicts between the extreme elements of both Islam and Hinduism had increased. In the end, these two separate and in some ways unrelated issues came to be brokered in the same agreement: on August 15, 1947, India received its independence from Britain and the partition occurred. As a result, an eastern section of India was cut off and turned into what would become Bangladesh, while a large part of western India was partitioned off into the country that is now Pakistan. The opposition to the partition of India was widespread and violent, with more than a half a million people dying in riots. With the creation of Pakistan, which was closer to Gopi Krishna's homeland, as many as ten to twelve million Sikhs and Hindus left their homes in what was suddenly no longer India, while millions of Muslims migrated in the opposite direction, making their way across the newly created border. Instead of celebrating the independence he had dedicated his life to, Gandhi is said to have spent August 15 pleading with his countrymen for an end to the violence and rioting.

While these riots marked a high point in the Muslim–Hindu infighting of that era, the number of violent skirmishes and the amount of general discord in Jammu and Kashmir continued for a number of reasons. One was that the Muslim population had grown and become a definite majority in Kashmir. Another was that Jammu and Kashmir now shared a border with the new country of Pakistan, and many Muslim supporters of partition believed that the entire province should have become part of Pakistan. Indeed, the controversy continues today, and Pakistan has not hidden its desire to annex Kashmir.[28]

It is interesting to note that these events and conditions are mentioned only briefly in Gopi Krishna's two autobiographical works. Given their momentous nature, it seems safe to assume that this must have been a conscious decision on his part. There could be many reasons for this, and one could be that he was writing material about kundalini and his personal experiences with this cosmic energy, and with the single-minded focus he exhibited whenever necessary in his life, he simply stuck with these topics. The role of a biography, on the other hand, is to provide context for the events occurring in the subject's life, and it can hardly be denied that Gopi Krishna's life would have been colored by these world-changing events during years that his autobiographies deal with, from 1937 to 1949.

Certainly the question of partition and the Muslim–Hindu conflict had relevance for Samiti. When Gopi Krishna formed it in 1946, the organization's goals were firmly fixed on economic reform with a particular emphasis on the unjust treatment of women. Given the overall background of what was happening in Kashmir in those days, however, it is easy to see that the organization would eventually occasionally become involved in specific situations that touched on the Muslim–Hindu conflict. In the early days, however, the members of Samiti focused on the goal of educating the public on the social ills caused by the dowries and excessively extravagant weddings.

Gopi Krishna soon had an opportunity to, as the saying goes, put his money where his mouth was. In the summer of 1947, not long before partition, his beloved daughter Ragya had reached marriageable age, and a suitable alliance had been found for her. In his autobiographies, Gopi Krishna states that his daughter "was married in an unostentatious manner" that was in complete accordance with the reform principles of Samiti.[29] He gives credit for this entirely to the groom, Radha Krishan Kaul, a young lawyer without parents or wealth. Not only was the young man willing to forgo having the showy, extravagant wedding that would have, according to custom, been a statement of his social standing, he was also willing to marry a woman without a dowry. This marked him as an exceptional young man, for as a yet-unestablished lawyer without parental backing, he could well have been expected to choose a wife with the kind of sizable dowry that would have given him a leg up in life.

According to custom, Gopi Krishna would have been responsible for finding a suitable husband for his daughter and for making all the arrangements for the marriage contract. Even in the normal course of events, this could be a long, drawn-out, and difficult process. In the case of seeking a potential groom who would marry in accordance with Samiti's doctrine, it might have been far more difficult than usual. In his writings, however, he has stated that a "family friend" took care of the arrangements. According to family history, it was one of Bhabi's brothers who spared Gopi Krishna this potentially arduous task in what he himself referred to as his "peculiar mental condition" at the time.

How this dedication to Samiti's goals might have been viewed through the eyes of a young woman who was still a few months from her eighteenth birthday is not mentioned, but Gopi Krishna does make a reference to "filial loyalty," which seems to indicate that Ragya, out of this loyalty to her father, was as keen to have a ceremony that met with Samiti's principles as he was.[30] Although she might well have agreed with her father's lofty ethical position, it cannot have been easy for a young woman who had probably, like many girls, fantasized about her wedding day.

When Ragya was interviewed for this biography on her father, she was in her eighties with a sharp, clear mind. Her memories of her wedding and the arrangements for it provide insight on a number of levels. In spite of her clearly expressed admiration for what her father stood for, there were still signs that she might well have once dreamed of a celebration that was not so subdued. Instead of the vast numbers of joyous, celebrating people, there was a quiet gathering of family and friends. Instead of a wide array of delicacies usually provided, the guests were offered a limited number of dishes. The food was delicious, wholesome, and plentiful to be sure, but it was nothing like the extravaganza that was provided at a typical Kashmiri wedding. What was perhaps most disappointing to her—and certainly without letting her father see her disappointment—was the state of her trousseau. In the normal course of events, it would have included any number of rich sari silks and intricately embroidered and beaded shalwar kameez.[31] Instead, she recalls going off to her new home with only a few simple saris.

It is also interesting to note that, while in Gopi Krishna's eyes the fact that someone besides himself arranged this very suitable marriage was a great blessing, Ragya expressed some regret that Gopi Krishna had not been able to take part in what was traditionally a father's tremendously important and almost sacred duty. What was most difficult for her, however, was her very clear memory that her father was present only at brief times during the ceremony itself and spent much of the time in his room while the festivities, such as they were, went on below in the garden of their home in Srinagar.

While it is always risky to extrapolate from a single event, Ragya's memories of her father's behavior during her wedding, combined with his own reference to his "peculiar mental condition," almost certainly provide some insight into Gopi Krishna's state of mind during this period. His autobiographical writings indicate that the years from 1944 up to Ragya's wedding in the summer of 1947 and on into 1949 were ones in which his life was proceeding fairly normally. He was able to fulfill his duties in the education department on a daily basis, and since 1946 he had been able to actively lead a dedicated social-reform movement that was continually gaining membership and momentum. On the other hand, he still had to pay an unusual amount of attention to the regularity of his diet:

the halo of expanded consciousness he experienced had grown, and the external and internal luminescence that he had been experiencing in varying degrees since the initial awakening had increased dramatically after his recovery from the experience he'd had at the end of 1943. Given all this, it can be fairly safely assumed that even though he was able to work and to lead and coordinate the activities of a growing social movement, he was not able to do everything, and a life that might have been viewed as fairly normal was in fact not.

When Ragya was interviewed, she expressed a profoundly loving admiration for her father. Indeed, like her two brothers, who were also interviewed, she said being Gopi Krishna's child was the greatest honor of her life. She also felt it was a blessing that had given her what was a wonderful and fulfilling life. She had been given two fine sons, and Radha Krishan Kaul had been a loving husband whose career took him from humble beginnings to the heights of being the joint registrar at the Delhi High Court, which had provided a more than comfortable living and an exalted social position.

Still, the years from 1937 to 1949 could not have been easy for Gopi Krishna's family, and he was the first to admit this. His deep love for them cannot be questioned. His description of his horror at losing all feelings of love for them during his ordeal after the initial awakening and of his profound relief when the feelings returned are evidence of this. He also communicated at numerous times during his life that his one great regret was over any suffering his wife and children might have endured during those unsettled years leading up to 1949. Gopi Krishna's comments on this, combined with those of Ragya and those of Jagdish and Nirmal that occur later in the book, provide insight both into their personal family's life and into life as experienced by the families of many of history's greats. It has often been observed that it is the spouses and the children of geniuses, revolutionary thinkers, and other historical figures who pay with their unwitting sacrifices some—if not a great deal—of the price for the achievements of the single-minded family member whose goal is changing the world and bettering the lot of all humankind.

Chapter Five

War, Poverty, and Emerging Cosmic Consciousness

While the political and cultural tension in Kashmir was terrible at the time of Ragya's 1947 wedding, the situation would actually become much worse after the August 15 pronouncement of Indian independence and the creation of Pakistan. In the partition agreement Pakistan was created out of the part of India that tended to have a predominantly Muslim majority in most areas. The princely state of Jammu and Kashmir—still at that time not a part of the official country of India—not only had a definite Muslim majority, it bordered the newly created country. In spite of this, it did not become part of Pakistan, and the Hindu Maharaja, Hari Singh, was firmly holding on to the independent status of the princely state he ruled.

The crisis for the princely state came in late October when it was invaded by a force of Pathan tribesmen that came over the border from Pakistan. Even as early as June that summer, the uprisings against Hari Singh had been led by Muslims in the areas along what would become the border. By September, anti-Muslim riots led by the more fanatical Hindu factions had broken out in the southern regions of the state. From the moment Pakistan became an official country, the problem became worse. Many of the more radical Muslims believed the entire state of Jammu and Kashmir should have become part of Pakistan, and they were willing to fight for it.

The instigators of the October invasion, the Pathans, are—and were then—an assemblage of clans and tribes who share a common language and history.[32] They are ethnic Afghans who only stopped being known by that name after it came to refer to the citizens of Afghanistan in general. Although Pathans have a history of being peaceful farmers, they have long been regarded as fierce fighters. This was indeed the face they showed on the morning of October 21, 1947, when convoys carrying about 2,000 of them were brought across the newly established border of Pakistan and into Jammu and Kashmir, where they stormed the city of Muzaffarabad. Armed with axes, swords, and some guns, they easily routed the Maharaja's army, which historians estimate to have been only about 500 strong. They then broke into the state armory, set fires, and shot people who could not recite the Muslim declaration of faith. Later reports described streets littered with dead bodies, including those of Pathans who were killed by the Hindus and Sikhs defending their homes. Women were also killed, and it is reported that many were taken as slaves. Others dove into the Neelum River to avoid this fate, and the river, like the streets, soon became littered with the dead.

The Maharaja, who had long waffled on whether he should cede his principality to India, was now in a position with little choice. Once the accession of the princely state to the Dominion of India was finalized, Indian ground and air forces were sent in to quell the invasion and, ultimately, to prevent the region from being taken over by Pakistan.[33] Tragically, this was not accomplished until after widespread death and damage had transpired.[34] The effects on Gopi Krishna's immediate family were also great. Before being stopped, the invading Pathans made it to Baramulla, Bhabi's family's home. Her father, Sudarshan Kuchroo, was shot dead in the street by the invaders, and the family's holdings were damaged, and their financial situation was gravely impacted.

Once Jammu and Kashmir was officially part of India, the Indian government sent in troops. It seemed evident to the government that the invasion by the Pathans was the first step in a concerted attempt by Pakistan to take control of Jammu and Kashmir and make it part of Pakistan, and the Indian government was determined to prevent this. The ensuing battle came to be known as the Indo–Pakistani War of 1947. The war lasted through the remainder of that year and through all of 1948. The final peace agreement was signed on January 5, 1949. While the whole of Jammu and Kashmir remained part of India, an agreement was reached that the northern portion—about a third—would be administered by Pakistan and the rest of the state would be administered by India.

To say this agreement did not solve—and never has solved—the problem is no exaggeration. Conditions during the war were horrific in the region, and the aftermath lingered. Food prices skyrocketed, and the relationship between the two religious/cultural groups was in worse tatters than it had been in recent history.[35] Gopi Krishna's family suffered terribly, as did the majority of people. There was little food and not enough money to buy it with. Tension between the cultures rent the air, and the peaceful Kashmir Valley that, which had always been such a homey place of security and safety for Gopi Krishna, Bhabi, and their children, was in shambles.

One immediate effect was that the office of the Department of Education could not make its usual November transfer from Srinagar to Jammu. Jammu, being located closer to the new Pakistan border, was suffering from even worse unrest. But even if his department had decided to make the move, Gopi Krishna would not have gone with them. He was determined not to leave his family in such a chaotic environment. Also, his leadership of Samiti had taken on more immediate urgency as the organization moved swiftly, for the time being, from focusing on the long-term goals of changing cultural values to the immediate one of providing relief efforts for the countless families whose lives had been destroyed by the invasion. It is worth noting here that, while the majority of members of Samiti may have been Hindu, Muslims also belonged: the organization was aimed at helping all people whose lives had been devastated by the invasion, regardless of their religion.

Throughout the winter and into the spring of 1948, Gopi Krishna continued to work in the Srinagar education office and to be involved with Samiti's relief efforts. This situation stretched through the late spring and summer, when the Department of Education office was in Srinagar just as it normally would have been. When the usual time for the transfer to Jammu came in November, it is unclear whether the department made the move. Regardless, Gopi Krishna did not go. At some point he had requested a leave of absence so that he could focus his attention on the work Samiti was doing. Thus, through the winter of 1948–1949 and into the spring and summer, he remained in Srinagar. Although the exact date of his return from this leave is not known, he was back at work by November of 1949 and made the annual transfer with the office to Jammu. Bhabi, confident now of his ability to take care of himself, remained in Srinagar with the boys. Mr. Kaul and Ragya were now in Delhi, where he was beginning his career in the legal profession, and she would become a teacher at a government higher secondary school for girls.

Over the many months Gopi Krishna had spent in Kashmir, there had been a gradual but very significant change in his experiences. Exactly how and when this progression occurred is not known; however, he writes about there being a marked difference by the time he was back in Jammu in November, this time staying with an old friend. The radiance and expansion of consciousness had increased yet again, and although he was still avoiding meditation, he would often sink into an altered state without any effort: "I sank deeper and deeper into myself, engulfed more and more by the lustrous waves of consciousness, which appeared to grow in size and extent the more I allowed myself to sink without resistance into the sea of consciousness in which I often found myself immersed." A transformation in the halo of awareness that surrounded his head made him continually conscious that he was breathing, walking, and acting in an all-pervasive and homogeneous life force that seemed neither to be affected by his actions nor to affect them. It seemed to him as if his consciousness had now transcended certain limitations and was able to be "in direct touch with its own substance on all sides, like a sentient dew drop floating intact in an ocean of pure being, without mingling with the surrounding mass of water."[36]

These gradual transformations kept occurring. By that December of 1949 he was noticing that these states were not only more frequent, they were becoming a source of joy and strength. These changes were so gradual that at first he assumed they were due to nothing more than the warmer, more pleasant climate in Jammu. By the third week in December, though, he was aware of another change: the lyrics and rhythms of his favorite mystic poets, which had often been floating through his consciousness during his transcendent states, remained more fixed in his mind. Slowly, an unexpected, unconscious impulse was rising up in him to try his hand at writing poetry. Even though he had never before evinced any talent or any inclination to do so, he sat down with paper and pencil on several occasions and made the attempt.[37] By his own admission the results were both sterile and puerile. Still he kept at it, writing in Kashmiri, for several hours a day over the next few weeks. In spite of his efforts, he could see absolutely no improvement in the quality of the verse he was attempting to write. Later in life he would look back on this dogged determination and the inexplicable impulse that had brought it on as an indication that he was being prepared—in a sense, schooled—by an unseen, internal force for what was perhaps the most extraordinary development yet in his ongoing transformation.

The defining moment of this aspect of the transformation came one afternoon when a young woman who was an active member of Samiti in Kashmir was visiting in Jammu. She had come by to visit Gopi Krishna to hear news of the group's efforts back in Srinagar. Walking her back to her destination after the visit, they came to the Tawi River, which separated the city of Jammu into two sections. As they crossed the Tawi Bridge over the river, an extraordinary sensation overcame him.[38] His awareness of his companion and his physical surroundings faded and was replaced by a blaze of light and the perception of a conscious presence that enveloped him and overshadowed the material world. Suddenly, out of this conscious presence, two lines of Kashmiri verse, written in luminous letters, floated into the air before him.

Although this couplet was not published in any of his books, there is fortunately a record of it. Decades later, in a discourse he was giving in Nishat, then a village near Srinagar, he quoted the verse:

> I will also, now, explain to you my own experience. I had absolutely no liking for verse, and I had never concerned myself with it. Years after the awakening, I suddenly felt an urge to write, and write in poetry. But it was a great difficulty for me to be able now to understand the rhyme and the meter. I had absolutely no knowledge of it nor had ever given any attention to it. Then one day, while I was crossing a bridge, a couplet came to me in a moment, complete, without any effort. And

that couplet was a beautiful Kashmiri verse, and that couplet was, "O, you doubter, who is depressed, don't lose hope. Stretch your hand to the Divine. Leave all your burden on Him and don't nurse this fear in your heart."

Although the English translation is lovely and profoundly meaningful, the actual Kashmiri verse is even more remarkable. Regarding it he said,

The construction, the music and the beauty of this work is, I should say, absolutely stunning. There is such a pun on words and such a combination of different sounds that I could never, even if I had worked hard on it for a month, I could never do it. And then I started to write in different languages, soon after.[39]

Coming out of the transcendent state that the couplet had come to him in, he found his young friend staring at him, nonplussed by how he had become so totally lost to the world. In his attempt to explain what had happened, he recited the verse that had come to him. She, in turn, was amazed by the beauty and depth of the words. Perhaps Gopi Krishna had mentioned his puerile efforts at writing verse, for when he tells the story he mentions that the young woman added that the sudden, seemingly effortless creation of this exquisite verse was made all the more astounding not only by how rapidly it had appeared but by the fact that it had been done by someone who "had never been visited by the muse before."[40] After he parted from his friend, he walked slowly home, immersed in gratitude not just for receiving the beautiful verse but for finally having something occur that was verifiable rather than being a totally subjective, internal experience. Although he didn't make the connection until later that night, it was also the first unmistakable example of the siddhis associated with kundalini awakening: as the Tantric texts say, poetry drips like honey off the awakened yogi's tongue.

He spent the rest of the day in deep thought and contemplation. Considering the myriad implications of all that had just happened, he became aware of two points in particular. First, the verse had not been the result of any deliberate mental effort on his part, and second, he could not by any means claim the artistic creation as being his own. Reflecting on these and other matters, he spent the evening aware to some extent of his surroundings, but in a state best described as a kind of a semitrance. He tried to eat, but the food was tasteless to him. Sitting at the table with the half-eaten meal before him, he suddenly and completely without effort or intention on his part found himself in the same state of wondrous cosmic awareness that he had experienced during Christmas in 1937. The only differences were that the glow that had encircled him on that day was replaced by the silvery, penetrating radiance that he had by now been experiencing for some time and that the sound of the roaring waterfall was now that of a melodiously humming glade filled with bees:

> The marvelous aspect of the condition lay in the sudden realization that, although linked to the body and surroundings, I had expanded in an indescribable manner into a titanic personality, conscious from within of an immediate and direct contact with an intensely conscious universe, a wonderful inexpressible immanence all around me....
>
> It was an amazing and staggering experience for which I can cite no parallel and no simile, an experience beyond all and everything belonging to this world conceivable by the mind or perceptible to the senses. I was intensely aware internally of a marvelous being so concentratedly and massively conscious as to out-luster and out-stature infinitely the cosmic image present before me, not only in point of extent and brightness, but in point of reality and substance as well. The phenomenal world, ceaselessly in motion, characterized by creation, incessant change, and dissolution, receded into the background and assumed the appearance of an extremely thin, rapidly melting layer of foam upon a substantial rolling ocean of life, a veil of exceedingly fine vapor before an infinitely large conscious sun....
>
> During this period...there were intervals of deeper and lesser penetration not distinguishable by the flow of time but by the state of immanence, which, at the point of the deepest penetration, assumed such an awe-inspiring, almighty, all-knowing, blissful, and at the same

time absolutely motionless, intangible, and formless character that the invisible line demarcating the material world and the boundless, all-conscious Reality ceased to exist, the two fusing into one; the mighty ocean sucked up by a drop, the enormous three-dimensional universe swallowed by a grain of sand, the entire creation, the knower and the known, the seer and the seen, reduced to an inexpressible sizeless void which no mind could conceive nor any language describe.[41]

After about half an hour of being lost in this cosmic transcendental state, he slowly began to come back to everyday reality, but before he did he found the couplets that would follow the verse that had come to him on the Tawi Bridge floating in his luminescent mind. Fully formed, the couplets dropped from the surrounding intelligence like snowflakes, indistinct on high but revealing their crystalline shapes and patterns when near. The beautifully worded lines came one after another, complete with rhyme and meter. Rising from the table, he went immediately to his room to try to capture the words before they were lost to him. Even though some faded immediately from his mind, after about two hours, he managed to get the verses down to the best of his ability.

Astounded by both the beauty of the words and their wondrous manifestation, he went to bed that night happy and excited. Throughout the evening he had been contemplating what had been happening to him. In all his years of considering whether his experiences could in actuality be related to kundalini, a major stumbling block had always been that he had had no inclination for what he referred to as the "supersensible" except for those few premonitory dreams he had had years earlier. While he had also certainly experienced the radiant cosmic Oneness that he felt sure was what the mystics and saints had written about, he had not—at least, not until now—experienced anything similar to what was described in the Tantric texts and in the stories about awakened kundalini yogis who had divinely inspired poetry drip like honey off their tongues or who achieved literary genius in spite of having only the most rudimentary of educations. While he realized he'd had only the merest taste of this, it was indeed a taste, and it was evidence of that very thing. After all the years of suffering and uncertainty, he had been given a glimpse into the supersensible reality; he had received a bit of the divine grace traditionally believed to be bestowed by kundalini-shakti. He was overwhelmed by his good fortune.

What was perhaps most astounding to him in all this was how undeserving he was of this grace. In the analytical, self-searching manner that never left him, he thought about his life that night. He examined how he had lived, what he had done, and what he had accomplished and found himself to be a very ordinary human being, certainly not one who had distinguished himself in such a way as to deserve such divine grace. But there he was. After years of rational observation and examination of both his inner and outer worlds, he could now come to no other conclusion but that he had awakened kundalini and reached the extraordinary, supernatural state written about in the Tantric texts. He fell asleep that night humbled beyond words.

If events of that day were astounding, the events of the next few weeks would make them pale. For the next fortnight, these exquisite couplets and verses, always in his native language of Kashmiri, would continue to flow unbidden into his mind, and he would attempt to write them down as quickly as he could. On one occasion during this two-week period, he had virtually the same experience as he had had on the evening of the Tawi Bridge incident. He was sitting in a chair reading a piece he had composed the day before when he felt an inclination to lean back, relax, and await what would happen. Without any effort on his part, he found himself back again in the indescribable, supreme, transcendental state, detached from the world, insensible to his surroundings, expanding in every direction, and enveloped in a sea of luminescence. He was lost in this "inexpressible void" for about half an hour, and in the moments of transitioning from one world to the next, he found another beautiful composition as if it were waiting for his conscious mind to become cognizant of it.

Toward the end of this period, the verses started to come in English. Since this was a language he was comfortable with, this change did not seem particularly surprising. A few days later, the language of the verses changed to Urdu. This again was not particularly surprising as he had a good working knowledge of Urdu and had little difficulty transcribing the verses as they came to him. After a few more days, another alteration occurred. This time the poetry came to him in Punjabi. This was now more difficult for him to transcribe as, although he had a good conversational knowledge and understanding of it from the friends he had in school in Lahore, he had never actually read any books in it. Still, he made every effort to capture the verses as best he could.

If he had been able to look at this from the perspective we have now and to see how the transmission and subsequent transcription of these verses was becoming increasingly challenging—almost as if he were being trained or taught a new skill—he might not have been quite so stunned by the next development. Nevertheless, he was indeed completely nonplussed when after a few days of writing in Punjabi, the verses began to flow into his mind in Persian—a language he could not read or speak. Still, the Kashmiri language is rich in Persian words, and he recognized some of the words and the poetic form the lines were taking as they appeared to him. Regardless, it took a great effort to capture the words, and many were missing from his final efforts on the Persian pieces.

Working with these few Persian verses took a toll on him: he became extremely exhausted, and he was having prolonged periods of restlessness each night before sleep. Fortunately, the lessons he had learned from the adverse effects of past forays into states of strain and overexcitement came back to him. As difficult as it was to turn his focus away from these alluring states and experiences, he forced himself to do so and gave himself complete rest for several days. After about a week, he was feeling restored and healthy, and he felt it was safe to allow himself to submit to the impulse to enter these elevated states of consciousness once again.

On doing so, he found himself the recipient of the most astounding occurrence in this train of events so far. In the passages where Gopi Krishna writes of this moment, there is a clear indication that he was aware, even before the words floated into his consciousness, that in a few moments he was going to be expected to transcribe a poem in a language he knew nothing about. Sensing this, he felt both a thrilling anticipation and some degree of fear. On feeling the inclination he should become prepared, he allowed himself to sink into the semitrance condition in which these transmissions occurred. Once he did, verses began coming to him in German, a language he had never studied, never learned, never read, and to the best of his memory, never even heard spoken.

To say he was amazed at this development is a gross understatement as he was aware that it was a "complete negation of the time-honored truth that language is an acquired and not an inherited possession." In a broader sense, it was a negation of our time-honored notions of a limited, compartmentalized reality that is bound on all sides by how we perceive time, space, and distance. As further evidence of this, in the following days verses came to him next in Italian and French. These were followed by a few verses in Sanskrit and Arabic. "Surely," he later wrote, "there could be nothing more convincing than the phenomena I had witnessed during the previous few weeks to bring the idea irresistibly home to me that I was in occasional contact with an inexpressible fount of all knowledge." It seemed to him that the only limiting factor in this foray was caused by his own limitations, so that if he had had the capacity to do so, he could have transcribed verses in any language at all.

Daily now he was now diving into these supernal realms of consciousness. With the advent of this inspired creativity (a term he would later use in the kundalini hypothesis he would eventually propose for scientific study), the doubts that had plagued him for years about whether his experiences were truly related to kundalini awakening and the worries about potentially developing mental illness vanished, and he was left with an immense and undying gratitude to the Divine.

Out of sheer determination and force of habit, he kept to his daily routine of going to his office. As much as he tried to prevent it, it was inevitable that his office mates would notice his altered behavior and the way he would unavoidably sink into moments of profoundly deep absorption. In spite of Gopi Krishna's best efforts to keep what was happening to him to himself, between what his colleagues at work and the friend he was staying with must have observed, word leaked out. Soon streams of people were coming to see him. At first, unwilling to appear rude or conceited, he tried to speak with them all, but it soon became apparent that this exertion was taking a great toll on his health. One of the first signs was that his sleep—as it had in the past when he had strained or overstimulated his system—became interrupted. Thinking this meant he needed less sleep, he erroneously concluded it was a sign he was becoming more detached from the physical world, more spiritual. As this sense of detachment became stronger, he felt the pull that had drawn mystics to renounce the world. He even began to toy with the idea that he could walk away from life as he knew it, becoming a complete renunciate. Concerned that this might actually happen, his host scolded him. This no doubt helped to remind him of his worldly responsibilities. His urge to become a renunciate was also tempered by an awareness of what he saw as a weakness in his constitution that would render him physically incapable of living the unspeakably hard life of a wandering ascetic. Looking back on this later, he would speculate that it was this very weakness that was at least in part responsible for him being able to observe so clearly the physiological aspects of kundalini awakening and how it was affected by external factors such as diet and regularity in lifestyle.

For about a month, Gopi Krishna lived in "a state of triumph and spiritual exaltation it is impossible to describe." Fortunately, he gradually became aware that the overstimulation was beginning to take the same toll as it had in the past. He stopped seeing the stream of visitors, he began to pay serious attention to his diet, and at some point he took yet another leave from his office. Once again he devoted himself to daily, worldly activities that helped him avoid falling into those states of utter absorption.

Around the middle of March, when spring would be blossoming in Kashmir, he realized it was time to return to Srinagar. Leaving the thought of ever becoming a renunciate, he returned to the home, wife, and family that had long been his source of refuge.

Gopi Krishna's adult children, when interviewed for this biography, told the tale of one such homecoming by their father in which he greeted them outside the house with the words in Kashmiri that could be translated to "I am divine" or "I am a god." Although exactly which homecoming this was could not be pinned down, it makes sense that it might well have been this one. What makes this moment so significant is that it contrasts so sharply with the human being that Gopi Krishna was. On relating this event, his family members stated that nothing like this was ever again stated or even implied by him. They, like everyone who knew him and has written about him, emphasized repeatedly how deeply and abidingly humble he was, how he stressed his ordinariness as a human being, and how he frequently pointed out that these experiences did not make him special or better or above anyone, for it was nothing less than the birthright of every one of us.

Perhaps this incident provides a brief window into his state during the first few months after the events that began that day on the Tawi Bridge. It certainly makes it sound as if there were instances when that state of utter "triumph and spiritual exaltation" came back over him. In those moments he must have been utterly awash and overwhelmed then by the realization of his Oneness with the incomprehensible vastness of a cosmic Divine that was not only infinite but intelligent and alive.

Chapter Six

When Poetry Drips like Honey from the Pen

Once Gopi Krishna was back in Srinagar, Bhabi could see that he was exhausted and needed rest. This was hampered by the fact that the news of his strange feats had reached the town and crowds had begun to gather outside his home. After a few days, he found he could see people for several hours a day as long as he spent the rest of the day in light activities and avoided becoming lost in deep absorption. In a few weeks' time, the crowds began to thin out, allowing him to get more rest. This, combined with Bhabi's careful attention to his diet, helped him resume apparent normalcy in about six months. For him at that point, this seems to have meant going about his daily activities without abruptly and unexpectedly diving into the ocean of supernal consciousness and becoming lost to those around him.

When his leave expired he decided not to return to his work. Even though this would cause a financial burden, he knew that in his present state of consciousness he could not possibly work in a busy government office, especially one where his conscience was in frequent conflict with the wishes of his superiors. Beyond this, both the recent military conflict and the governmental shift from being a sovereign princely state to being part of India had brought with them many changes. This resulted in any number of burning issues that needed to be handled with great care at a time when it was extremely difficult to do so. This situation ratcheted up the usual tension in the department to an even higher level. Aware of the strain this would put on his mental health, Gopi Krishna made an application for early retirement. Thankfully, it was accepted, as this meant his family would at least have a small pension to live on. Once this was finalized, his time was at last his own, and he was able to rejoin Samiti's efforts. Although he had not been active in the movement for several months, a few of the dedicated members had kept it alive.

The ravages created by the massive dislocation caused by the partition and the war continued. The cultural problems, social issues, and resulting suffering remained. Like others, Gopi Krishna struggled to take care of his family. At the same time he threw himself into his work with Samiti in response to the humanitarian cry that was resounding throughout the Kashmir Valley.

According to the descriptions in some yoga texts, the condition Gopi Krishna was now living in would make him a *jīvan mukta*, literally a person who has reached a state of perennial cosmic consciousness while still being in the physical body. In yoga, jīvan mukti—the state itself—is generally considered the same as the highest state of samādhi. Known as *sahaja-samādhi* or just *sahaja*, it is exceedingly rare. The renowned authority on yoga Georg Feuerstein describes it as a condition in which the yogi lives in essence in two worlds at the same time: in perennial enlightenment or liberation on one hand, and in the mundane world on the other.[42] Gopi Krishna used similar words to describe the state in a discourse he gave in Nishat, Kashmir, in 1977:

> ...there can be a state of perennial ecstasy, known as the sahaja, or jivan-mukti state. A man who has this state of consciousness lives in two worlds: the world of senses and the world of consciousness. In the world of senses, he sees the world as you see it. But in the world of consciousness he is totally different from you."[43]

Some contemporary Western definitions of jīvan mukti give the impression that anyone who can reach extended, profoundly deep levels of meditation—possibly the lower levels of samādhi—generally living in a peaceful state can be held to be a jīvan mukta. The references to this state in the sacred texts, however, make it inescapable that this is an extraordinarily singular level of spiritual attainment. A passage in the *Chāndogya Upanishad*, one of the earliest Upanishads, contains parallels to Gopi Krishna's descriptions of the internal sounds he heard and the ineffable luminosity he constantly lived in. The two verses below make it evident that a person who experiences this becomes worthy of renown. Another translation says that he becomes celebrated and then repeats it for emphasis, saying, "yea, he becomes celebrated."[44] This verse is also significant because while Gopi Krishna may have lived in this light, it reminds us—as he often did—that this light lives within each of us.

> Now the light that shines beyond the heavens, upon the backs of all, upon the backs of everything, higher than the highest—verily, that is the same as that is here within the person. It is visible…when one perceives (its) warmth in this body. It is audible when one closes one's ears and hears a kind of sound as of a bee, a bull, or a blazing fire. One should reverence that visible and audible light. He who knows this, he who knows this becomes one beautiful to see, one heard of in renown.[45]

Although Gopi Krishna had far too much humility to ever refer to himself as a jīvan mukta, it seems evident that this is the state that most accurately corresponds to the condition he lived in after December 1949. Historically in India, those spiritual seekers who managed to reach this state either became renunciates or had already left the material world to live in ashrams or as wandering mendicants. While Gopi Krishna had resisted the urge to take this path when he was a teenager and then again after that day on Tawi Bridge, he was again tempted now that he was experiencing the full, unfettered glory of perennial cosmic consciousness. He longed to take the renunciate's path so that he could remain totally absorbed in this state. In an ashram, where his condition would have been honored, all his basic needs would have been provided for so that he did not ever have to leave his state of supernal consciousness—just as throughout Christian history mystics who attained the union with the divine known as *unio mystica* often lived in hermitages, convents, or monasteries where the necessities of life were taken care of. In addition to having their basic needs supplied, the mystic or the yogi in the state of samādhi who lived in one of these sheltered places would have also been living in an environment free from the stressful chaos of the outside world. Further, the daily routine and activities in these settings would have been kept to a regulated schedule—a seemingly mundane factor but one frequently mentioned by Gopi Krishna in regards to the healthy awakening of kundalini.

Had Gopi Krishna decided to walk away from his family to live in an ashram or become a wandering mendicant, it would have been considered acceptable behavior. In one of the traditional Hindu views of a way of living there are four stages. They are *brahmacharya*, the student stage, from childhood until about the age of twenty-four; *gṛhastha*, the householder stage, a period until about the age of forty-eight during which one marries, raises a family, and enjoys the pleasures of the world; *vānaprastha*, the stage of retirement in which one gradually begins to withdraw from the world and its pleasures, turns responsibilities over to the children, and focuses more on the spiritual; and finally *saṃnyāsa*, when one becomes a renunciate, leaving all material goods behind in order to focus on obtaining *mokṣa*, or liberation. Although the saṃnyāsa would generally begin in a person's early seventies, it is acceptable at any time after one has completed the student stage.

Instead of becoming a renunciate, however, Gopi Krishna chose the more difficult path of living simultaneously in two very different worlds experienced by the jīvan mukta. Even though he alluded to there being a weakness in his nature—evidently a reference to his dietary sensitivity and susceptibility to extremes in temperature—that would have made it impossible for him to live the hard life of the wandering mendicant, he was much more concerned with the devastation his renunciation would wreak on his family. In fact, for the rest of his life he would counsel spiritual seekers against any path that would inflict harm on their dependents.

The culminating stages of his becoming a jīvan mukta certainly began that auspicious day on the Tawi Bridge in Jammu, and if the earlier reference to it taking about six months after that for his life to become more normal is correct, it seems reasonable to assume that by about May or June of 1950, this condition was fairly constant: he could look inward and enter the world of supernal, undifferentiated, cosmic awareness, and yet he could turn his gaze outward and function in the everyday world. And yet, even when he looked outward, the world he saw was bathed in the silvery luster of a luminescent radiance, surely making him perpetually aware of the state of divine grace in which he lived. That he was able to move so successfully between the states of ordinary and cosmic consciousness for the rest of his life was, at least in part, what allowed him to create such detailed, rational accounts of his experiences.

When Gopi Krishna himself described his condition after the events following the Tawi Bridge incident, he often spoke of it as having become stabilized. Certainly he no longer doubted that he had awakened kundalini as it was discussed in the ancient tradition or that he was experiencing the inspired creativity that is described in the renowned Tantric texts on kundalini. One of the texts containing such references that he was aware of, perhaps even early on, was *Saundaryalaharī*. It is attributed to Śaṅkarācārya, one of the most widely revered sages of Indian history. The very first lines of the text depict the union of Shakti with her beloved Shiva—the traditional imagery used to represent kundalini-shakti's awakening and rising to the thousand-petaled lotus in the brain. Inspired creativity and genius are both mentioned in verses throughout the text. One verse describes words "sweeter than the sweetness of honey, milk, and grapes" flowing from the yogi's lips; another says that the seeker becomes the "creator of great works of art"; yet another speaks of the way the "lotus-clusters of the great poets' minds" bloom with profound words that delight.[46]

Saundaryalaharī and similar texts, such as the previously mentioned *Panchastavi*, make it plain that this flow of exquisite words is a siddhi, a gift. In the poetic language of the texts, these gifts are bestowed by kundalini-shakti, as the Goddess, upon the awakened yogi. Throughout his life, Gopi Krishna stressed that his abilities were granted to him. Before that day on the Tawi Bridge, he says, he was a man with absolutely no poetic ability. Afterward, he was amazed to find lyrical words flowing effortlessly from his pen. As you will see in later chapters, this poetic ability and output did not decrease. On the contrary, right up until the time of his death he experienced prodigious outpourings of verse. But never once in all those years did he take personal credit for what he produced, saying always it was a gift of grace from the divine.

Unfortunately, in spite of his living most of his life in a state of luminosity and grace, it has been his suffering and the negative aspects that have attracted the most attention in some circles. Part of the reason for this is that his written descriptions of these difficult periods are so vivid that they capture the reader's attention. It may also be that the way *Living with Kundalini* was created has added to this issue. Before the book was produced, it was decided that it would combine the material in his first autobiography with supplemental material that Gopi Krishna had written years later in what was informally known as the *Autobiography Part II & Autobiography Part III*. The project was undertaken several years after his death when an experienced editor named Leslie Shepard, who had met and greatly admired Gopi Krishna, agreed to take on the editing. His task of trying to honor Gopi Krishna's words while combining two sets of sometimes overlapping material was made even more difficult by the fact that in telling his own story, Gopi Krishna used the more free-flowing style typical of his heritage rather than the more empirical style of his prose works on kundalini.

Because this style does not adhere to the strictly linear order that we tend to find in Western biographies and autobiographies, it is sometimes challenging for the reader to determine time frames. Before doing the focused research for this book, for instance, this author had the impression that the intense suffering characterized by burning heat and sensations of flames went on unabated for years. Indeed, lines such as "for years I was like one bound hand and foot to a log racing madly on a torrent"[47] contribute to such an impression. It is hoped that the preceding chapters help put this in perspective by showing that within that twelve-year span, two periods of horrible suffering stand out: the nine weeks after Christmas 1937 and the approximately twelve weeks following the same holiday in 1943.[48] To be sure, the entire twelve-year period was fraught with unimaginable challenges that required great self-control and tremendous discipline: he was never completely sure what was happening to him and was apprehensive about his mental health; he experienced bizarre, inexplicable, frequently painful physical sensations that were, as far as he knew, unheard of;

the slightest miscalculation in diet could disrupt his digestive system causing prolonged, excruciating upsets; subsequent disruptions of the flow of energy in his body could, in turn, cause virtually intolerable mood swings. In spite of these ongoing challenges, Gopi Krishna was able to work, raise his family, and seem—at least to all but his family—to be functioning fairly normally in the outer world, except for those extreme periods at the beginning of 1938 and in 1944.

Still, it cannot be denied that Gopi Krishna did in some instances place a degree of emphasis on the negative aspects of his experiences. Consequently, it is somewhat understandable that many people who have taken a cursory look at either of his autobiographies might have the impression that he was telling people that kundalini was dangerous and to avoid it all costs. Reading his other sixteen works or listening to the audios of his discourses makes it patently obvious that this was not the case.

While he does strike a cautionary tone about kundalini awakening, he is generally talking about the forceful and premature awakening of kundalini and not the gradual, healthy awakening that he believed was the basis for the ongoing evolution of consciousness in every human being. Because this fact has been widely missed and his emphasis misunderstood in some quarters, it is worthwhile to consider some of the reasons he might have handled this topic in this way. One is that, even today, there are yoga teachers who claim that because kundalini is a positive force, it can have no negative effects. It is evident that these so-called gurus are not familiar with the scriptures and Tantric sacred texts on kundalini. An individual who was indeed familiar with these texts was Lilian Silburn. A Sanskrit scholar from France, she was one of the earlier twentieth-century academics to research these works in India. After spending years on these efforts, she wrote *Kundalini: The Energy of the Depths*. An esteemed translation and commentary on some of the most important Kashmiri texts, it draws mainly on material from the *Tantrāloka* of Abhinavagupta. Born in Kashmir in 950 CE, Abhinavagupta was one of the greatest, if not the greatest, philosophers of Kashmiri Shaivism—the tradition of Gopi Krishna's homeland with its Tantric approach to the worship of Shiva, emphasis on the divine feminine Shakti, and detailed teachings on kundalini. Silburn's work opens with a description of the unimaginable power of kundalini, saying,

> Therefore, to probe her secrets, one must seek the help of a master belonging to a special lineage and endowed with unfailing knowledge.
>
> It cannot be overemphasized that without such a guide, or by following a powerless and ignorant teacher, the arousal of Kuṇḍalinī will have disastrous results. Very often, the serious troubles observed in some Christian mystics attributed to hysteria have no other cause than a defective ascent of Kuṇḍalinī.... When this is the case, one can better understand why the Śiva masters have been so careful in this matter and have kept all these practices shrouded in mystery.[49]

Works like this make it apparent that Gopi Krishna was on firm academic and sacred ground when he cautioned about the forceful, rapid, or premature awakening of kundalini.

His cautions about kundalini awakening may also have been spurred in part simply by the fact that he was an exceptionally caring and compassionate man who would not have wanted anyone to undergo any of the difficulties he had endured. That he had undergone them and ultimately succeeded in his quest was due in no small part to the self-discipline and control he had worked hard to develop in his earlier years. When he was making concentrated efforts to have writings published in the West in the mid-1960s, countless numbers of young people were flooding to India to ostensibly find enlightenment. Many were taking drugs and/or getting involved in extreme spiritual practices. In other parts of the world the interest in yoga, meditation, spirituality, and the occult was building in waves. In several places in his writing, Gopi Krishna refers to this yearning for the spiritual, misguided though it sometimes was, as an indication of the embryonic budding of the awakening of kundalini in those who felt it—a call, as it were, by the evolutionary energy urging us further down the path.

While many of these young people were no doubt sincere, it is safe to say that few of them would have appeared to have developed a great deal of self-discipline or self-control. Observing this as he must have, Gopi Krishna might well have sought to caution them. Certainly in his correspondence with those who over the years wrote to him because they thought they might be experiencing kundalini, he strongly advised against any extreme practice that might prematurely accelerate the awakening.

In spite of his sometimes cautionary tone, it can hardly be overemphasized that Gopi Krishna believed that the awakening of kundalini was a natural evolutionary process that was, ultimately, leading humankind to a higher state of consciousness. Although the day when the human race might reach what Teilhard de Chardin called the Omega Point and writers like the nineteenth-century physician and researcher Richard Maurice Bucke called perennial Cosmic Consciousness might be hundreds of years away, Gopi Krishna firmly believed we were on that road.

He also believed that kundalini could be safely awakened—and would be—by people on the spiritual path today. In fact, he also believed many people today were already undergoing an accelerated process—in most cases not as dramatic as his, but accelerated nonetheless. As will be detailed in later chapters, one reason he spent his life promoting kundalini research was so that the scientific and medical communities would correctly understand what these individuals were undergoing and, rather than prescribing drugs and treatments that could be harmful, would be able to give advice that would facilitate their processes.

When asked directly if kundalini could be awakened and states of higher consciousness reached, Gopi Krishna replied in the affirmative. In his Kashmir discourses, he discussed the dangers of real hatha yoga—historically, a practice developed to forcefully awaken kundalini—and then went on to refer to the types of yogas discussed in the *Bhagavad Gītā*:

> ...But, with [these] forms of Yoga, with a moderate life, in ninety-nine percent of cases, the arousal can be safe and healthy. The danger attends only violent methods where the body is not yet prepared for its arousal. But in the case of normal Yoga—moderate meditation, prayer and a temperate life, dedicated to a noble purpose, with a control over greed and ambition, with lust and anger subdued—there is no danger to the *sadhaka*.

This is how Lalleshwari expresses herself.... That is: "After coming into this world, I did not seek power or wealth. What moderate possessions, what moderate food, what moderate clothes Heaven provided me with, I considered to be sufficient for myself. I was content with the minimum needs supplied to me by Heaven. And all the pain and suffering that came my way I bore with patience. And by thus acting in my life I reached my Lord." A contented life, devoted to a noble cause, moderate wealth, moderate possessions, a temperate way of living, restraint in sex, truth, compassion, fortitude, strength of will and purpose, are the assets that you need to win to cosmic consciousness. There is no magical formula. The evolutionary impulse has been planted by Heaven into the body of each of us to lead to the emergence of a nobler, a purer and a loftier race, which can live in harmony and peace on this earth.[50]

Chapter Seven

Social Justice—Amid the Ravages of War

Life did not suddenly become easy for Gopi Krishna on his return to Srinagar in 1949 after what he would later come to call his "first experience of the unseen" in Jammu: even though the kundalini process within him had stabilized, the world around him had not. Countless people remained displaced from the exodus caused by partition or dispossessed by the vagaries of war, and these conditions would persist in Kashmir for a very long time. For Gopi Krishna's family, the situation would not become better for nearly seven years.

Bhabi's family, who had been supportive of Gopi Krishna's family in many ways in the past, had been devastated by the invasion. Not only had her father been shot dead, but her older brother had been imprisoned with other non-Muslims when the more northerly town of Bunji was captured by Muslim forces and held for a full year.[51] In Baramulla the family home had been plundered. Among the items of value taken was a five-kilogram gold statuette of the goddess Durga. Not only had the piece held great religious significance for the family, it had also been a means of preserving what wealth they had in a time and place where banking was not known as it is today. With Bhabi's father dead and her older brother in captivity, her remaining two brothers were left responsible for the survival of the wives and children in Baramulla whose lives had also been devastated by the war.

Without hope of help, Gopi Krishna, Bhabi, and the boys struggled on. Nirmal remembers a time during this period when the family went two days without food. Conditions like this were terrible for the growing boys, but also a tremendous strain on Gopi Krishna's system. Even though his kundalini awakening had now stabilized, he was still in an extremely extraordinary and sensitive state, and instead of living perhaps in a peaceful, regulated ashram where his needs would have been met, he was existing in the midst of the chaos and destitution left by war. While his need for massive amounts of food that had occurred during and after the Jammu experience had settled down, he continued to need highly nutritious food and to eat more than he had before. In the postwar turmoil, food prices came to be as much as ten times higher than they had been before the war, and now that Gopi Krishna had taken his early-retirement pension, his family was forced to live on half his previous income at a time when even his whole salary would have been inadequate. Not getting the food he required caused serious digestive upsets and other physical disturbances, sometimes lasting for months, and in one instance, for almost two years. On three separate occasions the impoverished conditions he was living in brought him close to death. One blessing was that even in the most difficult situations, the radiant halo and the vital energy he had experienced since the days after the Tawi Bridge remained constant and consistent. During the worst of times, however, other aspects of the sublime ethereal states of consciousness were temporarily lost to him.

Throughout all this, Gopi Krishna tried to function to all intents and purposes normally in the world. He says that only Bhabi was privy to how unusual his condition was and how dependent he was on his dietary needs. Yet his sons—Jagdish, who was fifteen by 1949, and Nirmal, who was ten—must have been aware of what happened when their father didn't get enough food, for Gopi Krishna later poignantly wrote of how these two hungry, growing boys would sometimes offer him portions of their own food at mealtime. Bhabi, it is needless to say, did the same.

It is heart-wrenching to imagine how this man, who was exceptionally kind and compassionate even before his awakening, felt when he saw his wife and sons suffering to make these sacrifices. And, much to his enduring pain,

Bhabi soon had to make even more sacrifices: as the political chaos in Kashmir continued for months and then years, and their own impoverished condition worsened, Bhabi was forced to sell the jewelry she had brought as her dowry to her marriage almost twenty-five years before.

Throughout his life and writings, Gopi Krishna credited Bhabi with saving him again and again. During interviews for this biography, Ragya, Jagdish, and Nirmal echoed this. While being Gopi Krishna's children was the greatest honor of their lives, the debt of gratitude they owed their mother was inexpressible.

When Gopi Krishna returned from Jammu in 1948 a changed man, Bhabi's role changed too, and she took it on with aplomb. She also had the intuitive depth to understand what was going on with her husband and to handle it accordingly. Word of Gopi Krishna's experience in Jammu and the poetry he had written in languages unknown to him had spread to his hometown even before he arrived. The result was that literally hundreds of people came to see him and lined up outside the door to his home. As he had when crowds had first come to see him in Jammu, he tried to see each person individually and listen to their stories, often ones of misery and loss. Many individuals were suffering from cultural tensions and the aftermath of the war even more than his own family was. Tragically, many of these people came to him believing that he now had miraculous powers and would be able to lift them out of their misfortune. In his autobiographies Gopi Krishna uses his description of this to discuss the widespread historical belief that visionaries had supernatural powers as well as a special connection to the cosmic intelligence that would allow them to intercede with fate or contravene the laws of nature, allowing them to save others from their suffering. However, no amount of denial on his part could convince many of his petitioners that he had no such power, and people continued to flock to him, petitioning him for help. Often their harrowing tales left him as shaken with grief as they were. Of the afflicted men and women who came to him, he wrote,

> ...my heart went out to them in sympathy. In their position, I too might have acted in the same manner. My utter inability to relieve their distress added so greatly to my sorrow at their misery that, unable to

bear it, I sometimes had to seek the sanctuary of my deeper being to gain assurance and strength to overcome it.[52]

He did not have the magic wand that could make their troubles fall away, but he did know from profound personal experience that the luminescent consciousness that he was now in touch with could do just that. That he could access that supernal world of radiant Oneness when others could not might well have been one of the factors that eventually spurred him to dedicate his life to trying to convince the world that this access to the divine was the birthright of every human being. At the time, however, it does not seem that his life's mission was quite so firmly fixed in his mind, and there is no doubt that he suffered along with those who came to him. The words *compassion* and *sympathy* have become so overused that we scarcely realize that they mean to literally share an emotion—passion or pathos—*with* someone. To experience, in other words, the pain they are experiencing right along with them. But this is exactly what Gopi Krishna was doing, and it was taking a toll on him. Lacking the miraculous powers the petitioners ascribed to him, all he could do was listen with a great depth of understanding and console them as best he could. Fortunately, in some cases this was enough, and the individuals left feeling at greater peace than when they arrived. Still, he was left weighted down with their grief and vividly aware that

> forming as we do the tiny individual cells of a mighty organism, we share alike the sorrows and misery existing in the world; but, debarred from realizing this by the wall of ego segregating each cell from the rest...[53]

This profound insight into the human condition and the realization that we are all One has been the message of mystics and visionaries from all traditions since time immemorial. While Gopi Krishna indicated that transcendental powers might well be attributed to some visionaries, he added that we are in error if we think they can contravene the laws of nature or alter a course of events that has been ordained. He later wrote:

The curative and other powers sometimes exercised by mystics and saints never went beyond the sphere of individual application, and it was left for people of genius who brought vision to the aid of intellect to devise universally efficacious remedies for scourges like smallpox and to make other discoveries in the physical realm, a task which was neither accomplished by nor fell within the province of prophets and visionaries.[54]

That he could not work miracles did not mean he was not experiencing siddhis in addition to the ability to receive inspired poetry. Even though displaying them would undoubtedly have gained him adulation and helped ease their terrible financial situation, he "refused to be tempted into making a vulgar exhibition or impious use of the priceless gift" he had been given.[55]

While there was no magic that could solve the suffering he saw around him, being the immanently practical man he was, he realized that social activism and reform could help a great deal. When the streams of people were coming to him with their problems, he noticed that in many cases their suffering had been caused by social ills. Since Samaj Sudhar Samiti was still functioning, he was now ready to throw whatever energy he could into its efforts once again. This had dual benefits for him. Now that he was no longer going into his government office, it gave him a place to work and be around congenial people without limiting his freedom. In addition, the realization that he was doing something very concrete to help ease the misery of others kept him from the temptation he occasionally felt to retreat totally into the world of the sublime: even though he had made the firm decision to never become a renunciate, the longing to lose himself permanently in cosmic bliss was sometimes intense.

In order to understand the importance of Samiti in his life after the stabilization of his kundalini awakening in 1949, it is worthwhile examining in more detail the role the organization—and his dedication to fighting social injustice—played in his life earlier on. When he had founded Samiti in 1946, Gopi Krishna was already familiar with social-justice work. In 1945 he had become chair of the Low-Paid Employees Association in Jammu and Kashmir, an organization that still exists today, actively fighting for the rights of workers and often staging protests and strikes when needed.

Shortly after its founding in 1946, Samiti acquired rented office space. In those early years of Samiti and before his retirement, whenever Gopi Krishna's department was in Srinagar his habit was to return home from work at about four in the afternoon, when he would have tea and a short rest. As long as his health would allow it, at about five o'clock he would return to the Samiti offices, staying until about eight o'clock. While there, he would make plans with the other association members and hear the stories of those who came to petition Samiti for help.

Unfortunately, with the exception of one or two events, it has not been possible to assign firm dates to many of the specific activities that Samiti carried out. As briefly mentioned in Chapter Five, due to the Pathan invasion and the ensuing war, Gopi Krishna stayed in Srinagar instead of making his customary office transfer to Jammu throughout 1948 and much of 1949—a period when Samiti, while still concerned with its founding principles, was focused on helping those people, especially women and orphans, who were suffering from the war and displacement. Ragya, Jagdish, and Nirmal all remember that their parents took scores of destitute women, including prostitutes, into their own home, where Bhabi helped them get clean, fed them, and treated them virtually as family members until other situations could be found for them. Other Samiti members may have also sometimes opened their homes, but there is some indication they weren't as willing as Gopi Krishna and Bhabi to take those who were considered to be "fallen" women, who had lost their caste, or who had become very dirty and disheveled. Bhabi had no qualms about such people, and even in situations when she was under great stress herself she took in the destitute. At some point in these early years Samiti managed to either purchase or construct a location for their offices. The area was enclosed in a compound, surrounded by a high fence. It was a large, pleasant space with grass and trees, a main building, a barn, and a few other outbuildings.[56] The main building contained an office area, rooms that could be used for meetings, and space that could sometimes be used as a refuge for the destitute women and orphans. Although it is not certain, it seems possible that having this area available for these women and children meant that Bhabi would not personally have to take people in so often.

Eventually the space in the Samiti compound was also used for teaching women to sew, embroider, and perform other tasks they could use to support themselves, and over time equipment like knitting and sewing machines was purchased for this purpose. A temple was also constructed in the compound, and the priest who cared for it was a member of Samiti. Among other members were a number of teachers. There were also medical professionals and lawyers whose expertise was especially valuable in the case of some of Samiti's more radical actions.

During Samiti's most active years, the site was also used to stage dramatic productions that illustrated the need for the social reforms the group promoted. For instance, plays would be written and put on that might reveal a family left in abject poverty by the dowry they had to provide for their daughter or depict the horrible plight of a woman who, already consumed with grief over the death of her husband, was thrown into the street, while all the wealth her dowry had brought to the home was kept by her husband's family. At times the group would also dramatize scenes from the *Mahabharata*, a great Indian epic that contains a tremendous amount of philosophical and devotional wisdom. These productions were very popular with the people of Srinagar.

One area where Samiti achieved exceptional success during these years related to the unjust treatment of widows. According to long-standing custom, widows were not allowed to remarry. It made no difference if she was very young or even if she was a child bride whose marriage had never been consummated. As mentioned in Chapter Four, a woman who was unfortunate enough to be in a marriage where the husband's family treated her cruelly would sometimes be put on the street, where begging and prostitution were her only options. Even in the best of situations, a widow was expected to essentially mourn for her dead husband until her own death. Customarily, she would have her head shaved and wear only rough-woven, plain saris for the rest of her life. These and other similar practices were meant to strip the woman of not just her beauty but her sexuality: in the Hindi language, the pronoun for a widow becomes *it* rather than *she*. All of these customs were indicative of an overall abhorrence of widows in general that had its roots, at least part, in an age-old superstition that if a woman's husband died, she was in some way at least partially to blame.

When Gopi Krishna's official retirement in 1950 allowed him to focus even more of his energy on Samiti, the group became increasingly concerned with the number of women who had been left widows by the war and the aftermath and were now living in destitution. It occurred to him that one rather straightforward solution to the problem would be for the women to remarry.

While a law was passed in British-ruled India in 1856 allowing for the remarriage of widows, such a ruling would have had little impact on the customary practices in Jammu and Kashmir, especially since the region was not under British rule. Even when the area did become part of India in 1947, a law that had come into effect nearly a century earlier would have made little difference in a land so steeped in its cultural traditions. Undaunted by this widespread, ingrained prejudice against widows, Gopi Krishna began to tackle the problem head on by actively recruiting single men who said they would consider marrying a widow. He found a surprising number of men who were willing, and over time the number grew. Some of these men were widowers themselves; others were men who had not been in a position to marry when they were younger, and some were young, eligible men who could have married a woman with a dowry but who were instead motivated, like other Samiti members, by a desire to do good in the world.

If, and only if, a widow was interested in remarrying, Gopi Krishna or other Samiti leaders would select a few men who they thought would meet the woman's criteria and be a suitable match. These men were carefully vetted by the organization. They had to be of known good character, have a solid means of support, and have a home for the new couple to live in. If the widow was a young woman with children, the leaders had to be assured that the man was willing to accept and care for the children as his own. Once these candidates were selected, the widow could then meet with them and decide if she might like to marry one of them. If so, the wedding would take place when she felt ready.

According to Margaret Kobelt, over 200 of these weddings took place. In albums she possessed, the bride and groom were seated in the center of the picture with Gopi Krishna seated between them, all three beaming and bedecked with garlands of flowers, with family members smiling happily around them. Although this process of selecting a group of potential husbands and having a woman simply pick one might seem strange to some of us today, it should be kept in mind that this was a society in which arranged marriages were the norm. These potential husbands were scrutinized and selected for the widow's consideration in much the same way a caring father would deliberate over prospective husbands for a beloved daughter.

Gopi Krishna's group sometimes took more imperative action. For example, one evening a young woman came to him in tears saying that her good friend was about to commit suicide and pleading with Gopi Krishna to find a way to stop her. The friend was a young widow who had fallen in love with a man who was a teacher, and she had discovered that she was now pregnant. Knowing that, as a widow, she was not allowed to marry and that her child would be shunned by society, she decided her only option was to kill herself. On hearing the story, Gopi Krishna immediately took action. He gathered a number of Samiti members, sending some to locate the young man, and took the doctor, the lawyer, and the priest with him to where the widow lived. After examining her, the doctor confirmed that the woman was indeed pregnant. The teacher soon arrived with the Samiti members who had located him, and the situation was explained to him. The couple was asked if they were both willing to be married. Although their culture had strictures against the remarriage of widows, it was not illegal. When they agreed that they did indeed want to marry, the ceremony was performed by the priest on the spot. The problem was solved, and the young woman's life was saved.

Samiti did not limit its assistance to widows. In a case that occurred during the chaos immediately following the Pathan invasion, a very young woman had been tricked into having sexual relations with a much older man. The man was a bus driver who had an opportunity to deal in the black market that was flourishing in the general disorder. Visiting the house where the desirable girl was staying with her aunt and uncle, he ingratiated himself by bringing hard-to-procure items. He then hired ruffians to watch the house and notify him when the girl was alone so that he could seduce her. Plying her with sweets and other gifts, he accomplished his purpose, and the girl became pregnant. Realizing her condition, she was terrified of telling her aunt and uncle. The man promised to help her end the pregnancy by bringing her an herbal abortifacient. Instead, hoping to force her into marrying him, he brought a harmless tonic. By the time she was aware of what he had done, it was too late to end the pregnancy. Appalled at his duplicity and finally realizing how she had been deceived all along, she began like so many others in her situation to plan her own death.

The girl was not only too young for the man, she was also of a higher caste. Knowing that in normal circumstances he would never be allowed to marry her, the bus driver went to Samiti. Lying, he said that the two were in love and were determined to live together. He asked Samiti to help them avoid the scandal of living together out of wedlock by marrying them. Before agreeing to help him, the organization began their customary investigation of the situation. A female member of Samiti managed to visit the girl and discovered that the girl wanted nothing to do with the man and was terrified about her situation.

The only solution seemed to be to find someone she would be willing to marry. Samiti began a search, and it was not long before a suitable, handsome young man who owned a house and large farm near the city came forward. He was also willing to care for the child as his own, and the girl agreed to marry him. The problem then became how to get the girl out of the house. In the postwar chaos and lawlessness still prevalent in those days, the obsessed bus driver had been able to hire a gang of thugs to watch the house the girl was in and attack anyone who tried to remove her. As the pregnancy became more advanced, the girl became increasingly desperate and suicidal. Realizing the urgency of the situation, Samiti members devised a plan to get her safely away from the house without the attackers realizing it. Setting the plan in motion, they sent a Samiti woman, who was dressed as a nurse wearing a burqa and who was accompanied by a man, to the house. Knocking on the door, they proclaimed loudly enough for the watchers to hear that she was a visiting nurse who was there to examine the girl. After spending an appropriate time inside, the woman and her companion left. Of course, this time it was the pregnant girl who was wearing the burqa. Because the danger of being discovered was still great, a small boat being steered by yet another Samiti member was waiting on a nearby river. After she was safely in the boat, the girl was transported to a waiting carriage, where another cautionary switch was performed. She was then carried to her wedding, happy and relieved for the first time in months.[57]

It might seem incomprehensible to us that a young woman would be so happy after being spirited away in complex subterfuge and taken to a wedding with a man she had never met. She obviously feared, however, a much worse alternative: either being thrown onto the streets by relatives who were incensed by her behavior or being forced into a marriage with a despicable man who she knew would never have her best interests at heart.

Chapter Eight

Radical Acts, Writing, and Rejection

Enclosing homes or other buildings inside a compound was not remarkable in Kashmir or the rest of India in those days, and it is still not unusual today. But it is no wonder that Samiti needed a compound enclosed by a high wall. The traditions and customs they were challenging with their head-on enthusiasm were deeply entrenched in the culture and, in some cases, held sacrosanct. Receiving a hefty dowry was considered the incontrovertible right of anyone who had been blessed with a son. Widows were unclean; prostitutes were worse. Women who lost their caste by marrying beneath their station or outside their faith were nearly as bad. By flying in the face of custom as he did in order to help these women, Gopi Krishna made enemies. In fact, according to Margaret Kobelt, there were three times when he came close to losing his life.

As an example of the dangers involved she tells the story of a woman who ran away from her husband with her sixteen-year-old daughter and came to Gopi Krishna for help. Margaret estimates that the event occurred at some point after Gopi Krishna's retirement from his government job at the beginning of 1950; regardless, by this time his reputation for helping must have been fairly widely known. The woman had come to him with her daughter because her husband was trying to force the girl to marry an elderly man whose only recommendation was that he was not asking for a dowry. Both the girl and her mother were resisting the idea and being beaten daily. Although the mother had gone to both a local government minister and to the police, neither would assist her. She now hoped that Gopi Krishna would not only give them sanctuary but also find a suitable young husband for the girl. While Samiti searched for candidates the girl might approve of, Bhabi took them into her home, keeping them close to her at all times in case the husband came to drag them back and beat them into submission. The husband eventually did arrive one morning after Gopi Krishna had gone to the Samiti office. Accompanied by a gang of men armed with sticks, hammers, and other implements, he began to pound on the door. Bhabi, who was at the back of the house, guessed immediately what was happening. Without hesitation she grabbed a flaming piece of wood from the fire, ran to the door, opened it, and brandished the firebrand at the men. They immediately backed off, giving the neighbors time to run to Samiti for help. When Gopi Krishna and the other Samiti members arrived, armed like the gang was, a violent battle broke out in the street. Many were injured, but the Samiti members did not give up until they had prevailed and the woman and her daughter were safe.

Events like this demonstrated the obvious need for Samiti to have a fenced-in compound. Not only would the woman and her daughter have been safer, Bhabi and the family would not have been put at such risk. While the exact date when the offices and the compound were built is not known, it seems to have been completed by some point in the early 1950s. What is perhaps most remarkable about this is that Gopi Krishna, as not only the founder of Samiti but the undisputed driving force behind its actions, had in effect created a shelter for abused women at a time and in a place that was revolutionary. Just how radical—and decades ahead of its time— this was can be put in perspective by considering the fact that the first well-documented, dedicated shelter for abused women in the first-world countries of the United States, the United Kingdom, and Canada was not built until 1971, when one was opened in England.[58]

In spite of the sometimes radical stance that Samiti took, Gopi Krishna was adamant that he did not want it to be a political organization. Given the unstable political climate, however, it was inevitable that Samiti would on occasion be drawn into issues that had political overtones. Certainly Gopi Krishna made enemies on both a personal and a political/governmental level. Margaret tells the story of how the same government minister who had refused to help the abused woman and her sixteen-year-old daughter had become increasingly aware of the influence Samiti's activities were having in the community. Aware of how it could boost his own standing, he determined to turn it into not only a government-run organization but also one under his own auspices. The way Gopi Krishna handled this onslaught provided an interesting insight into both his character and his rational, strategic thinking.

Just how the minister planned to execute this take-over is almost impossible for us to comprehend unless we keep in mind the general state of lawlessness and turmoil that was prevalent in Jammu and Kashmir in those days. As an example, the type of incident described above where two opposing bands of men, armed with sticks, shovels, and hammers, clashed in the streets was not unheard of. Given this climate, the minister who wanted to take over Samiti simply made a plan that involved gathering a gang of supporters that would surround the compound, occupy it, and take it over. The minister believed this would be particularly easy because the compound's fence had been observed to be weak in a number of places. He did not know, however, that Samiti had been secretly informed of the plot the day before it was to be put into effect or that Gopi Krishna had devised a plan of his own. Gathering a group of young, eager supporters, he had them hide themselves at the strategic points where the fence was weak as well as a few other places he determined the compound might be vulnerable.

Anticipating that a spy would be sent on the morning of the attack to ascertain any possible resistance, Gopi Krishna had the offices occupied that day with only himself and a few of the more elderly Samiti members. The spy duly arrived, ascertained no one was on the premises who would or could fend off an invasion, and informed the minister. The minister then confidently launched his attack, only to have his gang met with concentrated opposition at every possible entry point. In the ensuing melee the minister himself ended up sprawled in the dirt and never again tried to take control of the compound or any other aspect of Gopi Krishna's reform movement.

While the organization's primary mission was to ease social ills for women, Gopi Krishna also hoped to preserve and beautify Hindu temples in his area. This might seem like a straightforward goal; it was, however, fraught with complications related to the tension between Muslims and Hindus. Although the underlying tension between these two groups had come to a head during the First Indo–Pakistani War, the situation had its roots in centuries of history. Exploring this history and the complex, centuries-long interaction between these two vastly different cultures and religions is obviously far beyond the scope of this book. Still, in order to have some perspective regarding Samiti's dedication to preserving Hindu temples and, indeed, regarding some of the occasional references to Hindu–Muslim discord throughout this book, it is worthwhile to provide at least a little additional context.

In this regard, it is first important to keep in mind the unsatisfactory-to-both-sides agreement at the end of the First Indo–Pakistani War that saw about a third of the northern region of Jammu and Kashmir administered by Pakistan, with the rest of the province being overseen by the government of India just as the rest of the country was. Thus, Srinagar and the Kashmir Valley, which Gopi Krishna called home , were administered by the government of India and was, in essence, Hindu-run while the majority of the population was in fact Muslim.

Gopi Krishna was not just a Hindu Brahmin; as mentioned in Chapter One, he was part of the Kashmiri Pandits, an honored, esteemed, and highly educated ethnic group whose roots went back to the ancient days of the region, long before other religious groups entered the area or, in some cases, even existed. In spite of this rich Hindu heritage, throughout his life as a renowned author and public speaker, Gopi Krishna never promoted this faith, or indeed any other faith, over another. He wrote and spoke of Christ, Mohammed, Buddha, Guru Nanak, and all the other founders of the great spiritual traditions with equal reverence and tirelessly put forward the concept of the Oneness of the Divine with all creation—a belief coming not just from his personal experience of union with this ineffable divine, cosmic consciousness, but also from the main tenets of the Kashmiri Shaivism of his own background.

In spite of the ecumenical views Gopi Krishna would spend his life promoting, in those early days of Samiti he was Hindu in a time and place where Hindu–Muslim conflict simmered beneath the surface and still frequently broke out in varying degrees of violence and open discord. Reiterating that it is far beyond the scope of this book to put this conflict into context or ascribe blame in a situation where there was sometimes blame on both sides, it can be said that it is a historical fact that one way Muslims expressed their desire to spread their religion in the Kashmir Valley was to either desecrate or occupy Hindu temples. It is also a fact that when such an occupation occurred, Gopi Krishna and Samiti sometimes got involved and conflict ensued.

According to Margaret, one of the most noteworthy of these events occurred at a deeply revered temple in Srinagar. One evening the temple caretaker arrived at Gopi Krishna's in an extremely agitated state, explaining that a band of men had come to the temple, thrown him out, evicted the worshippers, and taken over both the temple itself and the secular building associated with it. Gopi Krishna, who was on the board of the temple, immediately went to the police to ask for help. Unfortunately, on his arrival he found the two men whom he suspected of being behind the occupation had beat him there and had already convinced police they were not going to be needed at the temple site because no crime had been committed. Faced with no other alternative, Gopi Krishna and a number of other Samiti members armed themselves with the usual sticks and ersatz weapons and made their way to the temple. Hoping not to have to use violence, they decided to first use noise as their weapon. Approaching the building where the usurpers were ensconced for the night, the Samiti members made a racket that suggested a much larger mob. Pounding on the doors with their hammers, they shouted at the top of their lungs. The commotion was enough to frighten the usurpers into fleeing. The caretaker was reinstated in his quarters that night, and the next morning the Hindu worshippers were free to pray in their temple.

Not all of Samiti's efforts to preserve and beautify temples had such political or religious implications. While some temples had been destroyed in the war or its aftermath, others had simply fallen into disrepair or were being misused in other ways. One that Samiti focused a great deal of energy on was Kheer Bhavani, one of the holiest and possibly the most beloved Shaivite pilgrimage sites in Kashmir. Located in a beautiful grassy area, surrounded by trees and with water nearby, the temple had originally been built on the site of a spring that had been considered holy since ancient times. The spring was said—and some historical evidence exists for this—to change colors. Dark-colored water signified that difficult times were ahead for the Kashmiri Hindus. A light, almost milky color signified the opposite. According to contemporary tradition, the spring's water became dark at the beginning of the Pathan invasion and remained so for three years. Even for those Kashmiri Brahmins who do not place any significance on the changing color of the water, it has been a sacred place for ages. For Gopi Krishna himself, Kheer Bhavani had special significance. Kheer, a traditional Kashmiri rice pudding that Gopi Krishna was particularly fond of, was the offering the pilgrims traditionally brought to the temple. It was offered to Bhavani who was also known as Ragnya Devi, the goddess Ragnya. Often also referred to as Maha Ragnya Bhagavatī, or the Great Goddess Ragnya, she is seen in Kashmiri Shaivism as a manifestation of Shiva's consort. As such, she is the form of divine consciousness that is immanent, in other words, with us here in the world, and she has been worshipped in this sense by the Kashmiri Shaivites from time immemorial.[59] The temple's special place in Gopi Krishna's heart was implied when he and Bhabi named their first child Ragya, a form of Ragnya, and continued to use Ragnya as a less formal name for her among the family.

One way a temple such as this can be despoiled is by merchants setting up stalls and hawking gewgaws and other tawdry memorabilia. Traditionally, it had been accepted that the poor and destitute should be able to place themselves near a holy shrine and either sell small items or beseech the pilgrims for aid. By Samiti's day, however, there were temples where prosperous merchants had taken over the area and were making great profits off the pilgrims. One of Gopi Krishna and Samiti's efforts was to fight to change the situation so that the already well-off merchants were no longer making profits and that any monetary benefit went either to the temple itself or to the poor. Needless to say, this was another reform strategy that made Gopi Krishna highly unpopular with some of the wealthy merchants—but equally beloved by the poor and the others he helped.

At Kheer Bhavani, Samiti took on another project that was one of its most ambitious in this regard. In those days the temple was about fourteen miles from Srinagar proper. This made it too far to walk back and forth to the city in one day, and many people—especially the poorer ones—had no choice but to sleep on the grass and shelter under the trees. When weather was fair, this was not so much of a problem. However, this is a mountainous region, and the altitude of the city itself is close to a mile. Weather changes rapidly at this altitude, and nights can be very cool even in the summer. Realizing that inclement weather was a problem for the pilgrims who had no other place to stay, especially the poorer ones, Gopi Krishna led his group to plan, oversee, and find financing for a row of small houses with balconies near the temple site that pilgrims could take shelter in.

Temple preservation was important to Gopi Krishna, but the area of social reform characterized as women's rights remained his, and consequently Samiti's, focus. In order to spread their ideas on this wide range of social-reform issues, the group—like many good radical movements—obtained a printing press. While the main purpose of the press was to print the flyers, brochures, and leaflets that informed the public about the good work they were doing, Samiti had also eventually printed a small booklet featuring several of the poems in various languages that had come to Gopi Krishna in Jammu in 1949. Entitled *From the Unseen*, it is known to have been printed by 1952, because in that year a seemingly insignificant, but in fact momentous, event occurred in the early summer of that year. A young man named James Hillman came across the pamphlet in a local fair in Srinagar.[60] Hillman would go on to become a renowned Jungian analyst and one of the most forward-thinking psychologists of the twentieth century. At the time, though, he was a twenty-six-year-old living in Srinagar with Kate, the Swedish woman he would eventually marry, struggling in vain to write a novel. Living in the apartment on the floor beneath them in their rented house was another young man, Frederik Hopman. Originally from Holland, he was known by the nickname Tontyn.

Discrepancies in published accounts make it unclear whether it was Tontyn or James who first had the idea of visiting Gopi Krishna. Regardless, after the two of them had read the booklet, they decided they wanted very much to meet the author. When this meeting with Gopi Krishna came about, it included Tontyn, James, Kate, and another friend, Gerald Hanley. The early summer day was so hot that even years later Hillman could vividly recollect how his sweat-soaked shirt stuck to the back of his chair as he spoke with Gopi Krishna in his small house in Karan Nagar in Srinagar.

Later Hillman would make the point that he was originally highly skeptical and went to meet Gopi Krishna only out of curiosity, but his opinion changed:

> Above all, I remember the eyes of the man: friendly, luminous, huge, softly-focused. They attracted and held my attention and somehow convinced me that what was happening in this room and with this man was genuine.... This meeting went deeper than I then realized. His eyes first led me to trust my own sight, my own convictions, beyond my trained, skeptical Western mind.[61]

Hillman also described Gopi Krishna as an "initiator" and a "signal person" in his life. In his comprehensive biography of Hillman's life, Dick Russell referred to Hillman's meeting with Gopi Krishna as a "fateful encounter," one that "would ultimately shift the course of Hillman's life and work."[62] For Gopi Krishna it was an encounter that would, if not shift the course of his life and work, certainly have profound implications for both. As you will see in the next chapter, Hillman not only eventually wrote a chapter-by-chapter commentary for Gopi Krishna's first published book, his autobiographical *Kundalini: The Evolutionary Energy in Man*, he and his friend Tontyn would become the driving force behind its eventual publication. Those events, however, would not occur for many years to come. In the meantime, Hillman paid several more visits to Gopi Krishna before he and Kate left Srinagar to travel higher into the Himalayas. According to Russell's biography, Hillman recalled Gopi Krishna telling him, "Go high in the mountains, that's very good to go high in the mountains, because that's where man meets God."[63]

While those words may be apocryphal, Hillman did indeed have a profound mystical experience on that trip—one that he stated would set him on the course his life was to follow. This path involved leaving the mountains and India, traveling to Switzerland, and enrolling in both the University of Zürich and the C.G. Jung Institute. In 1959 he finished with a doctorate in psychology and a diploma in Jungian analysis from the respective schools. The exceptional level of ability necessary for this dual accomplishment was obviously recognized by the institute as Hillman was almost immediately appointed Director of Studies. He held this position until 1969—in other words, virtually the entire time he was helping Gopi Krishna get published in the West. During this period Jung's work and Jungian analysis were becoming increasingly renowned, and Hillman was gaining widespread respect in the field of psychology. Without Hillman's commentary, it is quite possible that it would have taken far longer for the words of a completely unknown Kashmiri yogi to spread. Tontyn was also busy taking care of his family and his increasingly successful, stressful career. It was not until 1959 that Tontyn reconnected with Gopi Krishna—a reunion that would not only be the beginning of a lifelong, dedicated friendship but also the start of Tontyn's dogged, unrelenting effort to see *Kundalini: The Evolutionary Energy in Man* professionally published.

The years between his first meeting with Tontyn and their reuniting in 1959 were full to overflowing for Gopi Krishna, too. Not only was he needed on a daily basis to head up Samiti's multiple activities, he was occupied with his family: grandchildren came along, and he doted on all of them. His first grandchild, Ragya's son Rakesh, had been born in August of 1951. Within the next few years, his oldest son, Jagdish, married a young woman named Mohini Wazir, who would be a devoted wife and mother and an attentive, caring daughter-in-law. Their son Sunil, Gopi Krishna's second grandchild, was born in August of 1955. The following year another grandson, Ragya's son Rajiv, arrived. Another highly significant event was that Jagdish, who would eventually rise to a very high level in the aircraft-maintenance division of India Airlines, received his qualifications in aeronautical engineering, and in 1958 his and Mohini's daughter, Sunita—Gopi Krishna's first granddaughter—was born.

As was customary, Jagdish and his family lived in his parents' house in Karan Nagar in Srinagar for about two and a half years until he was transferred to Delhi in 1959. A reasonable assumption might be that at least one reason the family was not in such terrible poverty in the latter years of the 1950s was that Jagdish's income was now helping out the entire family. This sort of communal family assistance was certainly also customary in the culture. Ragya's husband,

R.K. Kaul, who had begun as a lawyer with few prospects or connections, was a gifted man. Even in those early days he had his feet on the rungs of a ladder that would eventually lead to the great esteem he would one day have in the High Court of Delhi.

Throughout his life, Mr. Kaul remained an unstinting supporter of Gopi Krishna's work, and it can safely be assumed that Ragya and her husband were also in some way instrumental in the improvement in Bhabi and Gopi Krishna's living conditions that took place somewhere in the mid-1950s. Regardless, this son-in-law was held in such high regard he was always referred to as Mr. Kaul even by those who might have used first names, or even pet names, for other members of the family.

In addition to Gopi Krishna's indication in his autobiographies that the family's living conditions improved about seven years after the momentous 1949 events in Jammu, other indicators exist. Perhaps the most significant one is that by 1957 he had been in a consistently good enough state not only to finish an entire book-length manuscript of verse but to polish it into potentially publishable condition. That he could afford the international postage necessary to send heavy manuscript copies to publishers and also pay someone to type multiple copies—neither an insignificant expense in that time and place—seems to indicate he had access to more funds than he had during the first half of the 1950s when he, Bhabi, and the boys sometimes did not have enough food. As he was not yet making money off his writing, it seems highly likely support was coming from the family members, like Mr. Kaul and Jagdish, who were earning good salaries.

Just how remarkable it is that Gopi Krishna was able to write this manuscript and polish it while he was spending more than full-time hours with Samiti's activities should not be overlooked. This extraordinary capacity to produce creative material and make a time-consuming effort to get it published while being occupied around the clock with other matters would prove to be one of the defining aspects of the rest of his life.

Piecing together when Gopi Krishna first began to write with an eye to publication and how that writing developed over the next several years is an extremely significant part of his life story. That he was thinking along the lines of publication in the very early 1950s is evinced by *From the Unseen* being in existence by that time. In order for Samiti to have printed it, Gopi Krishna must have first given a good deal of careful thought to selecting the poems that were eventually used out of the abundance of inspired verse he received in Jammu. After that, he would have had to make considerable effort to ensure the booklet's design, layout, and printing quality were all worthy of being made public.

There is ample evidence from the family's recollections that during these years Gopi Krishna produced a tremendous amount of written material, much if not all of it in verse. But when he began work on creating a cohesive, full-length manuscript is simply not known. What is certain is that by May of 1957 he had one completed and had managed to have a fair copy typed. This in itself was a frustrating, time-consuming process in the Kashmir of those days, where many of the typewriters were old, available paper was flimsy, and carbon paper was used to make copies—certainly for the copies that would have been good enough to send to a prospective publisher. By that point, Gopi Krishna would also have had to have spent a good deal of time doing research—another arduous process in that time and place—on which publishing companies might be interested, how to submit a manuscript, and how to write what we today call a query letter. This all had to be done not only decades before the internet but before there would have been any type of guide to publishing or to international publishers available in his remote area.

In spite of all these odds, he managed to persevere; on May 3, 1957, he began submitting those query letters to publishers. The work he described was entitled *Kundalini or the Evolutionary Energy in Man*. This manuscript was in a very different format from the book of that name that has gone on to remain in print for over fifty years, be translated into at least ten languages, and be published in thirteen countries. It was completely in verse. Over 900 quatrains long, it communicated the kind of complex, rational concepts that are normally reserved for works of prose and expressed the revolutionary ideas Gopi Krishna wanted to get across about kundalini as an evolutionary energy.

During the first two weeks of May 1957, he sent his queries to four publishers. In his letters he promoted the work as the first scientific treatise on the philosophy of esoteric yoga and how it related to modern science. Stressing that the manuscript addressed the burning issues of the day, he said it dealt with the current evolution of humanity, the true goal of yoga; the cause and cure for war; the meaning of dreams; the source of inspiration and genius; and the "superconscious" state. In conclusion, he wrote,

> Hence the work is in the shape of a scientific exposition of a very ancient but little known and less understood doctrine, which permeates the whole religious literature of India, now revealed and explained in the light of modern knowledge to the public at large both of the East and the West for the first time in this age.

Aware that such a statement might appear somewhat audacious, he added this subtle—or, perhaps, not so subtle—admonition in verse to the closing of his query letters:

> The wise do not unthinkingly condemn
> A thing, nor act in judgment formed in haste,
> For many a rough exterior hides a gem
> And many a seeming pearl is only paste.
> Th' impetuous, who without due thought opine,
> Forget that they too are to error prone,
> That every pebble is a hidden mine
> And every leaf of grass a realm unknown.

In his quest he sent material to Philosophical Library in New York, and George Allen & Unwin, Rider & Company, and Routledge & Kegan Paul in London. Routledge responded quickly saying they would never be able to sell a long book of verse in England. Philosophical Library and George Allen asked to see the manuscript but warned him that it was unlikely they would find it feasable to publish such lengthy verse. After some time, and a polite reminder or two from him, he received word that both had rejected the manuscript. Rider & Company also asked to see the manuscript. Although

Rider apparently rejected it too, they indicated they would be interested in seeing future efforts.

An all-verse manuscript entitled *Kundalini or the Evolutionary Energy in Man* that is apparently, but not positively, the one sent out in 1957 has survived the decades. It was, however, never published. One reason for this was apparently publishers' overall anxiety about issuing works of poetry. Publishers have always focused on the business of selling books, and poetry has never sold well. And this wasn't even a book of poems: it was over 3,600 lines of rhyming verse that made up a book in itself. Another factor in publishers' hesitation was no doubt that Gopi Krishna was virtually unknown outside Jammu and Kashmir and remained so for some time in spite of the extraordinary profundity of his awakening. Among the reasons for this was, as mentioned earlier, his refusal to use the siddhis, or gifts, he had been given in the tawdry demonstrations of paranormal abilities that many yogis or so-called gurus of the day were using—or feigning—to gain fortune or followers. Beyond this, Gopi Krishna adamantly refused to take followers. It might seem on the surface that the members of Samiti were followers, but they were friends, supporters, and colleagues, and he treated them as such. In order to take on spiritual followers, Gopi Krishna would have had to call himself a guru, and despite the number of people who sought him for spiritual guidance, he steadfastly refused to take on the role of a spiritual teacher and never let himself be called *guru*.

Given the profound respect for the spiritually awakened in India, it seems indubitable that if Gopi Krishna had either exploited his gifts or had taken on the traditional role of "awakened yogi as guru," his fame would have spread rapidly. That is not to say he wasn't renowned in Kashmir. He was. But it was a renown based on respect for a leader and a man of great wisdom.

Chapter Nine

How to Call for Research into Kundalini

Like a number of other literary works that have stood the test of time, *Kundalini: The Evolutionary Energy in Man*—a very different book from the one entitled *Kundalini or the Evolutionary Energy in Man*—traveled a very rocky road on its way to eventual publication. In spite of its painful naissance, this book has not only gone on to be published and translated an exceptional number of times, it has attained the remarkable distinction of remaining in print for nearly fifty years. It would, however, be an entire decade from when Gopi Krishna sent out that first manuscript in 1957 until the version known today would make it into print.

The story of this book's remarkable journey is intricately tied with Gopi Krishna's life during those ten years and reveals a great deal about his character. After he received the rejections in 1957, he took the comments to heart, and buoyed by Rider's expression of interest, he began to work on material in response to the criticism he received. In the early stages of his renewed correspondence with Tontyn that began in 1959, Gopi Krishna described what he had been writing and shared his unsuccessful attempts to find a publisher, not failing to mention that he had on hand a letter from Rider & Company expressing interest in his work. It may be that in this Gopi Krishna reveals a very human side of himself. By this point in time, the request from Rider was two years old.[64] Perhaps he was, like any still-unpublished writer, holding on to hope. Nonetheless, the fact that he had immediately begun working on new, improved material was indicative of the direct, rational action so typical of his character.

In describing his writing up to that point, he told Tontyn that he had now completed a third volume aimed at clarifying the obscure subject of kundalini. One of these three volumes was the material he had sent out to publishers in May of 1957. He explained that in their rejection, George Allen & Unwin had indicated the subject was too unfamiliar to their readership. In response to this criticism, Gopi Krishna communicated that he had been working on a version that would introduce the subject more gradually and be easier to understand. It is not clear from his wording whether this work is the third volume or a separate piece of work. Regardless, he stated that this material would make up a work of about 150 pages, with thirty or forty pages of prose introduction and the rest in verse. In the letter, Gopi Krishna wondered if Tontyn, and possibly James Hillman, might give him some advice on how to proceed before he sent it to Rider & Company. He estimated the manuscript might be done in a month or two and offered to send it to Tontyn if he were interested. In fact, he spent much longer working on this prose portion. Over the next several months, the correspondence continued with further discussions on Gopi Krishna's writing and repeated offers from both Tontyn and Hillman to read and help publish it. Little did they know this project would occupy a great deal of their time and energy for more than eight years.

In spite of ongoing, encouraging communication with Tontyn, it was not until December 26, 1961, that Gopi Krishna finally sent Tontyn the manuscript that he had once thought would be finished in a month or two. Describing the format the book was now in, Gopi Krishna wrote, "I have deliberately given it in the shape of a story of my life to make the otherwise obtuse and entirely new subject more intelligible to the reader." This is a very significant point. While the book known today as *Kundalini: The Evolutionary Energy in Man* is widely known as Gopi Krishna's first autobiography, he did not intend it as such: it was meant to be a book about kundalini, not about himself or his life.

Even knowing that his life was extremely busy, it is difficult for those of us who live in a world of lightning-fast data transfer to imagine how so much time could have elapsed between their first letters in 1959 and the dispatching of this manuscript unless we stop to consider the conditions in Kashmir at the time. While the conditions in the latter 1950s were better in Kashmir than they had been earlier, it was still a relatively isolated region that was far behind urban areas of India in development and many decades behind the industrialized West. Even seemingly simple matters such as having a handwritten manuscript typed could be an issue. Photocopiers were not available: duplicate copies had to be made with carbon paper, and fair copies needed for multiple submissions simply had to be typed a second or third time. Even more significantly, since Gopi Krishna's writing came from a state of inspiration, he had to wait for the proper mood to occur—a state that was affected by innumerable factors.

Unfortunately, no copy of the version Tontyn received from Gopi Krishna in December 1961 seems to have survived. Still, it can be assumed that this prose/verse manuscript contained a significant amount of verse. While Tontyn was waiting, he suggested that Gopi Krishna send a copy of the original all-verse version to him. He and Hillman then sent that original version out for review to a number of friends who had connections with the world of editing and publishing. The response to this poetic version was fairly unanimous: the reviewers generally felt the material was not at all suited for a Western audience. Reaction ranged from a literary critique of the verse itself to concern that such lengthy verse would never find an audience and/or that the material was simply too alien.

Even long before Tontyn and Hillman had sent this all-verse version out for review, Tontyn sensed the poetry would not go down well. In response to a letter in which Gopi Krishna has mentioned the prose/verse version he is working on, Tontyn comments:

> Judging from what I know of the average European reader who would be interested in your publications, I would say: the more prose the better. Few people read poetry and those who do more for the literary enjoyment and for aesthetic reasons and not for understanding the content. But of course I am in no position to advise you in these matters and my judgment cannot outweigh your intuition.

Throughout his work with Gopi Krishna on the manuscript, Tontyn also kept this deferential, respectful attitude. The esteem in which he held Gopi Krishna is apparent. Yet, he did not hesitate to give his straightforward opinion as he and Hillman went through the process of suggesting revisions. After receiving and reviewing the December 1961 manuscript, Tontyn wrote back saying in no uncertain terms that both he and Hillman believed it was unpublishable in its present state. Still, Tontyn stressed his and Hillman's willingness to help get the manuscript into publishable form and their enthusiasm for helping to bring Gopi Krishna's ideas to the West. Thus began a process of back-and-forth consultation, suggested revisions, and rewriting that lasted for several years.

Because no definite copy of that December 1961 manuscript exists, it is impossible to speculate from today's point of view on what made it so unacceptable to them. Tontyn was, however, unambiguous in his ensuing correspondence about the problems he and Hillman had with the work. In his initial letter suggesting the extensive revisions that would need to be made, Tontyn was careful to assure Gopi Krishna that he would not be doing any actual rewriting himself: neither he, Hillman, nor anyone else they found to help with editing would be putting words in Gopi Krishna's mouth. He added, however, that they would need to regroup material, putting it into chapters of specific interest. They would also need to delete material that was repetitious or, in some cases, problematic to Western readers. Tontyn added that, since one aim of the book was to attract scientific and intellectual readers, they would also need to make sure there was a very clear distinction between fact and opinion. Tontyn went on to pass on Hillman's desire for more information on dreams and visions, sexual stirrings, yogic experiences, and his daily life in general.

It was not long before Tontyn received Gopi Krishna's permission to proceed with his efforts on the manuscript. He and Hillman set to work immediately; however, due to their busy schedules it wasn't until April of 1962 that they wrote back to Gopi Krishna with a list of very specific requests for changes. Some of them involved fine points, such as asking for more detailed dates and more information on his education and career. Other requests were broader; for instance, asking for more scientific material and again for more information on his sex life and paranormal abilities. In his response a few weeks later, Gopi Krishna explained that he was working on another volume that would contain more scientific information and be aimed more specifically at the scientific community. Regarding his own sex life—a topic that was still obviously of interest—he wrote, "Sex, which is very intimately connected with the awakening of kundalini...should better be approached from a general rather than an individual point of view." He added that this, too, would be dealt with in the volume he was working on and that it would clarify many of the misconceptions about Tantra and Tantric practices.

At the beginning of October, Gopi Krishna mailed Tontyn and Hillman fifty pages of writing that responded to a number of their April revision requests. His family tells a story that certainly sounds like it might have occurred at this time of year. Bhabi, distressed that her husband was spending all his time writing, came into his room one day and interrupted him. Reminding him that the weather would soon be getting colder, she chided him because the firewood for winter had not yet been gathered. When she urged him to stop writing and start looking for wood, he looked up from his work and said, "Don't worry! When this is done, you'll have plenty of money to buy firewood!"

While it would still be many years until Gopi Krishna would see any financial gain from his efforts, serious progress was now being made on the book. Once Tontyn and Hillman received the revisions sent at the end of October, they began work on the book and hired an editor to do the copy editing—the corrections to punctuation and English usage. The man they hired was an experienced Swiss editor named Mr. Drake, who Tontyn later discovered had had kundalini experiences of his own. With Tontyn and the editor doing the bulk of the work and sending the material to Hillman for his comments and approval, they finished editing. Gopi Krishna received the manuscript in good order and responded at the end of December.

The one truly significant difference of opinion in the revision process was in regard to the use of verse. As mentioned earlier, even before any manuscript was available to him for editing, Tontyn was encouraging Gopi Krishna to minimize the use of verse as much as possible. Keeping in mind that the first manuscript called *Kundalini or the Evolutionary Energy in Man* that Gopi Krishna sent out in 1957 was entirely in verse and that the *Kundalini: The Evolutionary Energy in Man* that is still widely in print today contains no verse at all, it seems probable that this transformation was made in successive stages. While further scholarship may be able to determine when these successive stages were written and what they included, all that is certain today is that the manuscript that was finished at the end of 1962 still contained some verse. From viewing the versions of the manuscript that still exist—all undated, sadly—it can be assumed that this was essentially the penultimate version of the book and that it contained an introduction that was all in verse and had a certain amount of verse at the beginning of each chapter.

When Tontyn sent this manuscript back to Gopi Krishna, he stated very succinctly that he and Hillman felt all the verse should be removed. Gopi Krishna's response was a patent example of the extraordinary humility so many people remarked on in the course of his lifetime. Without any hesitation, he bowed to their opinion and said that they could remove the verse if they felt it was necessary. In one telling phrase he stated, "I submit to it."

Over the next several months versions of the manuscript flew back and forth between India and Switzerland with changes and suggestions made by both parties. There were now changes and additions that Gopi Krishna wanted made to the material that had been edited. Tontyn assured him they had not added words, "only using his own writing as a base," and they had only made deletions and condensations that would make the material more acceptable for Western audiences, which included the copy editor's corrections that were due to English not being Gopi Krishna's mother tongue. Still, Gopi Krishna felt the deletions left detrimental gaps and wanted to make suggestions concerning some of the other changes.

In the many letters exchanged in these days, the subject of inspired verse was often discussed. It seems that Gopi Krishna very much wanted Tontyn to better understand the difference between inspired verse and ordinary writing. After saying he submitted to the deletion of the verse, he wrote,

...inspired mystic rhyme is far different from the ordinary poetry to which people are generally accustomed.... Inspired poetry is always immortal presenting a condensed version of universal truths...I would not enter into a detailed discussion about the point at this stage nor insist on the insertion of the verses against the better judgment of your friends but I am certain that in the long run the poetic composition will have a more lasting appeal than my works in prose.

As the written discussion continued, he added,

I am as sure of the fact that Kundalini is the source of genius and the evolutionary mechanism in man as I am of myself, as I am of the fact that the sun will rise tomorrow at the appointed time.... The verses I have written, are, therefore, not to be judged from ordinary standards. Most of them are prophetic in nature or deal with cosmogonal truths. This poetry is not merely an effusion of words round ordinary mundane matters.... I am not writing to persuade you to insert the verses at this stage, I write this merely to emphasize the point that mystic poetry and writing are different altogether.

Still, as mentioned above, with characteristic humility, he yielded to his editors' wishes, and Tontyn and Drake were finally able to present their edited version to Gopi Krishna in March of 1963. When Gopi Krishna responded that he still wanted to make some changes, Tontyn was concerned that he was disappointed with the end result. The writer, whose precious work had endured the kind of editing that makes most writers' blood boil, responded with his typical humility and gratitude:

The labour devoted by you and Mr. Drake to the editing of the book has been of immense advantage to me by making me vividly conscious of the flaws in my writing. What I have learned would go a long way in shaping my next work on the subject. From this you can easily infer how your labour of love is helping me. This is enough to show that I have full appreciation for the work done by you in editing the manuscript.

Finally, in the spring of 1964 a version that was deemed acceptable by all parties was ready to go. Acting on Rider & Company's earlier interest in seeing another manuscript, Gopi Krishna sent it off to the London publishing company in early June. Rider & Company then passed it on to a literary adviser, G.J. Yorke.[65] It is evident that Yorke saw himself as being very knowledgeable about yoga and kundalini, and during their correspondence he challenged the yogi on many points with considerable pretension. Although Yorke's qualifications included having traveled in the East, written about his travels in China, and been associated with the Thirteenth Dalai Lama, seen from today's perspective on colonialist attitudes his questioning of Gopi Krishna's knowledge of yoga is truly cringeworthy. Another example of this condescension is found in the response of one New York agent to Gopi Krishna's work who begins his letter, "Dear Mr. Krishna: Your letter is a fascinating one. How in the world do you write in so professional a manner, English I mean." These brief glimpses provide insight into the attitudes many in the Western publishing world must have had about a totally unknown yogi from a remote part of India and what a difficult job Gopi Krishna had ahead of him in trying to find a publisher. It is difficult for us in a world today where yoga is part of everyday life to imagine how different the situation was at that time. To put these attitudes in context it is helpful to remember that in 1964 the hippie counterculture had barely begun to embrace yoga. Until 1965 it was even almost impossible for people from India to immigrate to the United States due to a highly restrictive immigration ban on people from that country. It wasn't until 1968 that the Beatles would make their famous trip to India, and it would take some time for news of their realizations to spread. If yoga was still foreign to the vast majority of Westerners in those days, the concept of kundalini was completely unheard of and totally alien.

Yorke, in his capacity as literary adviser, ultimately recommended that Rider & Company reject the book on the basis that it was not commercially viable. Although he made his interest in Gopi Krishna obvious by writing him in great detail and requesting a first look at his next manuscript, his final response still smacked of arrogance. He referred to the difficult periods Gopi Krishna had endured as being far too akin to madness and went so far as to intimate that this might make everything he had written questionable. In general, York also felt that the content was just too unfamiliar for Western audiences. After this rejection, the manuscript was sent to a number of other publishers. Eventually, all declined to publish the book. None of them had confidence that it would sell, and the refrain about the unfamiliarity of the content was often mentioned.

When a major British or American publisher was still not found over the next while, Tontyn decided to take a more active role in bringing the book out. Years earlier an Indian gentleman, Shri Ramadhar, who was the owner of a printing press but not a publishing company per se, had mentioned his interest in publishing some of Gopi Krishna's writing. Eventually he came into contact with Tontyn, and the two men entered into discussions about publishing the book in India so that an English version of the book would be in print.

By this time Hillman was becoming widely recognized. Jungian psychology had become increasingly popular, and Hillman's work with the Jung Institute was taking him to many countries. His many commitments notwithstanding, he continued to help. In hopes that an introduction written by a noted Western authority would aid in getting the book published, he wrote to several well-known acquaintances in search of a suitable person who would take on the task. One, Aldous Huxley, declined because of failing eyesight. Another, the renowned authority of the day on yoga, Mircea Eliade, declined because he said he had written so much on yoga and Tantra that he preferred not to be associated with anyone else's writing on the subject. However, a Stanford University professor emeritus of comparative religion and Indology named Frederic Spiegelberg accepted. Widely esteemed and considered a pioneer in his field, he was the author in the early 1960s of *Spiritual Practices of India* and of *Zen, Rocks, and Waters*. Spiegelberg grasped to a great extent the important implications of Gopi Krishna's proposed scientifically based explorations of kundalini, and the introduction he wrote served to add an academic authority for Westerners. Eventually it was decided that Hillman, with his growing renown, might also add something in this regard by writing a chapter-by-chapter commentary to Gopi Krishna's account. He and Tontyn felt this might not only add credibility— since Gopi Krishna was still so unknown outside of Kashmir—but also help put what was considered foreign material in context for a Western audience. In spite of his very busy schedule, Hillman took on this demanding task, adding almost 4,000 words to the original manuscript. He completed the work in the summer of 1965 in Sweden, his wife Kate's homeland, in the village of Botorp on the island Hemsö.

At the same time, the discussions between Tontyn and Shri Ramadhar were continuing. Eventually they resulted in a collaboration that created the publishing company Ramadhar & Hopman, which was listed as having locations in New Delhi and Zürich. In 1967, the company published *Kundalini: The Evolutionary Energy in Man*. Printed in India, the book was in English and contained the introduction by Spiegelberg and the commentary by Hillman. Its publication meant that Gopi Krishna finally had copies of his first published book in hand.

Although Gopi Krishna spent much of the decade between 1957—when he first attempted to find a Western publisher—and 1967 working on the publication of that first book, a great deal more was going on in his life. The activities with Samiti discussed in the preceding chapter continued through this period and were at times even more intense than previously. In order to further Samiti's humanitarian goals, he also became organizing secretary for the Jammu and Kashmir branch of a national organization called Bharat Sevak Sumaj, literally "a society that is India's servant." Founded originally by the renowned first prime minister of India, Jawaharlal Nehru, it still exists today. Its stated goals "Reaching the unreached, skill training for all without any barriers, and education for anyone, anytime, anywhere" were certainly compatible with Samiti's efforts to better not just society but the lives of specific individuals.[66]

Gopi Krishna was also continuing to work on the volumes in prose on kundalini that he had mentioned to Tontyn as early as 1959. Another project was a goal of making the life, poetry, and teachings of Lalleshwari known to the wider world. Also known as Lal Ded or Lalla, she was a twelfth-century saint cherished by the Kashmiri people. In spite of all that was going on in his life, he managed to write an ode to her that was over 1,000 lines long and was completed by 1964. The ode revered Lalla and at the same time used this veneration and her story as a device to illustrate the awakening of kundalini and the teachings of an enlightened yogini.

Gopi Krishna's personal life was also rich and full during this decade. Ragya and Mr. Kaul's second son, Rajiv, was born in 1956, and Mr. Kaul was continuing to rise in his profession. Jagdish's career with India Airlines was steadily advancing, and in May of 1960, he and Mohini's third child, a daughter named Anju, was born. During this decade, Nirmal finished his education. After starting his career, he married Chuni in July of 1964. Their first daughter, Jyotima, was born a year later. With her birth, Gopi Krishna and Bhabi had six beloved grandchildren.

If the successful men were helping the family's finances improve, the women were contributing in many ways as well. Both Chuni and Mohini not only took dictation and typed for their father-in-law, they also helped Bhabi make sure his strict dietary schedule was kept. But these were not their only accomplishments. Chuni took advanced degrees in Sanskrit, and Mohini became a particularly well-loved schoolteacher. What's more, it would not be long before Ragya's husband, Mr. Kaul, would emerge as a dedicated lifetime supporter of his father-in-law's efforts. It goes without saying that Gopi Krishna's family was bringing him great joy.

Chapter Ten

James Hillman and *Kundalini: The Evolutionary Energy in Man*

The significance of Ramadhar & Hopman's version of *Kundalini: The Evolutionary Energy in Man* was tremendous. Its publication was the first step in Gopi Krishna's ability to spread his ideas on kundalini to the wider world. Still, the book known today by that name did not begin its journey to wide renown in the Western world until it was published in Germany by Otto Wilhelm Barth Verlag in 1968 under the title *Kundalini: Erweckung der geistigen Kraft im Menschen* or, literally, *Kundalini: The Awakening of the Spiritual Power in Man*. This was the edition that lit the fuse that carried Gopi Krishna's light to the world.

A fascinating set of so-called coincidences and an equally intriguing group of people were the dynamic catalysts in this process. Certainly, Hillman was one. As can be seen from the chapter-by-chapter commentary he wrote for *Kundalini: The Evolutionary Energy in Man*, however, he was by that time in his life steeped in Jungian concepts. His profound spiritual experiences in Kashmir and Ladakh might have been no less important to him, but he was by this point seeing the world through a Jungian lens. Tontyn Hopman, who on the other hand had spent a significant part of his life in India, was particularly suited to comprehend the concept of kundalini.

Among all the fascinating people who helped publish *Kundalini: The Evolutionary Energy in Man* and bring Gopi Krishna's ideas to the West, Tontyn stands out to such a degree that it is worthwhile revisiting the years he spent working directly with him on the books, exploring Tontyn himself and their relationship in more detail. This is especially so because Tontyn's story is an eloquent example of how a person, through their own experiences of mystical awakening, could come to comprehend the profound importance of the information Gopi Krishna was toiling to bring to a generally unresponsive and unawakened West.

Born in Holland in 1914, Tontyn had training in engineering and architecture along with a remarkable facility with languages, which led to a lifelong career working for companies such as Swiss Air around the globe. He was also a gifted artist. In one sense, the story of Tontyn's role in Gopi Krishna's life begins even a few weeks before the discovery of that booklet of poems in the Kashmiri bazaar in 1952. At the time, he was in Delhi. He and his wife, Clara, who would become an internationally known sculptor, had been living in India.[67] Earlier that day Clara had left for Switzerland, taking their daughter Rhea to join her two brothers who were already in school there. That night Tontyn, as he had done each evening during the family's stay in Delhi, went out to walk around the grounds of their hotel to enjoy the cool night air. As he stood looking up at the full moon, he felt something unlike anything he had ever experienced in his life: a feeling rose up and burst in what he could only describe as an orgasmic sensation in his heart. It was an extraordinary experience, so incomprehensible, in fact, that he tried to put it out of his mind. Still, a few weeks later it happened again just as he was falling asleep.[68]

Around this time, he received an invitation from the Hillmans to join them in Kashmir. He did so, and soon the orgasmic heart sensations began to occur frequently, just as he fell asleep at night. His dreams also became exceptionally vivid, filled with profound archetypal imagery and concepts that stretched beyond the scope of normal consciousness. He became captivated by this astonishing internal play of consciousness and was eager to meet with the yogi that Hillman had heard about in the bazaar. As soon as that meeting drew to a close, Tontyn asked Gopi Krishna if he might meet with him for a private session. Gopi Krishna agreed, and the meeting took place soon after. In it Tontyn explained in detail what he had been experiencing since that night in the hotel garden in Delhi. In an interview done in his later years, he described Gopi Krishna's reaction with an enthusiasm that had him fairly leaping out of his chair. "When I described my own experience of orgasm in the heart, he said, 'Oh, you have kundalini!'"[69] It is perhaps unlikely that these were precisely Gopi Krishna's words. Still, there is no doubt that he felt certain Tontyn was undergoing a form of kundalini awakening.

Tontyn met a few more times with Gopi Krishna before he left Kashmir. He then stayed in correspondence with him for a while before falling out of touch. When Tontyn wrote him again it was February of 1959. In the letter, Tontyn thanked Gopi Krishna for the brief but "most important role" he had played in his life and for the "guidance and protection" he had been given. He indicated that he had been wanting for a long time to ask Gopi Krishna some questions, and he politely inquired whether it would be all right to do so. Gopi Krishna responded immediately, mentioning that Tontyn had recently been on his mind and that he would do his best to answer any questions he might have, adding that he remembered their meetings well. Although the phrase *You have kundalini!* was the one that stuck in Tontyn's mind for so many years, Gopi Krishna's actual words to him may have been more similar to the ones below, which were written early in the course of their resumed correspondence. In the letter previous to it, Tontyn had asked about the experience of what he referred to as an "inner woman," an inner feminine he experienced as part of himself. In response, Gopi Krishna wrote:

There is absolutely no doubt, as I mentioned to you at the start that in your case KUNDALINI has been partially awakened. The awakening has been spontaneous, assisted by you[r] artistic profession and your meditation. Perhaps you remember that I had told you that after some time your imagination would become more developed and sensitive. In fact by means of processes, which it will take long to grasp fully, the whole conscious structure begins to undergo a modification as soon as the awakening takes place. Some period according to one's temperament and physical efficiency is taken for adjustment of the nervous system. There may be different kinds of disturbances and disruption during this period. Ultimately the heightened consciousness expresses itself in some form or the other and gives evidence of supernormal and occult sensibilities. The experience of the inner woman is common in many cases of awakening.

It indicates the upward flow of seminal and Prana energy through the spinal cord to the various vital organs and the brain to strengthen and tone the nervous system and the brain cells.[70]

Tontyn's understanding of Hindu philosophies was deep enough that Gopi Krishna had no need to explain prāna to him. Although *prāna* can mean "breath," Tontyn would have known that the reference here was more closely related to its definition as *"life energy."* Just as the divine feminine Shakti manifests as kundalini-shakti in the body, in Tantric tradition she is also seen to manifest as prāna-shakti. In this role she animates all life and consciousness, running the biological life processes of our bodies and manifesting as the "power of awareness, illumination, or knowledge."[71]

Over the first few years of their renewed contact, Tontyn and Gopi Krishna communicated about both the progress on the book and Tontyn's own personal spiritual experiences. These experiences were at times becoming more intense. Scattered throughout his letters regarding the work being done on the manuscript in 1962 are Tontyn's descriptions of what he was undergoing and Gopi Krishna's advice to him. Toward the end of March that year, Tontyn began to have dreams that seemed to him to be foretelling a profound mystical experience. When it finally did occur one night, Tontyn was in a sense prepared for it and was determined to surrender to the experience. For a prolonged period that night, he had a powerful awareness of what he referred to as the "inner woman." Later that night this ongoing sensation grew and merged into "the wonderful experience of the golden, vibrating, loving, laughing light." He wrote that it was, "I believe, an experience of God."

He was physically exhausted the next day, but he was also intensely aware that something had changed in him. "I was much more open to people and nature. There was a renewal. Since then I have [the sense] that at night I am being taught. Something is drastically at work in me at night." In his response to Tontyn's letter about the experience, Gopi Krishna stated that he was greatly interested in Tontyn's description of the light:

> ...it tallies with the vivifying illumination created by Kundalini in a very active form. This light ultimately develops in the resplendence preceding the visions, the ecstasies, and the inspirations of mystics and yogis. It is in this light that in the condition of Samadhi, the Yogi becomes absorbed....

Unfortunately, Tontyn's work designing facilities in many parts of the world for Swiss Air was becoming increasingly stressful. This stress combined with his ongoing kundalini process was making his life difficult, and there were times when he needed to take leave from work. When Tontyn wrote to him asking for more specific advice on diet and exercise to deal with certain symptoms he was having, Gopi Krishna responded with a number of suggestions regarding food and activity. However, he couched any specific recommendations he made with these words:

> It is not advisable to prescribe a certain rigid course of diet and behaviour as every individual in whom the LIGHT is kindled must learn to regulate his food and conduct according to his environment and the demand and capacity of his system. There is every likelihood of the development of an internally guiding sense also. The most important thing to be remembered is that there must be moderation in everything. Please do not indulge in any practice which causes the stimulation of the activity already going on in the body, as that may result in putting a heavier strain on the system than it can normally bear. Too much mental application should also be avoided. Periods of mental activity should be alternated with intervals of mental rest. In fact a state of harmonized mental and physical behaviour is not only necessary for proper spiritual development, but also for longevity and health.

All this advice was placed within the context of a reminder that the "mode of conduct advocated by the founders of all religions of the earth is in fact intended to make this process of transformation easier and smoother for one who is on the path."

Throughout his work with Gopi Krishna on the manuscript, Tontyn maintained the deferential attitude that revealed the great esteem he held for him. In fact, he addressed his letters to him as *Maharaj,* which means *"great king."* It is easy to imagine Gopi Krishna reacting to this salutation each time he saw it with a smile and a shake of his head. Perhaps he recognized that Tontyn must have struggled a bit to come up with an acceptable way of addressing someone he came close to venerating. Tontyn knew, of course, that Gopi Krishna would not accept veneration. Even as Gopi Krishna's renown was growing in Kashmir, he steadfastly refused to be addressed by any of the pet names beloved gurus or spiritual masters are given, such as *guruji* or *babaji.* He also spurned honorifics such as *Sri* that can be used in a way that denotes special status. He preferred to be referred to as Pandit Gopi Krishna, the term *Pandit* being an honorific given to all respected Kashmiri Brahmins. He did seem to feel comfortable with those close to him calling him *Panditji, -ji* being a commonplace suffix used as a term of endearment that means something akin to *"beloved"* or *"greatly respected."* This term was evidently not quite enough for Tontyn who continued to refer to him as Maharaj throughout the years. It seems Gopi Krishna's friendship with this man was so special that he never compelled Tontyn to stop using it.

As seen in the previous chapter, this obvious respect did not keep Tontyn from giving his straightforward opinion, particularly when it came to the issue of verse. In spite of the fact that Gopi Krishna ultimately submitted to the removal of all verse from the book that would be the published *Kundalini: The Evolutionary Energy in Man*, he made a dedicated effort to get Tontyn to understand the importance of this literary form and that, indeed, inspired verse was something far beyond a mere literary form.

In addition to his comments to Tontyn in this regard in the previous chapter, Gopi Krishna introduced Tontyn to the work of the twelfth-century Kashmiri saint Lalleshwari and the research and writing he was doing on her at the time.

Using her as an example of a saint or mystic who had awakened kundalini, Gopi Krishna described how deeply beloved she was by the Kashmiri people and how her divinely inspired verses had survived through oral tradition for centuries. This verse, he explained, was an example of true inspiration—creative inspiration that came from a source far beyond limited human intellect. The ode he was writing about her was coming to him in the same manner:

> The work is entirely inspired. In my normal capacity I cannot write a few quatrains even if I labour for a long time over them.... True inspiration has its own peculiar way of expression, which is normally very difficult to imitate. The aim is to present Eternal Truths or Perennial Wisdom before the human intellect is in a readily intelligible form.

So that Tontyn could better understand what he was trying to express, he promised to send him a copy of the ode to Lalla as soon as it was finished. When it was, the two names it had been known by during the process, *Hymn to Lalla* and *Hymn to the Mother*, revealed that Gopi Krishna was praising Lalla as both a Kashmiri saint who had walked the earth and a representation of the Divine Mother, or kundalini-shakti, that she had awakened within.

It transpired that, even before this work was finished, he had begun to gain recognition for it in India among fellow admirers of the saint, and he was encouraged to have his work on her printed in the format of a small booklet so that it could be distributed. The booklet was created, and a few hundred were printed.[72] Right away Tontyn requested that a large portion of them be sent to Switzerland. On receiving them, he began to distribute copies and contact people in publishing and academia. In spite of his dedicated efforts, he was unable to find anyone who was able to truly appreciate the work or help with publishing it.

It seems likely that Tontyn, talented artist that he was, probably had some degree of appreciation for creative inspiration all along. Still, his efforts on behalf of the *Hymn to Lalla* indicate he was now willing to champion it, and he certainly recognized it as one of the siddhis described in yoga. He was also curious, as many people are, about siddhis in general. In one letter discussing possible additions to the material in the book, he asked pointedly about the siddhis Gopi Krishna had experienced since his awakening. He drew attention to the fact that in the current version of the manuscript, the only siddhi Gopi Krishna admitted to having was that of receiving the inspired verse. Tontyn then added:

> But in our conversations in 1952 you have given ample evidence that you had such gifts including telepathy, visions of the future, visions of a world war to come, that you could look into other people's past lives, etc.

Tontyn then asked if Gopi Krishna had, perhaps, denied these abilities in order to avoid encouraging those who might want to try to awaken kundalini simply to gain such powers. Gopi Krishna's response is significant.

> I have not denied the possession of supernormal gifts. Only I have not laid any emphasis on them in my writing. The real aim of the Yoga is not the acquirement of psychic powers but the development of the brain and the nervous system to a pitch of efficiency where one can respond to the all-knowing conscious world surrounding us at every moment of our life. In order to attain this condition of hyper-sensitiveness it is essential to keep the body in a state of health and equilibrium and the mind in a state of harmony and peace. If this condition is not achieved the extremely subtle other world remains concealed from our conscious observation. This condition of constant contact with the higher consciousness is in Sanskrit known as "Jnanam" the condition of transcendental knowledge.
>
> Dreams and visions, miracle-making and psychical gifts are but appearances met on every rung of the ladder that finally leads to the height where the individual spirit comes face to face with its own marvelous substance.
>
> There is a difference in the description of the conditions expressed by mystics of the east and the west—as also of the conception about them in the minds of the modern psychologists—and the ideal state described

by the inspired sages of India, the renowned seers of Upanishads and the Vedas. According to them, as also according to Patanjali, the famous author of Yoga Sutras, the possession of psychic powers and gifts does not by itself imply the highest stage of transcendence possible.... This is the supreme condition described in Gita and in all other authoritative spiritual texts of India. The acquirement of this condition is a miracle in itself. There is no doubt that one who attains to that condition possesses the other gifts but, if displayed blatantly, they act as impediments to the attainment of the real goal.

With his understanding of the profound significance of the role of siddhis in higher consciousness combined with his own mystical experiences, it is no wonder that Tontyn was poised to be one of the first Westerners to truly grasp the importance of Gopi Krishna's work. Nor should it be any surprise that he was willing to dedicate so much of his energy during those years between 1959 and 1967 to promoting what was, particularly in Western terms, a totally revolutionary view of evolution and consciousness.

Those who are at all familiar with Gopi Krishna's work, which has been before the public eye for many decades now, are so accustomed to the notion that kundalini is the evolutionary energy that it is easy to forget what a radical concept this is and, especially, what it was at the time. Although the notion that kundalini is an evolutionary energy is supported by digging deep into the age-old Tantric texts on Shakti and kundalini-shakti, it is couched there in intricate symbolic and allegorical imagery. These opaque, intricate esoteric allusions to Shakti as the cosmic divine feminine force who propels not just humanity but the entire cosmos along its continuously evolving pathway are light-years away from the kind of concrete concepts that can be investigated by science. So far away, in fact, that it would seem impossible to make the necessary connections. However, because of his profound understanding of his native spiritual traditions and, even more significantly, his rare kundalini awakening, Gopi Krishna was able to do just that.

It was unquestionably due to Tontyn's efforts that this revolutionary concept was introduced publicly in 1967 when *Kundalini: The Evolutionary Energy in*

Man was published in India by Ramadhar & Hopman. In the final section of his commentary in that book, Hillman refers to a passage by Gopi Krishna in the preceding pages that gives some clue as to the stage he had reached in his formulation of his theory of kundalini as the evolutionary energy—a cosmic, spiritual force functioning in the very physical human body.

> Contrary to the belief which attributes spiritual growth to purely psychic causes, to extreme self-denial and renunciation, or to an extraordinary degree of religious fervor, I found that a man can rise from the normal to a higher level of consciousness by a continuous biological process, as regular as any other activity of the body, and that at no stage is it necessary or even desirable for him either to neglect his flesh or to deny a place to the human feelings in the heart.... I have every reason to believe that mystical experience and transcendental knowledge can come to a man as naturally as the flow of genius, and that for this achievement it is not necessary for him, save for well directed efforts at self-ennoblement and regulation of appetites, to depart eccentrically from the normal course of human conduct...[73]

In the following pages of the book, Gopi Krishna stated clearly that this "evolutionary mechanism" was known as *kundalini* in India. Located at the base of the spine with the energy for its activity supplied mainly by the reproductive organs, it was the means of developing "spirituality, supernormal faculties and psychic powers" and was carrying all of humanity toward a "glorious state of consciousness" indicated by the mystics, prophets, and great geniuses of the past.[74]

Interestingly enough, a few seemingly insignificant lines in this chapter indicate that he had spent some twenty-five years trying to find a way to convince the rational mind of the reality of "the existence of the spiritual world and the possibility of development of a higher state of consciousness in normal man." He knew with every fiber of his being that this was true. But he was seeking a vehicle for verifying this concept that would be "as convincing to the anthropologist as to the man of God and as reasonable to the psychologist as the student of history."[75]

If the twenty-five years he referred to here began with his initial experience in 1937, it would seem to indicate that it was in about 1962 that he began to cohesively formulate his revolutionary theory about kundalini as the evolutionary energy. Possibly by around then, and certainly before the publication of the book in 1967, he was able to set it out in three succinct points: One, religion in human beings is an "expression of the evolutionary impulse" that springs from a normally functioning power center in the body. Known as *kundalini* in India, this evolutionary mechanism can, under certain favorable circumstances, be stimulated. Two, the transcendental states usually only ascribed to saints and visionaries are, in fact, the natural heritage of all human beings. Three, humankind's progress and happiness depends on following the universal laws associated with this evolutionary impulse.

Gopi Krishna's main motivation in getting his ideas out to the world was almost certainly his desire to make known kundalini's role as the mechanism that was propelling humankind along its evolutionary journey and, perhaps more importantly, the lifestyle and societal values necessary to make this journey a successful one. However, he was also profoundly motivated by his concern for individuals. He did not want anyone to suffer as he had. He believed we were at a time in history when an ever-increasing number of people would awaken kundalini to some extent, and he did not want anyone to have to face even a small percentage of the challenges he had endured. As mentioned earlier, he believed the best way to prevent this would be to avoid the forceful awakening of kundalini and to simply live the moderate, disciplined, ethical, deeply compassionate lives described by the great spiritual traditions that would, in turn, facilitate the natural, gradual fruition of kundalini in each of us. Repeatedly in his talks and writings he reiterated these teachings, often rephrasing or quoting directly the passage from the *Bhagavad Gītā* where Krishna describes the person who is dearly loved by him:

He who has no ill feeling for any being, who is friendly and compassionate, free from the desire to possess and the feeling of I-ness, even-minded in pain and pleasure and patient. (XII: 13)

The yogi who is ever content, who is always self-integrated, controls his senses and is unshakable in determination, whose mind and intellect are surrendered to me, who is My Devotee, he is dear to me. (XII: 14)[76]

Still, it is a truism that change is painful, and any awakening of a transformative energy is inevitably going to bring with it, depending on a wide variety of circumstances, a greater or lesser degree of upheaval in a person's life. Gopi Krishna believed that scientific proof of the existence of kundalini—regardless of what it is called—would be the way to convince the Western world that there was an actual, verifiable *reason* to follow those spiritual teachings. He also knew that without a proper understanding of how this transformative energy worked in the human body, the medical community would be misdiagnosing and consequently mistreating people who came to them with symptoms that neither they nor their patients understood. It is easy to imagine that at least a small part of Gopi Krishna's awareness and intense concern about such possible misdiagnoses had its roots in the fear he had in the early years of his awakening that he would be thought to be insane and that he was without the means of convincing anyone that he was not. Regardless, during his lifetime Gopi Krishna would never hesitate to help those who were going through a process of spiritual transformation. In an effort to provide assistance and guidance, he would come to answer letters from and meet with literally hundreds of individuals who were experiencing some degree of kundalini awakening. He knew, though, that these efforts were but a drop in the ocean and that widespread medical understanding of kundalini would be crucial in the years to come.

Chapter Eleven

Jailed! Leading the Hindu Resistance in Kashmir

Among the intriguing cast of characters that was instrumental in first
bringing Gopi Krishna's ideas to the wider world, perhaps none is more
fascinating than Barbara Rotraut Pleyer. By seeming coincidence, she met
Tontyn in 1967 on a flight to Japan; he was on an assignment for Swiss Air and
she on her extraordinary mission to bring about world peace. Eager as always
to spread the word about his beloved Maharaj, on that long flight Tontyn
introduced her to Gopi Krishna's ideas.

Born in Germany in 1929, Barbara studied law at the University of
Tübingen and would go on in her lifetime to receive not just that degree
but two additional doctorates and a medical degree and learn to speak some
fourteen languages. A truly exceptional and yet highly controversial person,
she achieved worldwide fame and notoriety prior to meeting Tontyn when
she gate-crashed the 1952 Olympic Games in Finland. By that time in her
life Barbara had become an impassioned peace activist and had taken on the
name Sinai (pronounced sĭn-ī in German). She had assumed this name as a
reference to Mount Sinai where she envisioned a council of nations occurring
that would bring about an everlasting world peace. Determined to make this
vision a reality, she saw the first postwar Olympics as a venue for bringing
her message of peace to the world and began to plot a way to break into the

opening ceremony of the games. Her plan was to grab the microphone and give an impassioned speech for peace in six languages.

Blonde and beautiful, she was dressed on the day of the event in a full-length white gown that resembled an angel's robe, and she carried a flaming torch. Somehow she managed to enter the stadium without a ticket or credentials. Then right after the athletes had entered, she burst onto the playing field and began to sprint around the track with her torch held high. Thinking she was part of the ceremony and suspecting she might be the Finnish beauty queen Armi Kuusela, who had recently won the first-ever Miss Universe pageant, the crowd went wild. It wasn't until she reached the podium, grabbed the microphone, and got out the first word of her speech that she was stopped. She had just managed to say *ystävät*, Finnish for *friends*, when the microphone was removed from her shaking hands. Then, gallantly and without fanfare, one of the elegantly dressed dignitaries on the podium gave her his arm and escorted her out of the stadium, where, without putting up any resistance, she was given over to the police. Because her shaking was pronounced—and no doubt because of concerns for her mental health—the police had her hospitalized. Later, the psychiatrist who examined her declared her to be a "charming and delightful girl" who was "somewhat overwrought, but highly intelligent."[77]

Although Sinai failed in her attempt to give her speech, the media had a heyday with her interference in the opening ceremony and soon dubbed her the Angel of Peace for the image she had created as she ran the track with her torch and flowing white gown. The massive attention she attracted led to her being asked to speak at many venues, and her fame spread. Of course, not everyone was impressed with her. It soon became known that she was the daughter and niece of two exalted Nazis. Her father, a professor and high-ranking officer, had been killed in Russia, but her uncle, a journalist, had made it through the war and continued to write from his far right perspective. In spite of her claim of having no association with her uncle or his ideas, her detractors used her family connections to discredit her.[78]

Nevertheless, she remained undaunted. The lesson she gleaned from her adventure was that she could accomplish anything: her original journey from Germany to Finland had been managed with literally only a few coins in her pocket; she had entered the games without a ticket or pass; she had sprinted to the podium with the roar of the crowds in her ears; she had managed to at least grab the microphone; and she had not received any punishment at all. What's more, she had become an overnight celebrity. Confident that nothing could stop her, she had parlayed her fleeting fame into being exactly where she wanted to be: on the world stage delivering her message of peace. For the next fifteen years she traveled the world and reportedly met with as many as sixty world leaders. They included King Faisal of Saudi Arabia; the Indian prime minister, Jawaharlal Nehru; the British prime minister, Sir Alec Douglas-Home; the Pakistani president, Iskander Mirza, and the prime minister of China, Zhou Enlai. It is even reported that she met with Mao Zedong.

During these years she was also exploring a spiritual path, becoming interested in both Buddhism and Catholicism. Her foray into the Catholic faith took her to St. Catherine's Monastery near Mt. Sinai, where she went on retreat for forty days at a time once a year for several years. As she had no visible means of support, questions were inevitably raised about how she managed to finance all this costly travel. When asked, she would only say that she was backed by two wealthy men who insisted on remaining anonymous and that there was an American millionaire who sometimes gave her the use of his private plane.[79] Although speculation was rife that certain authorities in postwar Germany were using her as a pawn, there was no indication that she was anything other than a dedicated, if obsessed, believer in world peace. Regardless, by 1967 her focus on attaining this goal shifted from the political arena to the spiritual. By this time, her years of traveling the world to meet political world leaders were seemingly over. Any financial support she may have had was also apparently at an end, for she frequently appeared to be scrambling for funds. After raising this question about financial sponsorship, a *Journal of Olympic History* article added that anyone following her accomplishments over these fifteen years might also wonder

...where she drew the inner strength just to be herself and to let adversaries just bounce off. In 1967 she founded a "Research Center for Kundalini" in Kashmir with the Indian scholar Gopi Krishna. Kundalini is, according to tradition, an ethereal strength which is to be awakened by the practice of yoga.[80]

While Gopi Krishna himself was no doubt the driving force behind the creation of that first kundalini research center, Sinai's role in this and other momentous events in 1967 can hardly be overstated. And the events of that year were indeed momentous.

On Tontyn's suggestion, Sinai went to Srinagar to meet Gopi Krishna in person. Exposed to the idea that the transformation of consciousness could be brought about by the awakening of the evolutionary energy—regardless of the name it was given in various spiritual traditions—she quickly grasped Gopi Krishna's contention that it was the key to world peace. Before long she threw her extraordinary determination into helping him with the creation of the Central Institute for Kundalini Research in Nishat, a goal Gopi Krishna had long had in mind. Nishat, then a village near Srinagar but now a suburb, was the location of a beautiful piece of property that had been purchased with funds from the sale of property that Bhabi had brought to the marriage.

Unfortunately, while Gopi Krishna's family life was more stable, the conditions in his beloved Kashmir were not. The tension between Muslim majority and Hindu minority had gradually been heating up, and in 1967 Kashmir once again became a hotbed of political and social unrest, and Gopi Krishna was in the thick of it. Samiti's efforts to help the downtrodden and improve social conditions had never waned, and although their goal was to remain absolutely apolitical, this became increasingly difficult. Although Gopi Krishna did not discuss his political activities at all in either of his autobiographies, in *Living with Kundalini*, there is a telling line:

> In spite of the deep desire of every member of the little group to confine their activities to the mission of service, they were drawn unwillingly into the troubled waters of political rivalry....[81]

These political activities reached a particular high point while Sinai was in Kashmir. To understand how Gopi Krishna was drawn into them—and the major role he eventually played—it is helpful to explore them a little more deeply. As mentioned in the context of the discussion on the First Indo–Pakistani War, as a Kashmiri Brahmin, Gopi Krishna was part of a religious minority in a land that had been the homeland of this ethnic and religious group long before any other group entered. Although Hindus had coexisted peacefully with Muslims for the most part from the time of their arrival, the antagonism brought on by Pakistan's creation and its open desire to annex Kashmir had continued to grow.

On the surface the outbreak of turmoil that occurred in Kashmir in 1967 was ostensibly religious-based, but it was to a great extent political. It also contained the elements that have historically characterized the conflicts between majorities and minorities. Indeed, some historical accounts of that period of conflict avoid the terms *Muslim* and *Hindu* completely by identifying the parties simply as the *majority* and the *minority*.

Throughout history many struggles between a people whose indigenous homeland is overtaken by a minority group who eventually becomes a majority have been documented. In these cases, minorities generally have felt—and often indeed been—persecuted. On the other hand, the majorities—sometimes with cause—have been afraid that the members of the minority would arm themselves, rise up, and wreak havoc upon them. They have then used this fear to justify any actual attempts at suppression they might undertake. These two groups inevitably tell their story from very different perspectives. Regardless, because Gopi Krishna was part of this Hindu minority, his story must necessarily be told from that perspective, and the fact remains that by 1967 the tension in Kashmir was at a height and this situation had undeniably been brought about to some extent by Pakistan's acknowledged desire to annex Kashmir. It is self-evident that, from Pakistan's point of view, annexing Kashmir would be much easier if there were few Kashmiri Brahmins left there to resist.

The political reasons that the outspoken members of the Muslim majority wanted to become part of Pakistan—and any justification they felt for their desires—are complex and far beyond the scope of this book. It can be mentioned, however, that while they may have become a clear majority in Kashmir, they themselves remained a minority in the context of India as a country. Fueling the discontent for both parties was the fact that life was easy for neither Hindu nor Muslim: food was scarce, and prices had remained extremely high.

Nonetheless, it is incontrovertible that Pakistan and many Muslims—at any rate, certainly the extremists among them—wanted to expel the Kashmiri Pandits. The evidence for this is that this goal was in fact accomplished in the early 1990s and that as of this writing virtually all Kashmiri Pandits still live in diaspora around the world. Although this expulsion occurred after Gopi Krishna's death in 1984 and is thus technically outside his life story, it provides necessary perspective on the conflict that was ongoing during much of his lifetime and that had such a significant flare-up in 1967. This is also true of an event that occurred two years after his death. In the midst of another intense wave of persecution in 1986, the extensive property north of Srinagar where he had founded the Central Institute for Kundalini Research was overtaken by Muslim extremists. The two Hindus who were guarding the property were shot and killed, and the land, the house, and the outbuildings were seized. Eventually the family home in Karan Nagar in Srinagar was also taken over. None of this property was ever restored to Gopi Krishna's family, and no compensation of any kind was ever provided.

Given this historical framework, it is easy to see why Kashmir was in turmoil in the mid-1960s and why Gopi Krishna was involved. He was still head of Samiti, and though there were indeed some Muslim members, most were Kashmiri Brahmins.

Most of the readily available historical accounts of this event are told from a fairly emotional point of view—it was, after all, a highly emotional time. However, by combining the bare-bones facts from these accounts with the rational, carefully considered references found in letters that Gopi Krishna wrote to a number of high-level state and national government officials, it is possible to piece together a fairly accurate picture of what occurred. In the annals of Kashmiri Shaivite history, this period in 1967 is referred to as *Bloody August*. By the end of Bloody August, the police had assailed the protestors with the heavy wooden batons known as *lathis* and had attacked them with tear gas and short-range shells. Over 1,000 men, close to 300 women, and 350 children were injured. Three Hindus were killed, and over 400 were arrested. Gopi Krishna was among them.

The event that lit the fuse in the powder keg that was the Kashmir Valley of the day was the alleged abduction of a young Hindu female—the question of whether she was a young woman or still a girl was a key point in the matter. According to her mother and the official school records her mother presented to the police when her daughter went missing, she was seventeen years old. The situation in Kashmir being what it had been for the last twenty years meant that no official birth certificate was available. The question of the girl's age was important because the man, a Muslim, who had her in his possession—and a woman really was a man's possession in those days—claimed she was eighteen and as such a woman of legal age who had come with him voluntarily. She had also, he said, converted to Islam and married him of her own free will.

By all undisputed accounts the girl, Kumari Parmeshwari Handoo, was exceptionally beautiful. Because her father had died and her widowed mother had no income, it had been necessary for her to get a job in one of the many Muslim-owned shops in Srinagar. The manager of the shop was a man who was widely known to have embezzled funds from a bank he had worked in, and his detractors believed he had gotten away with his crime because of corruption in the legal system.

According to the mother, the girl had been badly mistreated by both the manager and another employee—the man who eventually allegedly abducted her—by withholding her wages and forcing her to work late, miss the last bus, and walk four miles home in the dark. The mother's implication was that these men had used these and other forms of threatened mistreatment to coerce the girl—often referred to as the virgin girl in the emotional accounts—into doing their bidding. What is known for certain is that the alleged abductor had stolen a few thousand rupees from the till.

When the girl had not returned home by eleven o'clock on the night of August 3, the mother went to the local police. Within two days, the man and the girl were brought in by the police. Unfortunately, they were taken not to the station where the complaint had been lodged but to one that, like most in the valley, had no Hindu officials. The alleged abductor was freed the next morning, charged with neither the theft of the rupees nor the abduction. The girl, however, was kept in jail, where her mother was never allowed to speak to her alone.

Increasingly frantic, the mother was making the situation known and contacting higher-level government officials and anyone she thought might help. As the story spread through the Hindu community, a certain degree of tension arose, but the situation was not yet critical. Officials agreed that no action should be taken until more facts were gathered, especially related to the girl's actual age. It was agreed that, until she could have a medical examination, she should be turned over to either her mother or an agreed-upon neutral party. Instead, the police returned her to the alleged abductor.

When this mishandling of the situation occurred on August 6, the news spread through the Hindu community. By the next day, spontaneous protest rallies had arisen in the streets. According to press accounts, these demonstrations were peaceful. Regardless, newspaper photos of the day showed numerous badly injured Hindus, women, and teens among them.

By August 8, Gopi Krishna was involved. Whether through his work with Samiti or the widespread recognition of him as a yogi—most likely both—by this point in his life he was recognized as a leader within the Hindu community. On what must have been the morning of that day, he wrote a letter to Dr. Hridya Nath Kunzru, a member of parliament in the federal government, imploring him for help in the quickly deteriorating situation, stressing that the current situation with the allegedly abducted girl was not an isolated event. Without laying blame or referring to any issues of religion, he wrote:

> There is no doubt that certain anti-national elements are at the back of such conversions and abductions in order to pollute the secular atmosphere and to disturb the communal harmony in the State.

From the wording of the rest of the letter, it is clear Gopi Krishna hoped Kunzru would use his influence with the federal government to rectify the situation:

It is essential not only in the interest of the minority but also of the Government itself if they sternly discourage such conversions and marriages, but the Government has failed to do so and the Pandit community has taken the challenge very seriously. There is a hartal [a general closing of shops and businesses in protest] of Hindu businessmen and a mass gathering will be held at Shitalnath to protest this deplorable action of the Government. It is essential the Kashmiri Pandits should unite to stand against this and other similar affront[s] to their honour and injustice.

The letter was ended with the words "I am also participating in this movement."

Shitalnath was, and is today, a sacred Hindu site and temple ground going back as far as protohistoric times.[82] Unfortunately, demonstrators there and in other parts of the city were lathi-charged, several people were severely injured, and a dozen people were arrested at the events. It immediately became evident that an organized collective response was needed, and within short order the All Kashmir Hindu Action Committee was formed, with Gopi Krishna as its chairman.

The committee quickly became recognized as the minority's official representative body and as such took part in negotiating the settlement that was ultimately reached with the federal government for dealing with the situation. That agreement wasn't reached until the first days of September, and in the meantime the events of Bloody August unfolded. During the night of August 8, several people were pulled from their homes and taken to jail. Over the next few days, word spread that the Hindus who had been jailed were being treated inhumanely. Tensions increased, and another hartal was held. When no response to the Hindu Action Committee's pleas to the federal government came, it was decided to stage a *satyagraha*. Meaning literally "to hold firmly to the truth," satyagraha was a form of nonviolent resistance used widely during the Gandhi movement, often involving voluntary arrest. In order to get the government's attention, it was decided that five people a day would surrender themselves in this way. The satyagraha began on August 11 but still did not bring government action. More Hindus were injured and arrested. On August

14, Gopi Krishna was pulled from his home at three o'clock in the morning. Presumably charged at a police station that night, he was then transferred with other detainees to the Srinagar Central Jail.

Rumors of torture, or at the very least maltreatment, of the Hindu prisoners were spreading. On August 15, Independence Day in India, a Hindu who had been injured in the original protest died. Over the next ten days, protests escalated and the crowds of protestors were attacked with lathis, tear gas, and even short-range shells. Still, there was no response from the federal government.

From his jail cell, Gopi Krishna continued to write letters to high-level officials in his role as chairman of the Hindu Action Committee. In a letter on August 26 to Ghulam Mohammed Sadiq, chief minister of Jammu and Kashmir, he wrote that

[h]undreds of men and women have been injured, some seriously so....
Our people are smarting at the inhuman treatment meted out to them
in response to a reasonable demand.

As the violence escalated, Hindu shops were destroyed, and at least one home in Karan Nagar, Gopi Krishna's neighborhood, was burned. Two more Hindus died, and the mourners in their funeral processions were stoned. In spite of pleas from the Hindu Action Committee, it was not until September 2 that the federal government responded with a visit by Y.B. Chavan, the Union Home minister for India. By September 3, an agreement between Chavan and the Hindu Action Committee was reached, and the committee called off the protests and other aspects of what was called their direct action. Kumari Handoo was to be returned to a neutral party until the case made its way through the courts; a committee would be struck at the federal level to review the persecution and injustices the minority had long endured; and the satyagrahas and other detainees would be released from Central Jail.

Although the exact date is not known, Gopi Krishna was freed from jail probably sometime during that first week of September. That he was not released much earlier was not due to a lack of effort on the part of others—principally Sinai. From the moment he was incarcerated she began a campaign to have him freed. Naturally the Hindu Action Committee wanted him released, but those who knew of his sensitive physical condition and need to eat every few hours were even more anxious for his freedom. When it became evident his release would not be forthcoming, Sinai immediately pushed for special permission for him to receive the food he needed. Once the consent was obtained, Bhabi prepared his food at the usual times, and Sinai delivered these small meals several times a day to Gopi Krishna in Central Jail.

At the same time she continued to write letters and send telegrams to officials demanding his release. When her efforts had failed after the first two weeks, she went to Delhi to bring her appeal directly to the federal government. According to both Gopi Krishna's longtime secretary, Margaret Kobelt, and his family, Sinai managed to reach as high as Prime Minister Indira Gandhi herself. Gandhi, who was said to know of Gopi Krishna as a great yogi, sent word that he should be immediately released. However, in the spirit of satyagraha and like many incarcerated protest leaders throughout history, he refused to leave unless all his fellow protestors were also released. When this did not happen, he remained in Central Jail until the agreement with Chavan was struck. Tragically, over the next month, it became evident that many of the promises made by the government to correct the situation for the minority in Kashmir were not kept. Tensions and disputes continued to flare up over the next two months and break out time and again in the future.

In spite of the cataclysmic events in Kashmir, the work toward the publication of *Kundalini: The Evolutionary Energy in Man* was proceeding apace in Delhi, where it was to be printed. In November, when the actual printing of the book was close to being done, Sinai suddenly needed to make a return visit to Germany. She was determined to find a well-established European publisher for the book while she was there. Insisting that she needed a finished copy of the book to take along, before leaving India she flew first to New Delhi, where she bedeviled the printers into completing the run. When the first published copy of *Kundalini: The Evolutionary Energy in Man*, now containing Hillman's commentary and Spiegelberg's introduction, rolled off the press, Sinai grabbed a copy and headed to Germany.

As a German who had long been interested in spirituality, Sinai was no doubt aware of Otto Wilhelm Barth Verlag, a publishing company located near Munich that frequently published esoteric books. With her characteristically undaunted attitude, she was soon in touch with the company's publisher, Ursula von Mangoldt. A long-held, but possibly apocryphal, anecdote has it that von Mangoldt, a serious student of palmistry, took one look at Sinai's palm and said she knew that her company would publish Gopi Krishna's book. Be that as it may, that is exactly what happened: Otto Wilhelm Barth Verlag immediately agreed to publish the book in Germany. There were, however, two problems. The book had to be translated into German, and von Mangoldt insisted that she was only interested in doing the book if it could come out by March of 1968. Agreeing to do the translation herself, Sinai immediately began to work on the project so that von Mangoldt's deadline could be met.

As if 1967 had not been extraordinary enough for Gopi Krishna so far—what with living through political upheaval, heading the Hindu Action Committee, being incarcerated for weeks, having the first-ever edition of *Kundalini: The Evolutionary Energy in Man* published in his own country, and learning that his book was accepted by a major European publisher—there was one more astonishing occurrence to come. Ursula von Mangoldt, who must have been truly captivated by Gopi Krishna's work, wrote a letter on November 24 inviting him to come to Germany before the end of the year and to stay at least through February, assuring him all costs would be covered.

This would be Gopi Krishna's first opportunity not only to leave India but to go to Europe, where he could express his ideas in person to people there and where he hoped he could put the research he dreamed of into practice. Needless to say, he accepted the invitation. In 1967 Gopi Krishna had gone from being a writer who had struggled in adverse conditions for nearly two decades to get his work recognized to being a published author who was on his way to a two-month, publisher-funded, all-expenses-paid trip to Europe.

Chapter Twelve

Finally Published—Acclaim in the West

On Gopi Krishna's arrival in Germany, Ursula von Mangoldt took him to stay at her expansive villa that was located near Munich. It is easy to imagine how disorienting it must have been for anyone—let alone a yogi struggling to live in both the physical world and a higher state of consciousness at the same time—to leave the achingly beautiful, but poverty-stricken and strife-torn Kashmir and suddenly find himself not just in the comparative opulence of von Mangoldt's home but in bustling, modern-day Germany.

In preparation for his visit to Germany, Sinai and von Mangoldt had been busily organizing a series of talks for him to give that included lectures at the University of Munich, the University of Stuttgart, and the University of Hamburg. Although Sinai's focus during this period was on translating Gopi Krishna's book into German, she also accompanied him—a foreigner in what must have seemed a very strange land—on these trips to help him and make sure he arrived safely at all the destinations in Europe. While giving these talks, Gopi Krishna met a number of scientists who were extremely interested in his ideas and his work. The most significant of them was undoubtedly Carl Friedrich von Weizsäcker. At the time, von Weizsäcker was teaching in the philosophy department at the University of Hamburg. He had turned to philosophy, however, only after a career as one of the great German theoretical physicists.

As such he had been director of that field at the renowned Max Planck Institute in Göttingen from 1946 to 1957. In the war years prior to this he had been, like the other great German physicists such as Werner Heisenberg, recruited by Hitler to work on the development of an atom bomb. In May of 1945 he, Heisenberg, and the other leading physicists involved in the project were taken into custody and interned at Farm Hall in England. In later years, both he and Heisenberg would claim that the reason Germany—in spite of having many of the world's most brilliant physicists—did not beat America in the race to develop the atomic bomb was that they intentionally slowed the work on the project down so that Hitler would not have this cataclysmic weapon in his arsenal. While there have been critics who've felt Heisenberg and von Weizsäcker's claim was simply rationalization, the latter certainly spent the rest of his life trying to make the world a better and more peaceful place. After being repatriated to Germany, he taught physics at the University of Göttingen. After turning his attention to philosophy in 1957, he signed—and is said to be the initiator and main author of—the Göttingen Manifesto. The document, signed by eighteen German nuclear scientists that included Heisenberg and several other Nobel Prize–winning physicists, warned against nuclear armaments and made a strongly voiced declaration against Germany being allowed to reestablish work on developing them. The document attracted worldwide attention and was influential in denying Germany's return to nuclear armament development.[83] After this, von Weizsäcker would go on to found the Max Planck Institute for Social Sciences, and he spent the rest of his life teaching and writing over thirty books that considered the "moral, ethical, and environmental implications of quantum physics and atomic energy."[84]

When Gopi Krishna came to the University of Hamburg during that winter of 1968, friends encouraged von Weizsäcker to meet with him. Von Weizsäcker was, however, skeptical. This was the late sixties: the Beatles had now made their famous trip to India, and the fad for shallow interpretations of Indian philosophy and meditation was spreading. Having a great respect for Eastern traditions as well as a deep reverence for his own Christian tradition, von Weizsäcker had serious doubt about this superficial trend and suspected Gopi Krishna's visit was more of the same. Urged by friends, however, the renowned scientist overcame his reluctance. In describing this encounter, he later wrote:

> I felt in a fraction of a second: this man is genuine.... [H]e answered precise questions precisely, in a sometimes surprising way and with a deeply human sincerity that was often enhanced by a smile. His presence was good for me, and I could feel within me the traces of his simple and good emanations for as long as a month afterwards.[85]

Von Weizsäcker was only one of the people Gopi Krishna met on this trip to Germany who would play a major role in his life. Another was the Swiss woman Margaret Kobelt. Referred to earlier as Gopi Krishna's longtime secretary, Margaret was far more than that. In today's parlance, she might be thought of as a kind of combined personal and executive assistant and would become one of the most important people in his life. Both Tontyn and Sinai were, as they had already been in so many ways, catalysts in this fortuitous encounter.

Margaret, having formally studied home economics, used these skills to run a family-owned, five-story house on Gemsenstrasse in Zürich as a residence for students and others during her entire lifetime. But she broke with the Swiss conventional expectations for what she called "a proper young Swiss woman" to study astrology, apprenticing with one of the foremost teachers in Europe for several years. By 1967 her own reputation as an astrologer was growing, and she had become deeply interested in spirituality and Eastern thought. That year she traveled to the Swiss village of Gstaad to hear the renowned yogi Krishnamurti speak. Tontyn, who had long been interested in Krishnamurti's teachings, was also there. After inadvertently meeting with Margaret, he learned she lived in Zürich. Since he was often housed there for his work with Swiss Air, he asked her to do an astrological chart for him. When the two met again in Zürich, he began to tell her about Gopi Krishna. After this initial encounter, the two stayed in touch.

When Sinai decided to leave India and return to Europe, she not only wanted to find a major publisher for *Kundalini: The Evolutionary Energy in*

Man, she also hoped to meet James Hillman and become a student at the Jung Institute. As soon as Tontyn, who was still in India seeing to the final printing of the Ramadhar & Hopman edition of the book, learned Sinai was going to Zürich, he gave her Margaret's address. On arriving in Zürich, Sinai went to the house on Gemsenstrasse and asked for a place to stay for a few nights. Learning that Tontyn had sent her, Margaret immediately invited her in, and Sinai stayed not for a few nights but for over three weeks. During that time she told Margaret a great deal about Gopi Krishna and her goal of finding a European publisher for his book.

Once she had accomplished that objective, she contacted Margaret. Knowing that Gopi Krishna would be speaking in February in Stuttgart—the city on his tour closest to Zürich—Sinai invited Margaret to come to that city to meet Gopi Krishna personally. In spite of it being the middle of winter, Margaret accepted the invitation and, along with a friend, headed to Stuttgart in her tiny Fiat. Fortunately the roads, not as good as they are today, remained clear of snow, and they arrived safely at the house where Gopi Krishna was staying. Once there, they shared a meal with him and Sinai. Then the two women were each given a chance to meet with him individually. Because it was nearly dark by the time the meetings were over, the women were eager to begin their return journey. But just before they left, Margaret paused and spontaneously invited Gopi Krishna to stay at the house on Gemsenstrasse if he happened to have time to visit Zürich before going back to India.

In the car, the two friends remained in complete silence for a long while before speaking. Margaret later described it in this way:

> All at once we had to confess to each other that we felt we had been given such riches. We simply felt as our hearts, you know, had become more radiant and better somehow... that we had been given such a gift. It was as if a kingdom of riches had been given to us.[86]

The drive back to Zürich was not as uneventful as the trip north had been. A heavy snow had begun to fall and the roads to ice over. At one point the little Fiat spun out of control and went off the road. Margaret managed to get the car back on the road, and even this moment of drama did not dampen the feelings of love and peace that had filled their hearts earlier that day.

Before he left Europe, Gopi Krishna did have an opportunity to visit Switzerland. During that visit, he spent over two weeks at the house on Gemsenstrasse in Zürich. By this time Margaret had carefully read Gopi Krishna's book. She had a good background for understanding his ideas as she was not only familiar with Krishnamurti's work, she had also read a great deal of Eastern philosophy, including the writings of Ramakrishna and Vivekananda. Although she was impressed both by Gopi Krishna's ideas and the heartfelt impact he had had on her during their meeting in Germany, it was this period of time in close contact with him that convinced her he was someone she wanted to help. "While he was here," she would later explain, "I felt myself sustained by such a good, simply good, vibration, by a force—and that convinced me."

When he finally left for home at the end of February 1968, he presented Margaret with a Kashmiri shawl and told her no future trip to Europe would ever end without a stay in Gemsenstrasse, and this proved to be the case for the rest of his life. He often stayed for lengthy periods in one of the many apartments in the house, especially during the times of year when Kashmir was experiencing its seasonal extremes of heat and cold. Over the years Margaret not only provided him with a place to stay, she drove him around Europe to the various conferences he would one day speak at, accompanied him on trips to Canada and the United States, oversaw the publication, translation, and royalty distribution of his many books, and handled much of his voluminous correspondence. She also helped found the Swiss branch of Kundalini Research Association and kept an office for it on Gemsenstrasse. Through all this, she cooked his meals and, with regimental Swiss precision, made sure he ate on time. She even came up with a number of gracious techniques for interrupting important meetings when she felt it was time for him to eat. Margaret also spent a good deal of time in Kashmir, where she was accepted as a member of the family and where Bhabi taught her how to prepare Kashmiri dishes so Margaret could cook for Gopi Krishna when she herself could not be with him.

It is interesting that Margaret, in describing her first encounter with Gopi Krishna, used much the same wording as von Weizsäcker did in describing his.

It was some ineffable good and positive emanation coming from the yogi that first convinced both these rational, logical individuals that he was genuine. Margaret had needed both this personal experience of Gopi Krishna and the thorough examination of his ideas before she committed herself to helping him in any way. This was particularly true because Sinai, in spite of her obvious enthusiasm for and dedication to the yogi, had in some ways inspired more doubt than confidence. The complexity of Sinai's makeup was beginning to reveal itself. She was undoubtedly intellectually brilliant—she did, after all, attain three doctorates in political science, jurisprudence, and medicine—and there were many examples of extraordinary courage and fearless dedication in her life. But Margaret was discovering that, while Sinai's dedication to bringing about world peace had never faltered, her behavior could be not only extreme but erratic. Her dashing onto the field at the 1952 Olympics was not an isolated example of this. Margaret learned, for instance, that when Sinai was making her annual visits to the monastery on Mt. Sinai, she had once fasted for forty days and collapsed. On her initial visit to King Faisal, she had converted to Islam. Another time, after visiting a famous convent in Italy, she had converted to Catholicism. Now Sinai was dedicating her life to promoting Gopi Krishna's research. In addition, Margaret soon discovered that when Sinai had first arrived in Zürich and before coming to Gemsenstrasse, she had gone to meet with James Hillman. Once there, Sinai had demanded to be accepted into the Jung Institute's academic program. Her behavior during this meeting had been so troublesome that Hillman had decided not to admit her. These extremes and hints of erratic behavior gave Margaret pause, and she became very cautious about Sinai's opinions and enthusiasms. Ultimately, however, Gopi Krishna's writings and, especially, the character and demeanor he displayed during his visit won her over.

During the time he had been in Europe, his book had been translated and put into production with extraordinary speed and efficiency, and he had been back in Kashmir only a short while when he learned that von Mangoldt's March deadline had been reached. *Kundalini: Erweckung der geistigen Kraft im Menschen*, the first of Gopi Krishna's books to be put out by a major publisher, was done and, finally, after almost twenty years of unfailing and unflagging effort, his ideas were available to the wider world in not one but two major languages.

In spite of this success—or perhaps because of it—Gopi Krishna did not rest on his laurels. The hectic schedule in Germany and the homeward-bound journey to Kashmir, which was far more complicated and time-consuming than it is even today, had left him exhausted. He was, after all, soon to have his sixty-fifth birthday. Nonetheless, as soon as he had recuperated he began work on finishing another book he had begun before leaving for Europe. Entitled *The Coming War*, von Mangoldt had expressed interest in publishing it; this no doubt spurred him on. Unfortunately, it was never published, and exactly which version of the manuscript he was working on in the spring of 1968 is not known as more than one work bearing this name is found among his surviving papers. It was, however, most likely a version consisting of about 5,250 lines of inspired verse focused mainly on the premise of impending conflict and its possible prevention.[87]

While *The Coming War* seems to refer mostly to war in Kashmir, there is imagery that could refer to a wider, even worldwide conflagration—a theme that would recur many times during the span of his writing life. In addition to the various versions of *The Coming War*, he completed another all-verse volume in 1968 entitled *The Shape of Events to Come*. All of these manuscripts can be interpreted to be portending a third world war.[88]

It is no coincidence that all these works were written as inspired verse. Although Gopi Krishna never lost his hesitancy to claim to have any type of paranormal ability, it is difficult to read many verses in these works without thinking they are examples of prophecy. Gopi Krishna even occasionally made reference to this to those close to him, for example, in the 1963 letter to Tontyn quoted in Chapter Nine where he states that the inspired verses are often "prophetic in nature or deal with cosmogonal truths." The prophetic tone of passages in these poetic works, juxtaposed with the fact that, at least as of this writing, no third world war has occurred, raises a number of questions and issues, the most obvious being whether Gopi Krishna was simply wrong or a global conflagration is still on the horizon. While that particular question cannot be answered at this time, other issues related to the nature of prophecy cannot be ignored in an examination of the life of a man whose full-length works of inspired verse contain so much of what is apparently prognostication.

Gopi Krishna himself certainly made a great effort during his lifetime to explain the difficulties involved in receiving inspired verse, whether it was an attempt to predict the future or to express the essentially ineffable nature of cosmic consciousness and the divine. The opening lines of *The Coming War* express it this way:

> *Out of a luminous void encircling me*
> *And all the landscape seen, the earth and sky,*
> *A lustrous, all-pervading sea,*
> *Perceived by mind's internal cosmic eye,*
> *Like dim and distant objects drawing near,*
> *From but a blur assuming form and shape,*
> *These rhymes, impinging on a subtler ear,*
> *Arrive, a few to stay the rest to escape*
> *The memory as soon as the exalted mood*
> *Is ov'r, and I wake to the world around,*
> *In wonder on the marvel seen to brood,*
> *In wonder to recall the state profound...*

These words give a hint as to how indescribably difficult it must have been to be lost in a divine splendor and radiance so far beyond the human imagination that it was incomprehensible—and then to come back to this world and attempt to express what had been experienced in words the mundane world could understand. The great philosopher William James referred to this in his definition of *mystical experience* when he listed ineffable as its first characteristic. In other words, it could not, by its very nature, be expressed in the words we human beings have at our command.[89] To compound this, Gopi Krishna alludes in the quote above to how the words and images seen and heard in such a state might also be so indistinct that they were difficult to decipher, and in *Living with Kundalini* he likens the inspired words to rapidly falling snowflakes that crystallize before the eyes and just as swiftly melt away.[90] A further difficulty is created by the fact that, from Nostradamus to da Vinci, none of the great seers of history have ever received their visions stamped with time, date, or place.

All these and other issues aside, Gopi Krishna did have visions, and many were of war and devastation. Could some of these visions been of the countless wars that have taken place in the last few decades? The bombing of women, children, and other civilians in Iraq? The genocide in Rwanda? The 297 schoolgirls abducted by violent jihadists in Nigeria? The massacres in Tiananmen Square and Tibet? The flaming Twin Towers in New York? These and other horrific images from the last decades of the twentieth century and the first decades of the twenty-first are too numerous to mention, and there is simply no way to answer this question. It is also worthwhile to note that in some of his correspondence and conversations in the years after his first books of inspired verse were written, he explained that the coming troubles might take the form of either natural or environmental disasters that would be catastrophic enough to turn the attentions of the superpowers away from destroying each other with nuclear armaments to uniting in order to deal with the calamities involving Mother Nature.

Regardless, from his writings and further conversations on this topic it is abundantly clear he believed that the essential point was not the disasters themselves but the reasons for their occurrence. This cannot be overemphasized: for Gopi Krishna it was paramount. And it was a key factor in what motivated his undying passion to promote research on kundalini that would establish the evolutionary energy as a scientifically verifiable fact.

Although *The Coming War* was never published, *The Shape of Events to Come* did come out before the end of 1968. It was published in India by his Central Institute for Kundalini Research, in Srinagar, Kashmir. Although no hard copy of this book has been located as of this writing, another edition of it was published about a decade later that included, along with the verse, a ninety-six-page prose introduction. This introduction sheds light on the relationship between the evolutionary energy, its evolutionary goal, and the "warnings" contained in his inspired verse. For example:

The message contained in these writings is not a prophecy in the accepted sense of the term. It is an analysis of the present critical situation from the angle of evolution, brought about by our own neglect of spiritual laws. It is also a prognosis of the unhealthy mental conditions resulting from the evils rampant in society, which act as serious blocks in the evolution of the race.[91]

It is evident from the material covered earlier that the rampant societal evils referred to here are the prevalent greed, aggressiveness, and lust for power that cause social injustice and stand in diametrical opposition to the spiritual codes of conduct that range from the Ten Commandments of the Judeo-Christian tradition to the eightfold path of Buddhism and the yamas and niyamas of yoga.

In a discourse given in Zürich a few years after the Indian edition of *The Shape of Events to Come* had been published, Gopi Krishna expounded on this relationship between the prophetic tone found in his inspired verse and evolution.

...I had not been a believer in prophecy, generally speaking. And I had also not much thought about the future when the awakening occurred. But as soon as I started to write at the age of forty-nine, that is, fifteen years after the awakening, one of the first verses that came to me was:

"O, people of the world unite

And pave the way to peace sublime.

Divided you yourself invite

Disastrous wars, unrest and crime."

This was perhaps the first verse that came in English. And since that time, for all these nearly now twenty-five years, whenever I write, there is a reference to the coming events. I do not say that what I say is in the nature of a prophecy or a prediction. What I assert is that this writing is in the nature of a prognosis. I will explain myself a little further:

Let us assume, for the sake of argument, that human evolution is not a haphazard process, but is planned and designed. Let us also assume that a certain state of superconsciousness or I should say a God

> Consciousness is the ultimate target towards which human beings are evolving.... Let us again suppose that human beings are unaware of this process of evolution and they adopt modes of life and social or political orders which are diametrically opposed to the evolutionary drives in their bodies....
>
> What would be the result if, ignoring the revelation and ignoring the path of evolution about which the modern knowledge is still ignorant, we adopt a way of life which is not only opposite to evolution but also which is the path to degeneration and decay?

He often stated that either humanity would change its course or Mother Nature would change it with a blow. He described this blow as "a little buffet," and using an expression common in his time and place, he referred to this buffet as "a box on the ears, as a child has, to put it on the road, to put it straight. That is all I can foresee, that a calamity will come, but only to the extent of correcting us, not to destroy." In spite of these reassuring words, he also often reminded his listeners that the almighty power that would be delivering this slap on the wrist was one for whom billions of suns, millions of planets, and the infinity of time and space were mere playthings.[92]

In considering his predictive verses, it is also important to note that he frequently stated that he could not claim "finality" for the prognosis that was being made in them. He left all judgment to the future. He also made it clear, as stated above, that the events that unfolded in the visions were based on the condition of the world and humanity's collective consciousness at that time. Thus, it was possible that a massive change in humanity's attitude—for instance, a wholesale adherence to the spiritual rules of conduct or a concentrated, unified, focused prayer by enough individuals—could possibly change the way events would unfold, either mitigating them or even preventing them. Given human beings' tendency to stubbornness, this massive change in attitude may not seem likely. Still, it remained—and remains—a possibility.

Warning humanity about the potential for disaster and revealing the key for preventing them was only part of the reason Gopi Krishna worked on manuscripts such as *The Coming War* and *The Shape of Events to Come*. In a much broader sense, he was unveiling the incomprehensible cosmic intelligence's plans for humanity's evolution to higher states of consciousness and the mode of living that was necessary for us to attain this luminescent state.

Chapter Thirteen

Von Weizsäcker—
A Renowned Physicist Takes Up the Call

With his first trip to Europe, his meeting with von Weizsäcker, and the publication of his book in both English and German, Gopi Krishna's life would change dramatically. After the spring of 1968, the remote, northern Indian province of Kashmir would no longer be the only place he was known as a revered leader and a man of great wisdom. Now, at an age that was advanced for his time and place, world travel would become part of his life. Before he left for Europe again, however, he would once more focus on his writing. This, he believed, was the vehicle that would carry his message most effectively to the world. Accordingly, he pressed on with the momentum generated in 1968. By June of 1969, he had finished a revision of *The Coming War* and begun his second book that would be completely in prose, *The Secret of Yoga*. He also spent time revising a small prose volume called *Questions and Answers*. Produced while Sinai was in Kashmir, it had been conceived as a means of getting complex information about kundalini out to the public in an easy-to-understand format. To create the text, Sinai had carefully recorded the answers to a set of agreed-upon questions that she put to him in a series of interviews.

He must have been encouraged in his effort to produce written material by the spreading success of his first book. Earlier in 1969, Tontyn, who was steadfastly continuing his efforts on Gopi Krishna's behalf, had contacted the respected British publishers Vincent Stuart & John M. Watkins, Ltd., and by June they were expressing definite interest in publishing *Kundalini: The Evolutionary Energy in Man* in the United Kingdom. In conjunction with this, Gopi Krishna had come in contact with Leslie Shepard. Shepard was a filmmaker and highly respected editor who was also an author in his own right. In the late 1950s he had spent six months in India studying yoga and had a deep interest in spirituality. After coming into contact with Gopi Krishna's ideas through his first book, Shepard entered into correspondence with him and would eventually play a major role not only during Gopi Krishna's life but also after his death, when Shepard would edit and pull together material from three separate volumes of Gopi Krishna's autobiographical writings and craft the widely influential book *Living with Kundalini*.

Shepard was known for his own work as an author and was not a literary representative or agent for others per se. Regardless, he felt compelled to take on this role for Gopi Krishna's writings. Perhaps he did so because he felt this yogi, whom he greatly admired, from a rather isolated part of India, might need assistance navigating the shoals of the British publishing world. Whatever his reason, Shepard entered into negotiations with Stuart & Watkins on Gopi Krishna's behalf, and the British *Kundalini: The Evolutionary Energy in Man* was soon in production—an edition that had the potential for reaching a far wider audience than the English edition published in India could hope to.

Just as Tontyn was continuing to play a major role in Gopi Krishna's life, so was Sinai. In the second week of June 1969, Gopi Krishna received a letter from a Dr. Gerhard Wolfram, representing Die Gesellschaft für Religion und Wissenschaft, or the Society for Religion and Science. The German organization was sponsoring a seminar to be held from July 11 to 13 in Florence, Italy. Gopi Krishna was being invited to speak and once again to have all expenses paid. In spite of the rather late notice, he accepted the invitation: the meeting looked to be an opportunity to meet with more scientists and scholars. As the letter included an invitation for him to spend some time with Wolfram and his wife at their home in Munich, Gopi Krishna wrote to von Weizsäcker to see if they could meet while he was in Germany. Von Weizsäcker responded that he would not be available during that time but hoped to visit Gopi Krishna in Kashmir in the near future.

It eventually became apparent that Sinai was a driving force behind the organization of the seminar and that having it in Florence was no coincidence. The city and, especially, the neighboring village of Fiesole, had long been important in Sinai's life. This was the location of the Franciscan convent of Mother Giovanna Francesca. Mother Giovanna, who would one day be venerated by Pope Francis, was the founder of the Franciscan Missionary Sisters of the Incarnate Word. She had had mystical experiences and divine intuitions since early childhood, and it was said that she was radiant with divine love.[93] Unfortunately, neither Mother Giovanna's divine love nor Gopi Krishna's divine wisdom were enough to keep Sinai on an even keel during this period of her life. After translating *Kundalini: The Evolutionary Energy in Man*, she remained in Germany in hopes of beginning studies there that would add a medical degree to the two doctorates she already held. Having met von Weizsäcker in relation to her work on Gopi Krishna's book, she approached him in hopes of furthering her goal and possibly working closely with him in some capacity. At first, von Weizsäcker tried to assist her, but it eventually became apparent that he could not do so. The chinks in her makeup that had earlier troubled Margaret Kobelt were becoming more apparent and reached an extreme in her dealings with von Weizsäcker. She had somehow twisted his willingness to help her further Gopi Krishna's research into an obsession with the physicist, eventually becoming consumed with the notion that he should become not just her mentor but literally a "father" who claimed her publicly as his daughter.

It was becoming increasingly evident that Sinai's instability was at war with her extraordinary capacity to accomplish the near impossible. Her troubling obsessive tendencies had become apparent to Gopi Krishna fairly early on. Since that time he had been making a concerted effort to help her gain peace and heal these unhealthy aspects of her personality. With his guidance, she was often able to come to a deeper understanding of her behavior that helped correct misguided actions. She was eventually able to do so in the case of her obsession with von Weizsäcker, but not before the famous physicist was forced to break with her completely.

It is difficult not to speculate on whether Sinai's disruptive behavior in Germany might not have had some detrimental effect on von Weizsäcker's attitude about Gopi Krishna in those early days of their association and to wonder what his thoughts about her might have been. Regardless, those who knew Gopi Krishna personally often heard him say that he believed the people who helped him had been "sent by Heaven." That being so, he thanked heaven for each and every one of them, even though others would, like Sinai, prove to be mixed blessings.

Although the reason is not known, Sinai was not able to pull off the seminar she had tried to arrange in Florence. In the short time between the invitation and Gopi Krishna's arrival in Europe it had been canceled. Still, it was rescheduled as one to be held on the same dates in Munich. In order to attend it, Gopi Krishna flew first directly to Zürich. After his last trip to Europe he understood how vital it would be for him to rest for a few days after the grueling hours of flying and waiting in airports for transfers. When he finally arrived in Zürich, he was met by both Tontyn and Margaret and taken to the house on Gemsenstrasse, where he could recuperate before traveling to Munich to make his presentation at the seminar.

Entitled simply *"Religion und Wissenschaft,"* the seminar was evidently aimed at individuals with an interest in cross-cultural spiritual traditions: the scheduled speakers included not only Gopi Krishna and two other Hindu yogis but also representatives from Islam, Buddhism, and Christianity. One of the yogis was Swami Chidananda, who was the son of the widely respected Swami Sivananda Saraswati, the revered founder of the Divine Light Society in Rishikesh. After attending the seminar, Gopi Krishna stayed in Europe until the first part of September 1969 and continued his efforts to make contact with the scientific community regarding kundalini research. Although his complete itinerary is not known, he did stay first with the Wolframs and then later again in Zürich. Once he arrived back in Kashmir, he spent some time recuperating before tackling the correspondence that had accumulated while he was gone. Even though he had to spend an ever-increasing amount of time answering letters as his renown grew, he did not neglect his writing. Very soon he was working on *The Secret of Yoga* again, continuing with this project through the end of 1969 and into the next year.

While he was doing so, a number of other events were weaving together in ways that would have great significance for Gopi Krishna's future. Unbeknownst to him, in faraway Kootenay Bay, British Columbia, Canada, a woman named Sylvia Hellman had somehow obtained a copy of the Ramadhar & Hopman Indian edition of *Kundalini: The Evolutionary Energy in Man.* Born in Germany in 1911, Hellman's experience of war had motivated her to move to Canada in 1951 and then later go to India, where she studied with the Swami Sivananda. After she proved to be an extraordinarily adept pupil, the renowned Swami initiated her into his lineage in 1956, giving her the title Sivananda Radha Saraswati. This was a time when initiating a non-Indian woman into a sacred Hindu lineage was virtually unheard of, and after receiving this great honor, she returned to Canada, where, at Sivananda's suggestion, she founded the Yashodhara ashram that still exists in British Columbia. Eventually she became widely known as Swami Radha and renowned not only for the ashram but also for writing the book *Kundalini Yoga for the West.*

Although in 1969 her teaching and her ashram were still in the fledgling stages, a man in New York named Gene Kieffer heard of her and became interested in her work. About this time an invoice from the bookstore associated with the ashram shows an order for two dozen copies of the Ramadhar & Hopman edition of Gopi Krishna's book. It is perhaps one of these books that Swami Radha sent to Gene Kieffer, for he did indeed receive a copy from her, and it quite literally changed his life.

At the time, Gene was the married father of four children. With a background in journalism, he had been the owner of a highly successful advertising agency in his home state of Iowa but had recently packed up his family and moved them to New York City, where he started up a color graphics company. Just when the company was becoming successful, Gene received the copy of *Kundalini: The Evolutionary Energy in Man.* Reading it, Gene became so impressed that, before he had even finished, he wrote to Gopi Krishna. After exchanging only a few letters and receiving a piece of Gopi Krishna's recently finished writing,

Gene made a commitment to dedicate his time, energy, and whatever finances he could to furthering the yogi's work. Extraordinary as it may seem, Gene Kieffer—alive as of this writing at ninety-seven years of age—never faltered in keeping this promise.[94]

By October 1969 Gene was enthusiastically sending copies of *Kundalini: The Evolutionary Energy in Man* to absolutely anyone he thought might be interested. A noteworthy example of the responses came from a woman named Pauline Harden, who was associated with a Florida branch of the Friends of Teilhard de Chardin. After reading the book, she wrote directly to Gopi Krishna. After saying that Gene had informed her about Gopi Krishna's work and the research planned to verify his findings "to the satisfaction of scientists," she added:

> This is all very important to me—it bears out beautifully the predictions of Pierre Teilhard de Chardin, French scientist-mystic, of whom I am sure you are aware. I have felt for some time it is my mission to spread the word of Teilhard's writings as widely and as quickly as possible. Your work is *vital* at this time.

It is evident from this that even Gene's earliest efforts to promote Gopi Krishna's work were making inroads almost immediately. In spite of her obvious issues Sinai, too, was continuing her efforts during that autumn of 1969: she was already beginning to think about organizing another conference in Florence. By the final days of December the conference was beginning to take shape. In a new year's greeting card she sent out, she claimed two major accomplishments that had occurred just before and on New Year's Day. The first was the founding on January 1 of the Institute for the Practice and Scientific Observation of Meditation, which included a special branch for research on Kundalini and the spiritual energy in man, to be headed by Gopi Krishna. As the observing scientists for the foundation, she listed Dr. Johann Kugler, of the Neurology Clinic at the University of Munich, and physiologist Dr. Hans Reichel. A number of other interested scientists were listed, including Werner Heisenberg. (Whether Heisenberg actually ever had any direct interest in this is not known; however, there is evidence that Sinai did meet with him at some point, and Gopi Krishna met with him at least once.)

Sinai's second proclaimed accomplishment was a meeting she organized just prior to New Year's Day in Starnberg as a first step in planning a major conference to be held in Florence in 1970 from October 25 to 31. To be called "Religion and Science, Statesmanship and Virtue," its purpose was to bring together a number of leading scientists and religious leaders, including Gopi Krishna. A subsequent invitation sent out to potential speakers stated:

> The main purpose of this Florence conference is to bring about a coordinated movement amongst the scientific, spiritual, political and other interested peoples of the world to promote mutual understanding, cooperation and peace between all people of all countries.

This call for speakers was signed by Sinai, as president of her Institute for the Practice and Observation of Meditation, along with Swami Chidananda and Johann Kugler. Naturally, an invitation to speak went out to Gopi Krishna. It would have a profound effect on his life.

While Gopi Krishna was still in Kashmir, Sinai was in the process of organizing an additional European gathering on the theme of religion and science. This one would be held prior to the Florence conference in Nicosia, the capital of Cyprus. Upon receiving Sinai's invitation to this meeting, Gopi Krishna agreed to attend. At it he was scheduled to meet with Archbishop Makarios III. Considered the Father of Cyprus, Makarios was not only archbishop of the Greek Orthodox Church there, he had also been elected the country's first president when it obtained independence in 1960.

Gopi Krishna left Kashmir around the middle of October, attending the gathering in Cyprus with Sinai as planned. Although little is known of Gopi Krishna's meeting with Makarios, the Cyprus event was by all accounts a success. When it was concluded, Sinai accompanied Gopi Krishna to Florence, where he was to stay at the Yoga Centro on via dei Bardi. The Yoga Centro, founded by Antonio and Marcella Naim in 1964, was one of the first two yoga studios in Florence. Today the Centro is considered part of the city's yoga history, and the Naims are remembered as the master yoga teachers who were instrumental in bringing yoga to Italy. But even as early as 1970 they were widely known.

Gratified to meet the Naims, Gopi Krishna was more than content with the simple accommodations at the Yoga Centro. However, as happened several times during these early trips when very few people understood how assiduous he had to be in keeping a regular schedule of eating and resting, he was left to his own devices in a strange land. In his later writings he would point out how the regular, virtually rigid schedules kept in ashrams, monasteries, and other religious enclaves provided the structure needed to support the healthy awakening of the spiritual energies. This was, of course, not yet widely known, and the Yoga Centro was simply a yoga studio and not an ashram.

For years after his stay there, he would tell a story about it as an example of how Heaven could come to our aid in even small ways. One night after he'd arrived in Florence, he had been invited out for the evening by some of his new acquaintances. When the evening was over, they drove back to the Yoga Centro, dropped him off on the street, and drove away. When he tried to use the key he'd been given for the door to the now-shuttered Centro, it would not work. There he was, a sixty-seven-year-old man with a delicate constitution, on the streets of a foreign country on a late October night. He did not have enough money on his person to go to a hotel, and indeed he did not know where to find one. At the time he was worried not so much about himself per se as about how a night spent on a cold, damp doorstep might affect his ability to deliver his talk and interact with the important scientists he was hoping to meet. After trying again and again to open the door, he stood in consternation on the street. Just then a car pulled up, and a complete stranger asked him if he needed help. Overcoming the language barrier as best they could, Gopi Krishna managed to explain the situation. After failing to open the door himself, the stranger bundled Gopi Krishna into his car, took him to his home to eat and sleep, and brought him back when the Centro was opened the next morning.[95]

Eager to give his presentation and, especially, to speak with the internationally known scientists in attendance, Gopi Krishna was stunned when Sinai suddenly canceled the conference shortly before it was to begin. Neither Gopi Krishna nor Margaret, who had been in ongoing contact with

Sinai about the arrangements, was ever able to discover what had led to this last-minute cancellation.

In spite of the actual conference being called off, a number of smaller talks and gatherings had somehow been arranged. Speaking at them, Gopi Krishna managed to meet with a number of doctors and scientists. At this time he also met with a woman named Evelyn Ferrantini. An Italian translator whose languages included German and English, Ferrantini would remain a good friend and supporter for the rest of his life, just as the Naims would. After meeting Gopi Krishna they would all, especially the Naims, have a major role in founding an Italian branch of the Kundalini Research Foundation—one of the first international branches of the Central Institute for Kundalini Research that Gopi Krishna had started in Kashmir. Evelyn Ferrantini and the Naims were also eager to see Gopi Krishna's work translated into Italian, becoming instrumental in the eventual publication of both *Kundalini: The Evolutionary Energy in Man* and *The Secret of Yoga* in Italy.

Nonetheless, the small talks and meetings in Florence were a far cry from what he had hoped to accomplish toward his research goals at a formal conference including internationally known scientists and spiritual leaders. On leaving the city, he went immediately to Zürich to recuperate at the house on Gemsenstrasse, where Margaret was now planning to set up a Swiss branch of the Kundalini Research Foundation. Margaret described him as being, on his arrival, terribly let down that the Florence conference had been canceled. Disappointing as this might have been, he received other news that his efforts were not in vain. During his stay in Italy, the Stuart & Watkins edition of *Kundalini: The Evolutionary Energy in Man* had been officially launched in Great Britain. Although he had no way of knowing this at the time, this publication would ultimately be the catalyst for a cascade of translations and international editions.

That October, another fortuitous event was occurring in the United States: Gene Kieffer was making plans to travel to Zürich. In response to a request for more information made during their brief correspondence prior to Gopi Krishna's trip to Europe, the yogi had sent him a draft of the talk he was preparing for the Florence conference. Thunderstruck by the document, Gene became determined to meet Gopi Krishna in person. Aware that it would be much easier to do this in Europe than in Kashmir, Gene cast his serious concerns about the expense aside, bought his ticket, and arrived on November 5—a day that was coincidentally Gene's birthday and one he would often say in the future was the most important of his life. After spending four days in Zürich, Gene was overwhelmingly convinced—as countless people had been and would be—by Gopi Krishna's demeanor not only that he was utterly sincere but that he had attained a virtually inconceivable state of cosmic consciousness.

Shortly after Gene's departure, Gopi Krishna went to Munich in order to meet with von Weizsäcker and a number of other scientists. Sinai had also arranged for a lecture by Gopi Krishna to be put on in Hamburg on November 18 by the Society for Religion, Science, and Peace. The title for that evening's lecture was "The Spiritual Power-Center in Man, the Necessity of Its Research, and the Responsibility of Science." There, Gopi Krishna spoke along with Hugo Enomiya-Lassalle, who was one of the many important people the yogi would cross paths with during his life. A German Jesuit priest, Enomiya-Lassalle had been sent to Japan as a missionary in 1935. After being wounded in the atomic blast in Hiroshima, Lassalle spent years attempting to establish a cathedral in that city that would be a testament to world peace. After accomplishing this goal in 1954 with the completion of the Memorial Cathedral to World Peace, Lassalle became a serious student of Zen and eventually one of the earliest and one of the foremost teachers in the world to embrace both Roman Catholic Christianity and Zen Buddhism, and it is fascinating to imagine what the conversation between the two men might have been that night. Clearly Sinai, in spite of her issues, was still making a concerted effort to promote kundalini research and, ultimately, help bring about world peace.

By the final week of November, Gopi Krishna was back in southern Germany, staying in Starnberg with Karl Friedrich Basedow, an acquaintance of von Weizsäcker's. Plans were now underway for the creation of an organization dedicated to furthering kundalini research named the Forschungsgesellschaft für östliche Weisheit und westliche Wissenschaft, or the Research Foundation for Eastern Wisdom and Western Science. An association had been formed to oversee the foundation, with Basedow listed as general secretary. Von Weizsäcker, with only limited time to commit, agreed to be the nominal head of the organization, while Basedow became the person expected to head up the foundation and its actual work.

Exactly what the foundation was considering in terms of future research is not certain. Gopi Krishna had evidently not yet formulated his kundalini hypothesis. The crux of this premise would eventually maintain that kundalini—known by many names in different spiritual traditions—was responsible for mystical experience, inspired creativity and genius, and paranormal phenomena. Gopi Krishna had by this time, however, made clear his contention that the activity of this transformative evolutionary energy, while profoundly spiritual in nature, operated in the human body, where it brought about certain physiological changes that would be detectable by the science of the day. Although this premise would not be stated in print until the release of his next book, *The Biological Basis of Religion and Genius*, he had definitely been making it known. Given this, it seems likely that it was a study of the biologically based changes associated with the awakening of kundalini that was of interest to the scientists associated with the foundation early in its inception. Regardless, the formation of the foundation was a major step in advancing his goals.

Following this highly productive time in Germany, Gopi Krishna traveled back to what had become his European home base on Gemsenstrasse in Zürich. The year 1970 was coming to an end. During the extraordinary year and a half that had begun after his return from his first trip to Europe, the pivotal British edition of *Kundalini: The Evolutionary Energy in Man* had come out and interest in an Italian translation and publication was high. Plans were now underway for kundalini research foundations of one sort or another in Germany, Italy, and Switzerland. Two lengthy trips to Europe had been made, and Gopi Krishna had made contact with an exceptional number of people who would be important to his life and work. But perhaps most astounding was the amount of writing he accomplished while all this other activity had been going on. He had finished up the all-verse book *The Coming War*; he had revised *Questions and Answers*; he had completed the writing of his second all-prose book, *The Secret of Yoga,* and sent it out to potential publishers; and he had composed a speech that was ninety pages long.

It is easy to imagine that Gopi Krishna contemplated all this as he sat in the house on Gemsenstrasse on Christmas Day 1970. On Christmas Eve Margaret had carried out the Swiss tradition of covering the Christmas tree with small white candles and setting them alight that evening. Recalling this beautiful image the next day, Gopi Krishna wrote in a letter:

> From the little study I have made it is obvious that the cult of kundalini was known all over the world in ancient days. The almost universal symbol of the Sun and the Serpent in use from as remote a period as the Neolithic age clearly points to the conclusion that in one form or another the Serpent Power was known and worshipped from very ancient times. There are clear references to this fact even in the Bible....
> One of the names of Kundalini is Shakambari, i.e. one that has branches of a tree. You can clearly see the resemblance when you see a chart of the human nervous system. The spinal cord is the trunk of the tree. Illumination of the tree with burning candles is symbolic of the inner illumination experienced on the awakening of Kundalini. Christ was an illumined prophet with an awakened Kundalini.

Chapter Fourteen

Exploring the Biological Basis
of Religion and Genius

After spending Christmas and New Year's Day in Zürich, Gopi Krishna was so eager to get home that, against Margaret's advice, he booked the earliest flight he could get in spite of its less than favorable connections. On January 3, 1971, he left for India. As Margaret had predicted, the trip took a toll on his health. After spending a short time in Delhi with family, he flew to Kashmir where he began to improve, gaining strength for a year that would see advancements on as many fronts as 1970 had.

Much of January and February was spent recuperating and answering the many letters that had piled up during his absence, including correspondence that was now flowing in from the supporters who were setting up foundations to promote his work abroad and from potential publishers. Interest in publishing *Kundalini: The Evolutionary Energy in Man* was about to take off. Not only did the progress begun in 1970 on translating and publishing the Italian edition continue in the early months of 1971, Tontyn had found a Dutch translator and was working on finding a publisher in Holland. Before the end of 1971 both these editions would come out, making the book available in Great Britain and Europe to speakers of English, German, Italian, and Dutch. Important as these European developments were, another was taking shape in the United States that would have even farther-reaching effects.

With the polished edition produced by Stuart & Watkins in hand, both Gene Kieffer and Leslie Shepard had begun to search for a US publisher. Shambhala was an obvious choice. Getting the work accepted by them, however, represented a serious challenge. Not only was Shambhala arguably the top spiritual-book publisher of the day, the company had been founded with a definite leaning toward publications related to Buddhism. The odds against getting the work of an unknown Hindu yogi accepted seemed insurmountable. Nevertheless, both men remained undaunted. Gene Kieffer, in particular, was tenacious in his pursuit of the spiritual publisher. Although editors there expressed some initial hesitation, Gene convinced them to take the book on that spring. Although the German, British, English, Dutch, and Italian versions of the book were extremely important, it is fairly safe to say that Shambhala's international reputation for excellence made this company's edition the single most important development in the book's publishing history, given that it remains in print some five decades after its release.[96]

If the worldwide publication of *Kundalini: The Evolutionary Energy in Man* was the most consequential factor in introducing the man Gopi Krishna to a vast audience, the publication of *The Biological Basis of Religion and Genius* was the most influential in bringing his ideas to the attention of the scientific community, and this was, after all, the goal he pursued with unremitting determination throughout his lifetime. The story of the book's creation and its being ready for international publication by the close of 1971 is one rich with intertwining events and so-called coincidences.

It all began with Sinai's decision to hold that eventually canceled conference in Florence in the fall of 1970. By the time that conference had been officially confirmed, the speakers included an impressive list of scientists, political figures, and religious leaders. Given her background as the woman who had flown around the world meeting with many of the most important heads of state of the time, there was no reason to doubt her being able to bring some of the world's top scientists and spiritual leaders together for a conference, and Gopi Krishna undoubtedly saw this as a priceless opportunity to express his theories to individuals influential enough to make his proposed research a reality. His presentation to them was therefore of paramount importance. The ultimate result was a ninety-page essay on the topic of the shortfalls of religion and science that detailed how research into an evolutionary energy—responsible for both spiritual and scientific genius—could overcome the shortfalls in these two seemingly disparate domains and, in doing so, usher in an era of peace.

Exactly when he began work on his written presentation for the conference is not certain. According to Gene Kieffer's recollections, however, Gopi Krishna had originally been planning to give an extemporaneous speech and did not begin writing out his talk until shortly before he left Kashmir for Europe, when he received Gene's request for more information mentioned in the last chapter. With his extensive background in advertising, Gene had wanted the information to create a brief brochure he could send out to scientists and other influential people. What he received instead was a draft of the document that would be ninety pages long by the time it was finished. Even though it was far too much material to use in a brief brochure, Gene thought it was the most extraordinary piece of writing he had ever read. In spite of the fact that he had spent considerable time in deep and earnest spiritual pursuit, he had not come across anything that answered the spiritual questions that beset him in the way these words did.

After actually meeting with Gopi Krishna, he became determined to make the document into a book that would be called *The Biological Basis of Religion and Genius*. Building on his successful advertising career, on his arrival in New York he had started a burgeoning graphics company. Producing a book and promoting it seemed like something well within his capabilities. By February of 1971 he had formed a publishing company called New Concepts and had begun the work of turning the essay into a book. His goal, however, was not just to create the book; it was to get it out to people who mattered. Using every contact he had and all of his promotional acumen, he put together a list of over 200 scientists, professors, and influential people to send the finished book to. During this period of time, he had also received a copy of the manuscript for *The Shape of Events to Come*. Convinced that research into the premise proposed by Gopi Krishna could contribute to an intellectual and spiritual climate that could help prevent the potential calamities described in that manuscript, Gene was fired with a sense of urgency. He set himself a specific date to get *The Biological Basis of Religion and Genius* in their hands and to reach that goal.

In spite of Gene's skill and resolve, however, both the production of the book and his promotional efforts were fraught with setbacks and delays. On the last day that it would be possible to meet his deadline, Gene received printed copies and pressed his family into service. Inspired by his enthusiasm, they zealously labeled over 200 envelopes and stuffed them with books just in time for Gene to rush to a New York City post office before the 11:00 p.m. closing time. When he arrived and placed the books on the counter, the postman refused to take them, saying items being mailed at book rate had to be in by 8:00 p.m. Gene argued but to no avail. Defeated, he carried his bags of books back to the car. And then he had an idea. He would stuff them into mailboxes; they would be picked up in the morning and go out as planned. He and his son Tom spent much of the rest of the night driving around New York City cramming copies of the New Concepts edition of *The Biological Basis of Religion and Genius* into mailboxes.

By April replies to Gene's mass mailing had begun to come in. He received a number of thank-yous, but only a couple of responses that indicated, in Gene's opinion, a deep grasp of the concepts expressed in the book. Over the next while, New Concepts published a hardcover edition with a more polished design and continued to contact scientists and important people. Even those respondents who did seem to comprehend the profound implications of the theories seemed to have little idea how they could further the research. And many were frankly skeptical of the notion that legitimate science could or should have any interest in concepts propounded by an unknown Kashmiri and rooted in yoga—a tradition that was not widely known among the mainstream in 1971.

The production of the book in the United States was, however, soon to get a tremendous boost from another series of events. The first had been underway for some time in Germany. Basedow's efforts to develop the Research Foundation for Eastern Wisdom and Western Science were continuing, and von Weizsäcker's interest in Gopi Krishna's proposal for research was high. For some time, von Weizsäcker had been hoping to make time in his busy schedule to go to Kashmir and visit face to face with the yogi. During the first part of 1971 he became increasingly determined to make the trip, ultimately doing so in April.

During these early months of 1971, Ursula von Mangoldt had also been presented with a copy of the ninety-page essay. Although exactly how this occurred is not certain, what is known is that von Weizsäcker was given a copy of the essay at a time when he had a deep desire to promote kundalini research, and after reading it, he agreed to write the formal introduction to the essay. Fully aware of the respect von Weizsäcker commanded in Germany, von Mangoldt knew that combining a commendation by von Weizsäcker with Gopi Krishna's powerful essay would make an eminently publishable book. Approached with the suggestion, von Weizsäcker agreed to write the detailed introduction for the book.

In the United States, Gene was becoming discouraged by the lack of response he was getting from the scientific community and wrote to von Mangoldt. Replying to him at the end of March, she commiserated and suggested he include an English translation of the introduction von Weizsäcker was doing for the German edition in any subsequent editions he wanted to produce. She added that, unfortunately, due to the physicist's busy schedule, she wasn't expecting the introduction to be completed before late summer or autumn.

Armed with the knowledge that the introduction from the famed physicist was in the works and realizing how it would both add scientific authority to Gopi Krishna's ideas and counteract his lack of renown in North America, Gene decided to approach a major publisher. Through his extensive contacts in the publishing world, he knew a woman named Ruth Nanda Anshen. An esteemed author in her own right, with a background and interest in spirituality, Anshen had been put in charge of putting together and editing a *Religious Perspectives* series for Harper & Row, a series that would include books by thinkers as renowned as Paul Tillich, Erich Fromm, and Martin Heidegger. With an introduction by von Weizsäcker promised, Anshen accepted the book on the behalf of her Harper & Row series.

Von Weizsäcker apparently began work on the piece somewhat earlier than von Mangoldt expected and completed a draft of it during his visit with Gopi Krishna. After the trip, he returned to Germany determined not only to polish the introduction but to have Basedow organize a seminar in July where Gopi Krishna could meet and discuss his ideas with other German scientists and influential people. Unfortunately, von Weizsäcker became extremely ill after his trip to India. When he did not recover quickly, both his work on the final draft of the introduction and the plans for Gopi Krishna's July trip to Germany were postponed.

In spite of his illness, von Weizsäcker managed to polish his introduction in time for Otto Wilhelm Barth Verlag to publish the German edition of the book, *Die biologische Basis der religiösen Erfahrung*, in 1971 as von Mangoldt had originally planned. For Ruth Nanda Anshen's purposes, however, the final draft of von Weizsäcker's section still had to be translated into English for the American edition. This was completed by the winter of 1971. By the end of the year *The Biological Basis for Religion and Genius* was virtually ready for publication in her prestigious series.

In this book Gopi Krishna laid out with unfailing, step-by-step logic the reasons kundalini research was needed. For the first time he also had the opportunity to explain the aspects of kundalini awakening that made it so amenable to scientific examination. While kundalini awakening was the profoundest of spiritual experience, guided by an all-pervading, omniscient cosmic intelligence, its method of working in the human body was biological in nature. Therefore, it could be detected—and thus verified—by scientific examination.

> With the awakening of Kundalini, an amazing activity commences in the whole nervous system from the crown of the head to the toes.... Whenever an awakening of this kind occurs, the normal biological rhythm of the body immediately experiences a drastic change, entirely beyond the power of control of the *sadhaka* [in this case, the successful yogi]. His body is now transformed into a miniature laboratory, working at high speed day and night.... This entirely biological operation is carried out in such an unmistakable way that even a novice in physiology cannot fail to notice it.[97]

Ruth Nanda Anshen's grasp of the significance of this revolutionary proposal for research must have been great, for on receiving Gopi Krishna's manuscript for *The Secret of Yoga*, she accepted it, too, for inclusion in her eminent *Religious Perspectives* series. While the acceptance of both *The Biological Basis* and *The Secret of Yoga* by Harper & Row and the Shambhala publication of *Kundalini: The Evolutionary Energy in Man* can be seen as the crowning events of 1971, a great deal also happened on other fronts throughout that year. The piled-up correspondence that Gopi Krishna had to deal with when he got back to Kashmir in January indicated not only the increased interest in the publication of his autobiography and the development of kundalini centers in various countries mentioned earlier but also a noticeable increase generally in his international renown. During the late winter and early spring of 1971 he received letters from doctors associated with Indian universities and other important organizations. For instance, in March he received a letter from Dr. A.S. Ramaswami, a scientist who had organized a Kundalini Research Group at the All India Institute of Medical Sciences—a foundation that would come to have a pivotal role in Gopi Krishna's research efforts later in the 1970s. Another letter received that month indicated that the widely respected French philosopher Maryse Choisy, who was both a professor at the Institut Supérieur d'Hiérologie in Paris and founder of the journal *Psyché*, had received a copy of *The Biological Basis* from Gene Kieffer. She was now offering to translate the work into French because, she said,

the author's age is an urgent challenge to humanity—a spiritual bomb. Every scientist who is horrified at the possibilities of nuclear calamity in the hands of the unregenerate owes it to himself to investigate this evolutionary psychophysiological power.

This mass of correspondence also included an invitation from Amrit Desai, the founder of Kripalu Yoga, to speak at a World Congress for Enlightenment along with himself and other Indian spiritual teachers that included Yogi Bhajan, Swami Satchidananda, and Swami Vishnu-devananda. To be held in August in Oregon, the conference was expected to have massive attendance as each of these speakers was considered a guru with an extensive following of his own. One newspaper article of the day said organizers were hoping to attract a quarter of a million young people.[98] In spite of the opportunity to speak to such a huge audience, Gopi Krishna politely declined the invitation. This was neither the first nor the last time that he would turn down invitations and opportunities that would have widely increased his fame. Over the years, he would often repeat his preference to instead meet with smaller groups of people, especially scientists or others who might further his research goals.

In this regard, there was undoubtedly no other event in that spring of 1971 that came closer to fulfilling this particular heart's desire than the visit von Weizsäcker made to Kashmir. After spending about a week with associates in New Delhi, the renowned physicist arrived in Kashmir on April 21. During the week the physicist and the yogi spent together in the Himalayan foothills, their discussions ranged over a great many topics, undoubtedly including how Eastern wisdom and Western science could best further world peace and prosperity. According to a letter he wrote afterward, they also discussed an issue that had been on Gopi Krishna's mind for some time, namely, how he might better "adjust his writings to the temper of the Western mind" and express the research he was proposing in the terminology used in Western science and scholarship. To further this goal, von Weizsäcker strongly advised Gopi Krishna to spend more time in Europe so that he could meet with more scientists and scholars, enter into in-depth discussions, and exchange ideas with them. This, Gopi Krishna agreed, would not only broaden his knowledge of the outer world in general, it would help him better know the Western mind and, thus, how to get his ideas across to the scientific and medical communities of the West. An added benefit of spending more time in Europe would be that he would be able to pick up some knowledge of languages such as German and Italian.

It is apparent that von Weizsäcker was serious about his suggestion that Gopi Krishna spend more time in Europe, for he left Kashmir with plans in place to have Basedow organize a gathering of scientists and scholars who could meet with Gopi Krishna in the later part of July, when he hoped his own schedule would allow him to participate at least to some extent. That Gopi Krishna took von Weizsäcker's advice to heart was also apparent. On April 30, the day after the physicist left, Gopi Krishna wrote to Basedow and Margaret telling them of his plans to arrive in Europe before July in order to spend several months there dividing his time between writing and the types of meetings von Weizsäcker had recommended.

In Germany, however, it soon became apparent that von Weizsäcker's illness was going to be debilitating for longer than first thought. Basedow quickly informed Gopi Krishna of this, saying that the proposed gathering of scientists would certainly have to be put off at least until the fall. In spite of this setback, Gopi Krishna decided to go ahead with the trip as planned. At the end of June, he arrived at the Zürich airport to find Margaret and Tontyn eagerly waiting for him. Never one to arrive without gifts, Gopi Krishna greeted them with a huge bag of mangoes. Even years later Margaret could vividly recall eating the fruit in her kitchen with Tontyn and Gopi Krishna and being amazed by its luscious color and delicious savor. After staying about a week in the house on Gemsenstrasse, Gopi Krishna left for Starnberg, Germany, where von Weizsäcker had during the previous year established yet another *Max Planck Institute*, this one for *Erforschung der Lebensbedingungen der wissenschaftlich-technischen Welt*, or roughly translated, Research on Living Conditions in the Modern World. Even though von Weizsäcker's illness prevented Gopi Krishna from seeing him at this time, Starnberg was Basedow's home. It was also now the location of the Research Foundation for Eastern Wisdom and Western Science. Other scientists associated with von Weizsäcker's branch of the Max Planck Institute were also located there, providing the likelihood of discussions that could broaden his understanding of Western thinking.

One such person who was very eager to meet with him, but who was unable to do so at the time, was Swami Radha. On learning of Gopi Krishna's plans to be in Europe, she had been hoping the dates would coincide with a late-spring trip she was planning to make from Canada to her homeland. Unfortunately, she was not able to extend her stay in Germany past May, and as Gopi Krishna was unable to arrive any earlier, the two did not meet. Swami Radha did, however, meet with Basedow on that trip to discuss kundalini research. She also connected with Margaret, with whom she formed a friendship, occasionally staying in Gemsenstrasse on future visits to Europe and keeping in touch with

Gopi Krishna, whom she finally managed to meet face to face just over a year before his final illness and death.

On his arrival in Starnberg, Gopi Krishna found that some of the living arrangements made for him were conducive neither to his writing nor to his health. In one arrangement, he was billeted with two elderly ladies where he had to do his own shopping and cooking; in another he had to walk directly through someone else's living quarters to get to the bathroom.

Fortunately an opportunity for a better situation soon opened up to him. Evelyn Ferrantini was now living in Berlin. She invited him to that city, found him an agreeable place to stay, and introduced him to some of her medical and scholarly acquaintances. By the 1970s, postwar West Berlin had become a clean, orderly, vibrant city, and although there seemed to be few noteworthy developments in terms of furthering his research, Gopi Krishna enjoyed his stay there immensely.

In Starnberg, Basedow had continued his work with the Research Foundation for Eastern Wisdom and Western Science. It is unclear, however, whether Gopi Krishna was able to attend the small conference that had once been planned for the fall. If this is so, there is no evidence that Gopi Krishna was upset by this turn of events. Margaret's family chalet in the Swiss alpine village of Engelberg had become available to her, and she urged Gopi Krishna to come there, where he would have ideal accommodation and be able to work on his writing surrounded in the beauty and healthy air of the Alps. By the end of September, he had accepted her invitation. Remaining there until returning to Zürich close to the end of the year, he accomplished a great deal of writing.

His intense occupation with spreading his message while he was in Europe did not make him forget about the work that needed to be done in Kashmir. Before he had left there, he hired Mr. K.N. Koul, a loyal Samiti supporter, giving him permission to hire any additionally needed staff. Once Gopi Krishna was in Europe, scores of meticulously detailed letters began to flow from Kashmir. One area of focus was the further development of centers and offices for kundalini research. Now that two of his books would be coming out in the prestigious Harper & Row series, he knew he would need formal office spaces for conducting meetings as well as comfortable accommodations for the important visitors who might be arriving to discuss his work. Having also discussed these needs with von Weizsäcker, he instructed Mr. Koul to turn the ground-floor room in the house in Karan Nagar that had been his writing space into a proper office and to create letterhead, etc. for the Kundalini Research Centre in Srinagar. For the center that was already built to some extent in Nishat, he directed a number of specific improvements. These included extensively detailed directions on gardens that specified the fruits and vegetables that should be grown for the visitors' meals and flower beds that would beautify the grounds, turning an already extraordinarily beautiful place into a virtual paradise for the scientists and scholars who would come.

Accomplishing these improvements took far more of Gopi Krishna's and his helpers' time than those of us living in an efficient, contemporary society can easily imagine. For example, something as seemingly simple as getting a telephone installed in the Nishat center took months of effort and numerous letters, written with increasingly frustrated urgency. In the end the phone was only installed when an influential friend intervened, pulling strings to get the task accomplished.

The other task based in Kashmir that Gopi Krishna began to oversee while he was in Europe was the translation of certain ancient Kashmiri Shaivite texts with their wealth of knowledge about kundalini-shakti, her potential awakening, and her role in the ultimate transformation and evolution of individual consciousness to God Consciousness. As Gopi Krishna became increasingly familiar with these texts over the years, he saw that few of them had been translated from Sanskrit even into an Indian language, let alone into English. Many of these texts were written by yogis who had reached higher states of consciousness through the awakening of kundalini. Realizing the immense value of these works, Gopi Krishna determined to have several of them translated from Sanskrit into English so that they could be published and reach a wide audience. While in Engelberg that autumn, he set to work hiring translators and transcribers.

The published editions he envisioned would contain the original Sanskrit text along with an English translation. In the time-honored tradition of the sacred texts of India, these translations would include an introduction and lengthy commentaries that elucidated the meaning of each verse. Many of these verses were written in highly poetic language. What's more, they contained information on kundalini awakening that had been purposely obfuscated by the original composers of the verses. Over the centuries this cloaking of the deeper meaning of the texts has been widely held to have been done in order to ensure that the intentional activation of kundalini was undertaken only by initiates who had learned gurus to guide them. Aware of the intricacies involved, Gopi Krishna hired first-rate Kashmiri Sanskrit scholars to do the translations. He then worked on the commentaries himself, knowing that his experiences with kundalini had given him unique contemporary insight into the meaning and interpretation of the texts.

Repeatedly, he stressed how essential it was for these texts to be made available to the public. In one letter from Engelberg to his helpers in Kashmir, he wrote of the tremendous pride they should be feeling for taking on this endeavor, for

> [this] is the first time we are taking up the great work of translating for the world the spiritual treasures left by the sages of Kashmir.... [C]are should be [taken] that every subtle shade of meaning is clearly brought out for they are of great scientific importance.

The two texts he focused his energy on at the time were the *Vijnana Bhairava* and *Panchastavi*. The *Vijnana Bhairava*, possibly written in the eighth century, is framed as a dialogue between Bhairava, a fearsome form of Shiva, and his beloved, Shakti. It contains 112 brief, encapsulated descriptions of meditation/breathing techniques for the awakening of kundalini and the reaching of enlightenment. *Panchastavi*, also probably eighth century, is a paean to Tripura, one of the names given Kundalini-Shakti when she is personified as the supreme Goddess. Within its exquisitely beautiful and poetic language can be found descriptions of the characteristics of the kundalini awakening, from the mystical experience itself with its splendorous light and bliss to the charisma and siddhis attained by the enlightened yogi and the onset the yogi experiences of inspired creativity and genius.

"With the grace of Heaven," Gopi Krishna would one day write in a letter, "this ancient literary treasure will become known through all the world."

Chapter Fifteen

Julian Huxley, Edgar Mitchell,
and a Challenge Set to Verse

G opi Krishna remained in Europe through the rest of 1971 and well into 1972. During the last months of 1971, he continued his long-distance efforts to ensure the readiness of the Nishat and Srinagar locations in Kashmir for the expected foreign visitors and to encourage work on the translations. Before the end of the year he made one more trip to Starnberg where he stayed with Basedow and was back in Engelberg around the middle of December. During these early weeks of December, he also had personal worries. Throughout the year, tensions between Pakistan and India had been building once again, and by November accord between the two nations had broken down, and his correspondents in Kashmir were sending him reports of border skirmishes. On December 3, the Second Indo–Pakistani War was officially declared, and the letters from home mentioned strikes on airfields. Fortunately the actual war lasted less than two weeks, and Srinagar was not affected in the way it had been in the First Indo–Pakistani War.

By early December in New York, plans were well underway for Gene Kieffer and George Tompkins, a businessman with an interest in the newly developing field of video production, to bring their families to Engelberg for a Christmas holiday that would combine a ski trip for the children—Gene's four and George's five—with an opportunity for George to meet Gopi Krishna in person. Several years after Gopi Krishna's death, George would describe that first meeting in a magazine article he wrote:

> In 1971 my life took a dramatic turn following my initial meeting with Pandit Gopi Krishna in Zürich, Switzerland. It was at that time period when Gopi Krishna was introducing the subject of Kundalini to the West. There is a Greek term *Kairos* which aptly describes this meeting—a decisive moment, dense with the possibility of grace.[99]

Throughout the two families' stay, Gopi Krishna divided his time between the chalet and Zürich, where he could work in more solitude, returning to Engelberg to spend time with Gene and George and to meet with Barbara Connell. A filmmaker from London, Connell had recently gained a good deal of recognition in England for her work and wanted to discuss the possibility of doing a film on Gopi Krishna and kundalini. In spite of the fact that a friend who had accompanied her was apparently suffering from some type of psychological disturbance, the talks concerning the potential film went well. Barbara also had time for a personal consultation with Gopi Krishna. Tragically, it was learned that after she and the friend landed in England on their way back, the car they were traveling home in crashed, and Barbara was killed. Decades later, an audiotape of her interview with Gopi Krishna would be found, showing that much of the conversation focused on issues surrounding life after death. In it Gopi Krishna discusses the nonphysical aspects of our being and on the immortality of the *atman*—a concept in the Hindu system that is generally described as the inner essence or true Self and sometimes translated as "the soul." It is difficult not to wonder whether her having this discussion with an enlightened yogi shortly before her death was chance or, if it was, like George Tompkins's reference to kairos, a moment in time steeped in grace.

For Gopi Krishna, the new year of 1972 dawned with promise. Although Harper & Row had not met their December 1971 publication deadline, there was every indication their *Biological Basis* would be launched soon and that *The Secret of Yoga* would follow. In Germany, *Die biologische Basis der religiösen Erfahrung* was beginning to attract a good deal of positive attention.

Throughout these first months of 1972, Gopi Krishna alternated between Germany and Switzerland. When he was in Switzerland, Margaret made the best use of the time she had with him by setting up lectures for him to give for groups and societies interested in yoga and Eastern thought. Two of these talks, in Basel and Bern, were organized by Peter Oswald. Now recognized as one of the earliest pioneers of yoga in Europe, Oswald founded the Ashtanga Yoga Studio (*Astanga Yoga Akademie*) of Switzerland in 1960. By 1972 when he met Gopi Krishna he was already well-known. One of the talks Oswald arranged was held at the University of Basel where a large lecture hall was filled to overflowing with students who enthusiastically responded to his ideas.

In Bern that year Gopi Krishna also met with the renowned philosopher Jean Gebser, whose work on the evolution of consciousness had had, and continues to have to this day, widespread influence. Gebser was seriously ill at the time. Unable to travel to Zürich, he had asked if Gopi Krishna could possibly come to visit him at his home. According to Margaret, Gebser was tremendously pleased to meet Gopi Krishna and honored by the visit. Although Gebser died the following year, the two men remained in contact by correspondence for the brief remainder of Gebser's life, and the philosopher promoted Gopi Krishna's work in many ways, for instance, insisting that the great yoga authority Georg Feuerstein be sent a transcript of the talk Gopi Krishna had given in Basel.

In spite of being extremely busy giving lectures, meeting with people whose interest they generated, and carrying on extensive correspondence not only with his small staff in Kashmir but with interested European contacts he had previously made, Gopi Krishna produced an extraordinary amount of writing before he left for home in April. The year before he had begun a new book tentatively titled *Some Questions Answered* that was apparently a different manuscript from the one he had created with Sinai. Gene and others agreed that a major work in this format—one that doled out information on kundalini and the relevance of the research in small doses—might make this complex, foreign concept more easily comprehensible and acceptable to the Western mind. During the early months of 1972, he continued his work on this project.

Of all the writing he did during this period, the most astounding involves correspondence with two famous individuals from very different walks of life: Julian Huxley and Edgar Mitchell.

Born in England in 1887, Julian Huxley was the older sibling of Aldous Huxley. He became known as the preeminent evolutionary biologist of the early twentieth century primarily for synthesizing Darwin's theories with Mendel's work on heredity—a synthesis that was seen as a major advancement in the understanding of natural selection. A confirmed atheist, he was highly critical of organized religion. He was also a humanist who did an extensive humanitarian work during his life.

His entry into the sphere of Gopi Krishna's life work came when Huxley was eighty-four years of age and Harper & Row sent him a copy of *The Biological Basis* for review before its final publication. As a known and vociferous nonbeliever, he was certainly an interesting choice as a reviewer. Although he would later say he preferred to be labeled *agnostic*—a term he said his father had coined—rather than *atheist*, in a letter accompanying his review he categorically states that neither God nor any type of intelligent life force exists. From this position, he scorned the book. He roundly disparaged von Weizsäcker's views on science, even though he admitted that he had no idea who von Weizsäcker was or what his scientific qualifications might be—a surprising admission given the latter's renown for both his work in physics and the Göttingen Manifesto.

On receiving a copy of the review Huxley had sent to Harper & Row, Gopi Krishna decided to write a response. Instead of a simple letter of rebuttal, however, the effort triggered an outpouring of inspired creativity that culminated in just over 2,000 lines of verse. While it is not known exactly when during the first few months of the year Gopi Krishna received his copy of the Huxley letter, the poem was completed on March 1, and according to a number of people's memories, the entire work was done in a matter of a few weeks. Even if the work had taken much of January and February, it would have been an exceptional accomplishment, especially given the other extensive demands on his attention.

Huxley responded to his receipt of Gopi Krishna's verse by way of a letter to Gene Kieffer, calling it a "remarkable achievement." He maintained, however, his certainty that we could know nothing about the "divine" and that evolution could be completely explained by the theory of natural selection. Still, he did agree with Gopi Krishna that the world was on the brink of peril and believed there was hope that disaster could be averted:

> We are now at a crucial point—the world population will double in about 30 years, and pollution increases, interesting wild animals and lovely wild flowers are being destroyed. And so anything that helps this is important.... Please give my best regards to Mr. Krishna—and say that I think we are partners in the great adventure, even if we don't agree over details and methods.

Amazingly, by March 15, Gopi Krishna had completed another 1,328 lines of verse, this time as part of an ongoing correspondence conversation with Edgar Mitchell. An aeronautical engineer, Navy test pilot, and NASA astronaut, Mitchell gained fame in the 1970s as a member of the Apollo 14 mission to the moon. Along with astronaut Alan Shepard, he spent a record amount of time on the lunar surface doing research. Later, he raised eyebrows in some scientific circles because he was a firm believer in UFOs and the possibility of alien life-forms. On the return flight from the moon, he had a profound mystical experience that would change the course of his life.

Mitchell's life crossed paths with Gopi Krishna's in 1972 through a connection with John White, a journalist who had become known in those days for his writing on meditation and other aspects of the human-potential movement. From those early days onward, White's writing focused on various aspects of consciousness research, and he would eventually become the author of fifteen books, including *Kundalini, Evolution, and Enlightenment*. Published in 1979 and again in 1990, the book is still well-read today. In 1971, John White was one of the people who received a copy of *The Biological Basis* as part of Gene's mass mailing. Although he had been familiar with the concept of kundalini for some time before receiving the book, he found Gopi Krishna's presentation powerful and persuasive and became interested in promoting his research.

1971 was the year of Edgar Mitchell's Apollo mission and the accompanying mystical experience. In attempting to describe what occurred, he would later say that, while his eyes were fixated on the floating blue sphere we call Earth, he had a transcendental experience of the connectedness of everything in the universe and an awareness of an intelligent cosmic, creative force. He came to this conclusion:

> I realized that the story of ourselves as told by science—our cosmology, our religion—was incomplete and likely flawed. I recognized that the Newtonian idea of separate, independent, discrete things in the universe wasn't a fully accurate description. What was needed was a new story of who we are and what we are capable of becoming.[100]

After his return from the mission, he retired from the Navy and began working to develop the Institute of Noetic Sciences (IONS), a research organization that would take these higher concepts into account and help move science in a new, much broader direction. Aware that he needed a communications expert to help him get the organization off the ground, he hired John White to do the job.

The similarities between Mitchell's desire to move science in a new, more spiritually inclusive direction and Gopi Krishna's research goals did not escape White's notice, and he soon had the two men corresponding. Early on, it seemed obvious that IONS would be the perfect place to conduct kundalini research. Mitchell's goal for the institute, however, was to focus on research into psychic phenomena, or *psi*, as it was known in the slang of the day. In his correspondence with Mitchell, including the nearly forty pages that were in verse, Gopi Krishna tried to convince Mitchell that while research on the paranormal had been going on for years, it was no closer to understanding its root causes than when it started. Research on kundalini would, in contrast, reveal not only the biological but the spiritual and evolutionary basis for these phenomena. Indeed, the kundalini hypothesis that Gopi Krishna eventually set out for research would certainly included paranormal phenomena.

Although Mitchell maintained his position that IONS should focus on psychic research, according to John White, Mitchell's hesitation about taking on a major kundalini research project was not only because of his determined interest in psi, it was also due to the fact that the scope of Gopi Krishna's proposed project, as described later in the chapter, seemed simply too large and all-consuming to him. Regardless, even if Mitchell had been willing to set up the kundalini research project in those early days, it would not have happened. Only a few years into the early development, the institute's main patron had a financial crisis, most of the financial backing was lost, and it was quite some time before the institute as it exists today came into being. Regardless, Mitchell maintained a deep respect and admiration for Gopi Krishna, writing a superlative review of *The Secret of Yoga* when the book finally came out.[101]

By the middle of March when Gopi Krishna sent his poetry off to Mitchell, he had written a total of almost 100 pages of inspired verse in a matter of weeks. To put this in the context of how truly remarkable this was, these 3,400 lines of verse all rhymed and represented well almost 29,000 words written in the tight, uncompromising, structured rhythm of iambic pentameter. What's more, this is not all he had written by the end of March. In addition to his lengthy correspondence with European contacts and staff in Kashmir, he completed a 2,000-word essay as part of his preparation for an appearance on a German television show. The interest triggered by the release of *Die biologische Basis der religiösen Erfahrung* was mounting in Germany. This, combined with the growing enthusiasm of the day for meditation, resulted in increased media attention. The essay he prepared for the show that spring was entitled "Meditation as a Means to Self-Knowledge." An accomplished piece of writing, it contradicts popular thought of the day on meditation and encapsulates several of his complex ideas in simple language. No recording of the interview seems to be available, but a copy of the written essay is. Here are the final paragraphs:

> ...There is no magical formula or mantra or secret method of meditation that can work miracles and carry us to higher states of consciousness by the momentum of our own efforts without Grace Divine....
>
> Viewed from this angle, meditation becomes a part and parcel of our lives, a life-long occupation, a permanent duty that we owe to God. We have not to hurry, we have not to find magical methods, but

we have to tune our mind so that the thought of God and the Divine is never far from it.

We can attend to all our occupations and duties without the least hindrance and, perhaps, even more efficiently if divine thoughts always occupy a place at the back of our minds. This is Sahaja Yoga, the easiest and most effective form of spiritual discipline. It is prescribed by every great religious teacher of the past. This is what Christ means when he says love your God with all your heart and soul, because a beloved object occupies a permanent place in the thoughts of the lover. When we are able to think of a beloved sweetheart a hundred times a day, without impairing the efficiency of our work, we should also be able to do it with the Divine if our thirst is real. The same is taught by Buddha and the *Bhagavad Gita*. Keep the Divine always in your mind.

This is the safest method, for no force is necessary. The mind can become habituated to it with slow, gradual practice. As I have said, this has to be a life-long practice and search. The constant remembrance of God, the holiest of the holy, is to be followed by purity in thought and conduct. The world has not to be given up, the desires have not to be totally denied. They are a part and parcel of human life. But moderation has to be exercised to keep the thought on God. Otherwise, desires and passions consume all our energy and time. Moderation and purity of mind are therefore essential and form an integral part of meditation.

But wherefrom comes this desire for meditation, this urge to attain to an inner state of peace and beatitude or to experience God? This is because our brains are still evolving, because mankind has to reach a higher state of consciousness for which there is a special arrangement in the brain and nervous system of man. This mechanism is not yet known to scholars. It is my earnest wish to make this divine power-reservoir known to the world of science. It is because of this possibility in our brain that our meditational exercise succeeds. It is necessary that this knowledge should become well known, because once it is known, meditation for gaining a higher state of consciousness by stimulating this centre in the brain, known as *Brahma-randhra* in India, will become an integral part of human life, leading to a glorious state of consciousness, conducive to peace and happiness of the world.[102]

Margaret recollected that on the day that Gopi Krishna was getting ready for the taping of the show, he discovered that his churidar, the tight-fitting leggings traditionally worn with the long, Kashmiri jacket called a *kurta*, had been left behind in Zürich. Without them, he was forced to wear loose-fitting trousers that did not look nearly as good. While he later said that of course it did not matter at all, Margaret knew he would have much preferred to appear on German television looking as elegant as possible.

On April 11, 1972, he left Europe for home, having spent the first few months of the year producing a truly extraordinary amount of writing, making important contacts, and promoting the concept of kundalini research. It can also be said that he greatly enjoyed his time in Switzerland, especially in Engelberg, and that, in spite of all he accomplished, he was in some ways refreshed and rested. This would stand him in good stead, for the pace of his work did not slow at all when he reached home. As usual, however, the journey was hard on his system, and on his arrival in Delhi, Ragya insisted that he spend five days resting with her and her family.

When he returned to Kashmir he was met with many tasks, from answering accumulated correspondence to overseeing the work on the centers to make them ready for foreign visitors. These two activities were closely related as some of the most important correspondence dealt with some very significant visitors. In addition to a visit planned by Gene and George, a number of scientists and psychologists interested in kundalini awakening wanted to come for consultations and to do interviews. The first of these were Gay Gaer Luce and Erik Peper, two individuals who were on the vanguard of the research into biofeedback, a field that was still in its infancy in the day. The two arrived in Kashmir around June 20, set up their recording equipment, and proceeded to interview Gopi Krishna for several days.

Even fifty years after the event, the biographical data on Luce's website recognizes the time she spent with Gopi Krishna in Kashmir as part of her spiritual initiation. By the time of that meeting in 1972, Luce had already distinguished herself on a number of fronts. She had not only obtained her PhD from Stanford and become one of the early researchers on biofeedback, she had earned an outstanding reputation as a science writer. Her journalism had appeared in many publications, including the *New York Times*, and she had already had three books issued by leading publishers: *Biological Rhythms in Human and Animal Physiology*; *Body Time: Physiological Rhythms and Social Stress*; and *Insomnia: The Guide for Troubled Sleepers*. As if these accomplishments weren't enough, prior to the trip to Kashmir she had been honored with the American Psychological Association 1971 Award for Science Writing.

Luce also had yet another book to her credit. Entitled *Sleep and Dreams*, along with *New York Times* articles on biofeedback, it had been co-authored by Erik Peper. Although Peper was not as well-known or widely published as Luce at the time of the trip, he also had his PhD and had already been researching biofeedback and other factors related to holistic healing, making him a pioneer in these fields. Since those early days of his career, he has gone on to author several books and become an internationally recognized authority on holistic health, self-healing strategies, and stress management.

Luce and Peper spent about two and a half weeks with Gopi Krishna, interviewing him daily and recording many hours of their conversations. A transcript of their talks numbers in the hundreds of pages. The pair had many detailed questions about kundalini awakening, especially what its biological effects might be and how exactly it might transform consciousness. While much of this specific material can be found in the books Gopi Krishna later wrote and the talks he gave, one of the great values of this conversation is its detailed description of Gopi Krishna's principal proposed research project. While he had certainly been discussing his ideas for kundalini research with scientists such as von Weizsäcker for some time, no written description that sets out exactly how he saw the project unfolding seems to have yet existed. *Kundalini: The Evolutionary Energy in Man*, being autobiographical in nature, does not contain a detailed description of the research project. But neither do *The Biological Basis of Religion* or *The Secret of Yoga*.

Although this omission seems surprising at first glance, it was in fact consistent with the steps that are revealed over the course of his discussions with

Luce and Peper, and it is clear that his initial goal was to spread information about kundalini. His desire was not only to increase awareness of the fact that it existed but also to foster the understanding that it was in fact a universal force known by different names in different cultures. Specifically, he wanted to elucidate kundalini's role as the evolutionary energy and its relationship to genius, inspired creativity, mystical experience, and ultimately higher consciousness. Each in its own way, his first three internationally published books certainly did this.

Once this groundwork for the research project was sufficiently laid, the second step could begin. This would involve advertising for volunteers who would be interested in being part of the experimental project and in committing to taking on and being guided through a set of spiritually oriented disciplines that were aimed at awakening kundalini. Although his thoughts on the number of necessary applicants varied somewhat at different times during his life, one estimate was that out of 1,000 applicants, he felt he might be able to select 200 suitable candidates. During this process he would be looking for young people between their late teens to early thirties who possessed sattvic qualities and were drawn to a lifestyle that embodied these traits. These were the very characteristics he talked about when quoting his beloved poetess Lal Ded and the *Bhagavad Gītā*. They included a dedication to goodness, truth, compassion, serenity, strength of will and purpose, and a lack of greed, combined with a willingness to live a moderate, temperate life, dedicated to a noble cause. The project would ideally take place in a location with a moderate climate. While undertaking the disciplines prescribed, the candidates would live their normal lives. However, they would also need to do some service-oriented work, be willing to exercise sexual restraint at specific times during the process, and be agreeable to undergoing the physical tests and examinations the scientists doing the research wanted to conduct.

In spite of the fact that it may, even now, be many decades before equipment will be developed that can actually measure pranic activity, Gopi Krishna was confident that even in those days equipment and tests existed that could measure physiological and biochemical changes related to the awakening of kundalini. In order to have these tests conducted, the next stage in the research project would be to recruit a team of scientists from various disciplines, for instance, medicine, neurology, biology, and biochemistry. Although some estimates suggested that the project might go on for several years, Gopi Krishna was sure that, given a likely group of candidates, there should be one or two that would show signs of biologically based changes that were demonstrable and quantifiable within the first year or two. These early successes, he believed, would be enough to convince the scientists involved, and ultimately the scientific and medical communities at large, of the validity and critical importance of doing this research and having it adequately funded until the ultimate goal of having some of the candidates reach the higher states of consciousness described in the yogic texts and be able to demonstrate the same type of staggering, undeniable transformation in consciousness and in intellectual and creative abilities that he himself had undergone.[103]

After spending three or four hours a day for over two weeks learning about the possibilities for kundalini research and gaining a massive amount of detailed information about the awakening itself, Luce and Peper left Kashmir on around July 8. Once they were back in the United States, as is related in the next chapter, they began to speak about kundalini research possibilities to other scientists.

Chapter Sixteen

LSD, False Gurus, and the Real Nature
of Mystical Experience

Several weeks prior to Luce and Peper's arrival in Kashmir in July of 1972, Gopi Krishna had received the good news that the Harper & Row edition of *The Biological Basis of Religion and Genius* was finally launched in the United States. By the time they arrived, the publisher's edition of *The Secret of Yoga* was also out, and Gopi Krishna was able to give them a copy of the book.[104]

The increasing number of publications and translations of his work undoubtedly contributed to the number of people who wanted to meet with him, and Luce and Peper were just the first two in a line of visitors who would flow into Kashmir over the summer. Gene was the next to visit, bringing George Tompkins along with him. Arriving shortly after Luce and Peper left, they stayed for two weeks consulting with Gopi Krishna and, in general, enjoying Kashmir and the open-armed hospitality offered up by his family. The two men departed on July 22, leaving just enough time to prepare for the next set of visitors from the United States, who arrived a week later. This group, headed by Dr. Carmi Harari, consisted of twenty-two members of the Association for Humanistic Psychology (AHP). A noted psychologist, Harari served a term as president of the American Psychological Association. He was one of the principal early advocates of the humanistic psychology movement and that year was president of the AHP. His group met with Gopi Krishna for an afternoon at the center in Nishat. The psychologists peppered the yogi with questions and impressed him with their enthusiasm and interest. One, a Dr. Arthur Brodbeck, who was founder of the Human Potential Institute in New York, sought a private meeting the next day to discuss in more detail how he could use Gopi Krishna's ideas to further his goals of unleashing untapped human potential. Another visitor that summer was the renowned journalist, philosopher, and international award–winning poet William Irwin Thompson. Influenced by the ideas of thinkers such at Teilhard de Chardin, Thompson was increasingly interested in the concept of the evolution of consciousness on a planetary scale. Thompson was accompanied by Robin van Löben Sels, a woman who would go on to become a noted Jungian analyst, poet, and author.

The influx of visitors continued into early autumn. They included his Italian friend and translator Evelyn Ferrantini, along with interested supporters from the United States such as Eleanore Berg, who made tapes of her interviews with him that were later published.[105] A number of important Indian visitors also arrived. One was Hridya Nath Kunzru, the highly influential federal politician whom Gopi Krishna had been in touch with during the uprisings in 1968. By the early 1970s, Kunzru had risen to even higher national political prominence as president of the Indian Council of World Affairs under Prime Minister Nehru. His paying a personal visit to Gopi Krishna was a significant event.

By the autumn of 1973 the activity in Kashmir was continuing on a number of fronts. One of the highlights for Gopi Krishna and his family was Margaret's first trip to India. Arriving in mid-October, she was soon accepted as a member of the family. Along with the lavish amounts of Swiss chocolate and other gifts for the family, she brought a new typewriter and a top-of-the-line Dictaphone purchased by Gene. Although Gopi Krishna often wrote material out himself by hand to have it typed later, he also often dictated to one of the local women who could both take dictation and do the typing. Gene hoped the Dictaphone would make the final transcription of the prodigious amounts of material that poured from the yogi easier and more efficient. While Gopi Krishna accepted the gift with deep appreciation for the thought behind it, after a few tries he made it clear to Margaret as politely as possible that the clicking on buttons and the noisy whir of the machine were not at all conducive to the receipt of divinely inspired creativity. He greatly preferred, he said, to have a human to dictate to.

The secretarial and general office help that Margaret was able to provide during her visit made it possible for Gopi Krishna to accomplish a great deal, especially on furthering the work on the Kashmiri Shaivite texts during these autumn months. Just how important he felt the publication of this material would be is reflected in a letter to Kunzru regarding the plans for the politician's upcoming visit:

> I am busily involved in Research now and have a regular office for it. Our ancient culture lies deeply buried under a mass of superstition and inertia. Even the works of our great philosopher and mystic Abhinava Gupta are unknown to the world. I have started translations of his works as well as of other books that have great scientific implication in the light of present day knowledge about altered states of consciousness brought about by yoga and other religious disciplines.

By the time Margaret left in November, the translation the *Vijnana Bhairava* into English was completed, with only Gopi Krishna's introduction and a few more of the commentaries on the verses to be finalized. The work on the translation of *Panchastavi* into English had also proceeded well, and Gopi Krishna was frequently expressing his hope that these two volumes of age-old Kashmir Shaivite wisdom regarding kundalini would soon be made more readily available to the West.[106]

During these final months of 1972, Gopi Krishna was also receiving invitations to participate in various forums in the coming year. One came from the Swiss yoga teacher Peter Oswald. He was planning to come to India to conduct a yoga retreat in Varanasi, and he very much hoped that Gopi Krishna would participate. Another important invitation came from Gay Luce. In charge of organizing the fifth annual Council Grove Conference, Luce invited Gopi Krishna to participate in the gathering which was scheduled to begin April 30, 1973, in Kansas. Established by Dr. Elmer Green at the Menninger Foundation, the purpose of these Council Grove conferences was to bring together philosophers, scientists, spiritual leaders, and practitioners of both allotropic and alternative medicine. Although the participants were from very diverse backgrounds, a common thread was an interest in the exploration of consciousness, and the gatherings had been attracting some of the most prominent alternative thinkers of the day. Prior to Luce sending the invitation to speak, Green had also personally written to Gopi Krishna inviting him to the foundation. Developed by the Menninger family in 1919 in Topeka, Kansas, it had come to be known as one of the leading institutes, if not the leading one, focused on psychiatry in the United States. Green, who held degrees in physics and biopsychology, had joined the Menninger Foundation in 1964 and had developed a psychophysiology laboratory there. Credited with being one of the inventors of biofeedback, he was one of the earliest researchers into the ability to intentionally control normally involuntary, autonomic physiological processes, such as heart rate, blood pressure, and skin temperature. Both he and his wife, Alyce, who worked with him, were highly interested in the reputed abilities of yoga adepts to control these functions and believed ordinary people could learn to do the same with biofeedback. Much of the Greens' seminal research explored how this ability could be used to improve health and even heal certain diseases.[107]

By the end of 1972, Gopi Krishna had decided to turn down the invitation to Oswald's 1973 event in Varanasi as he thought he might be in Europe or the United States by then, but he was still debating attending the gathering in Council Grove. In December, Gay Luce wrote him again, virtually pleading with him to attend. As he had not yet made an appearance in North America, he was also being urged by others to come, making his trip to Kansas just one stop on an extended tour of the United States.

The discussion about whether to make the trip was centered to a great extent on the question of what was more important: his writing to produce more material for publication or his meeting with well-known, influential scientists. The Council Grove Conference would certainly have provided the latter. It was not so much a conference in the way this term is usually used as a select gathering of people who would make presentations and confer among themselves. The individuals slated to attend in 1973 were indeed among the leaders in the growing so-called New Age movement toward alternative medicine and science. Several of them were involved in research into consciousness and, specifically, altered states of consciousness. In addition to Elmer Green and Gay Luce, participants whose names are still widely known in the history of this crusade included psychologists Stanley Krippner, PhD; Charles Tart, PhD; and psychiatrist Stanislav Grof, PhD, MD. If Gopi Krishna came to the United States to attend the conference, he would also be able to meet with a number of important thinkers Gene had made contact with, including the leading psychologist Rollo May and the controversial but brilliant psychiatrist R.D. Laing.

In opposition to his desire to meet scientists who might be interested in kundalini research was his need to produce publishable material that would build on the momentum created by his current success. He had recently received the encouraging news from Otto Wilhelm Barth Verlag in Germany that their first edition of *Die biologische Basis der religiösen Erfahrung* had been doing well enough for them to bring out a second edition. Harper & Row, in addition to their North American edition, had now authorized a British version that was being published by Turnstone Press. In the United States an article by William Irwin Thompson on Gopi Krishna's work appeared in the prestigious *Harper's Magazine,* entitled, "The Common Ground of Mysticism and Science."[108]

In order to meet this growing demand for his work, by September he had finished a tentative final draft of the book that was now called *Questions and Answers*. He was also revising an earlier book-length prose work called *From Human to Transhuman Consciousness*. For him to be able to continue these efforts in an inspired state, he needed to maintain good health, particularly by avoiding becoming fatigued or stressed. Experience had shown him that his ideal state was unlikely to be obtained for any significant amounts of time while he was traveling. In a letter written during the debate over whether he should make the trip, he expressed this:

I can only write effectively when I am entirely free of diversions. My stay in the States can only be fruitful if I have a calm life and a quiet environment. Pressure and tension are never conducive to right expression in a spiritual undertaking. In fact when I repeatedly mention in my writings that too much storm and stress, involved in the modern way of life, is inimical to the evolutionary progress of mankind[,] I, at least, should not be the person to follow methods of working which I myself condemn.

In the end Gopi Krishna decided that continuing to write was the more important of the two goals. He remained in Kashmir instead of going to the United States in 1973. This decision had certain consequences. Looking back from the perspective of this biography, it is tempting to wonder how things might have turned out differently and how much more widely his work might have been promoted if he had indeed gone. From Gopi Krishna's perspective, on the other hand, any progress made in spreading his ideas was due to the "will of heaven," and no evidence that he regretted or ever questioned his decision has been found. According to letters from Swami Radha and John White, however, he was very much missed at the Council Grove Conference. An additional upshot to his absence was noted by John White. The author felt strongly that Gopi Krishna's absence from the United States and, more specifically, his not submitting himself to Elmer Green's biofeedback equipment at the Menninger Foundation had raised questions about the validity of his having reached a state of higher consciousness.

In order to understand how these questions might have arisen—and to explore the possibilities of why Gopi Krishna chose not to go to Council Grove—it is necessary to understand the contemporary climate regarding consciousness research. At that time, this concept almost always referred very specifically to research into altered states of consciousness. One facet of this research focused on psychedelic drugs such as LSD and psilocybin, also known as magic mushrooms. While the most widely reported research in this field was being done by Timothy Leary, Council Grove participants such as Dr. Grof were also becoming well-known for their research on psychedelics.

Psychedelic drug experiences were also becoming broadly equated with true mystical experiences. Part of this was based on works by authors such as Carlos Castañeda, whose first book, *The Teachings of Don Juan: A Yaqui*

Way of Knowledge, made the claim that it was an ethnographic account of his association with a Yaqui shaman who had trained him in the use of naturally occurring psychedelics such as peyote to attain profound mystical states and shamanistic powers. While these books are today widely considered to be works of fiction, they were so convincing that the counterculture embraced them as gospel truth. While many participants in the counterculture did drugs simply to tune in and tune out, another segment of this population was heavily influenced by the spiritual aspects of these types of books. This, combined with what they were hearing about the laboratory experiments on psychedelics, convinced them to quite consciously experiment on themselves in an attempt to reach altered, expanded, and/or mystical states of consciousness.

Another aspect of the climate in the West related to attitudes about consciousness was the appearance on the scene of Indian supposed gurus such as Maharishi Mahesh Yogi, the founder of Transcendental Meditation (TM), and Maharaji, the head of the Divine Light Society. The popularity of such teachers was growing at a phenomenal rate. In the United States, literally hundreds of thousands of people were taking to these paths and other forms of meditation on the promise of reaching alternate states of consciousness that engendered bliss, peace, and eternal happiness.

TM was becoming known worldwide for its successful sale of supposedly personalized mantras to individuals who wanted to learn to meditate. The Maharishi claimed that the repetition of these mantras would lead to transcendental states and, for the advanced practitioners, even to the paranormal powers known as *siddhis* in the yoga tradition. Gopi Krishna was continually receiving information from the United States about the Maharishi's influence there. Tens of thousands of people, mostly young people, were generally paying $125 or more for initiation, as it was being called, and given a mantra that was said to be especially chosen for them. While this might not sound like an excessive amount of money, its equivalent in current US funds today is close to $1,000. Initiates were warned that they must keep their mantra secret, for if they told anyone, the mantra would lose its power. Since then, it has been widely accepted that the single-syllable mantras were given out based on a simple combination of gender and age group, so that there were, in fact, only a limited number of mantras being given out.[109]

These mantra-induced states along with other meditation and non-drug-related altered states were being researched just as psychedelic-induced states were. News on these findings, especially those related to biofeedback, was making a stir in the media. Gay Luce's writing along with the Greens' biofeedback research at the Menninger Foundation were receiving an ever-increasing amount of attention. Closely related to this was the fact that with the invention of the EEG in Germany in the 1920s, the existence of different levels of brain waves had been discovered. Designated *alpha*, *beta*, and *theta*, these waves were held to be related to different states of consciousness, with beta prevalent in normal waking, and alpha and theta prevalent in sleep and certain altered states of consciousness. It was widely believed that some advanced yogis in India could use their ability to meditate to enter these altered states of consciousness at will and control many normally autonomic functions.

The Greens' work in this regard had received a huge boost three years prior to the Council Grove Conference that Gopi Krishna was invited to attend. An Indian yogi, Swami Rama, allowed himself to be studied at the Menninger Foundation. During these experiments the Swami stopped his heart from pumping blood for seventeen seconds, changed skin temperature on two locations on his hand by 10°F, and produced theta waves at will. These results received widespread media attention and got even more notice among the practitioners of alternative medicine and the scientists who would be attending the Council Grove Conference. The Greens and many other biofeedback enthusiasts were convinced that this process could be used to train ordinary individuals to control physiological processes just as these yogis did. In fact, the Greens often used the phrase "biofeedback—the yoga of the West."[110]

When Gopi Krishna decided to neither attend the conference nor visit the United States at the time, John White was concerned that the questions about Gopi Krishna he had first noticed at the conference were beginning to circulate. Part of this was based on the erroneous assumption that Gopi Krishna's not visiting the US meant that he was unwilling to be tested and, in turn, that he had not reached the states of consciousness he was claiming. If he had indeed reached these states, the critics claimed, he would gladly submit to being tested and be able to produce the same results as Swami Rama. This was all made even more significant, they argued, because Gopi Krishna was supposedly promoting scientific research.

Although Gopi Krishna did, in fact, later consent to be tested by Green, he certainly had grave doubts about the entire issue. The crux of the problem was clearly related to the way the concept of altered states of consciousness now permeated the mishmash of the alternative movements that ranged from research on mind-expanding drugs and altered brain waves to meditation techniques and biofeedback training. The grave difficulty in all this, from the point of view of someone like Gopi Krishna, was how altered states had become widely synonymous with *higher* states of consciousness. Psychedelics were believed by many to produce the same type of mystical experiences written about by the great saints and mystics of the world's spiritual traditions; the peaceful feelings produced by repeating mantras were being mistaken for the reaching of samadhi, the rarely attained eighth limb of Patanjali's classical yoga. In the field of psychology, the transpersonal psychology movement was recognizing the rapid growth in people reporting spiritual experiences—and sometimes the spiritual emergencies associated with these experiences. They were also widely discussing the importance of these experiences in terms of personal growth.

The problem was not that these experiences were invalid. Mantras and meditation, for instance, could produce positive effects. The critical issue from Gopi Krishna's standpoint was that altered states of consciousness were quite simply not the higher states of consciousness he was writing about. He was even more adamant about the stark differentiation between psychedelic drug experiences and higher states of consciousness. These were *cosmic* states of consciousness where one's ego dissolved, melding into Union with the vastness of ineffable, incomprehensible Divine Intelligence that created and controlled not only the Earth but the billions of planets that existed in galaxies stretching out into infinity.

This melding with the cosmos was clearly not the same thing as the blissful feelings one might attain after meditating or chanting a mantra for a lengthy amount of time, and it was certainly not equivalent to the phantasmagoric visions of an LSD trip. The same was true for the ability of a yogi like Swami Rama to change brain waves or skin temperature at will. While being able to measure these states might well have been useful for the medical science of the day, in Gopi Krishna's view these experiments were light-years away from research on higher, cosmic states of consciousness. Possibly even worse, they were a distraction. He had no doubt he could demonstrate the same ability to control autonomic functions that Swami Rama had shown, but he was painfully aware that this would do nothing more than draw attention to himself and away from the vital research he believed needed to be done.

While his decision to cancel any plans to travel to the United States in 1973 was made primarily so that he could stay home to write, it might also be speculated that it had the added advantage of allowing him to avoid, at least for the time being, landing in that country in the midst of the alternative scene that included everything from drug-fueled experimentation and the mass craze for false gurus to the growing conviction that entering an altered state of consciousness was, if not enlightenment itself, then at least the kind of true mystical experience that was well on the way to it.

In addition to canceling those plans, he set aside any trips to Europe so that he spent the entire year of 1973 in India. It proved to be a very fruitful year. Part of this was due to the fact that the family had by now obtained a home in New Delhi. Located in Sarvodaya Enclave, a residential community which was then mostly encircled by open land, the house remained a family home until well into the twenty-first century, when all the enclave had become surrounded by the bustling expansion of the city. The two-story house was large enough by the standards of the time to accommodate all the members of the extended family who came and went, as well as providing a space for Gopi Krishna in which he could write.

Having the home in Sarvodaya Enclave meant that he had an established place to work in both Kashmir and New Delhi. Now he, Bhabi, and the other members of the family could move between the locations, avoiding the seasonal extremes of the two climates. Having this option was a great benefit to Gopi Krishna's health and his ability to write. Accordingly, he spent the winter months of 1973 working in Sarvodaya Enclave. When the temperature there grew too hot, about 104°F in the middle of April, he and Bhabi returned to Kashmir, where he continued his work. He was also busy making new and renewing old connections with important people. Among his correspondents during this period were R.D. Laing and the renowned French authority on Eastern traditions Amaury de Riencourt. Although neither of these celebrated authors made it to Kashmir that summer, they both hoped to do so in the near future. Among the many visitors who did arrive, one of the most anticipated was Margaret, in August.

Quite possibly the most important person Gopi Krishna communicated with that summer was Dr. Karan Singh. He was the son of the Maharaja Hari Singh who had still been the Maharaja of the princely state of Jammu and Kashmir at the onset of the First Indo–Pakistani War. When the Maharaja stepped down, Karan Singh was appointed Prince Regent and, for a brief time, Raj of Jammu and Kashmir. With the princely state's accession to India, Karan Singh became its governor and eventually its official member of the Indian parliament. During Indira Gandhi's rule of the country, he would rise to the vaunted position of minister for health and family planning. In that capacity he would play a crucial role in Gopi Krishna's crusade for kundalini research. By that July he had already been appointed by Gandhi to the somewhat lesser rank of federal minister of tourism and civil aviation. As such he had traveled to Europe, where he had learned of the widespread impression Gopi Krishna had been making there. Karan Singh had briefly met Gopi Krishna years before, and on returning home he sent him an invitation to meet in order to renew their acquaintance. This would be the beginning of a long and fruitful association.[111]

The final month of 1973 brought the personal joyous news that Gopi Krishna's son Nirmal and his wife, Chuni, had brought their second daughter, Jyotsana, into the world. This would be the last of the seven grandchildren, all of whom Gopi Krishna and Bhabi would adore and treasure for the rest of their lives. So, while in most respects 1973 was an extremely positive year in Gopi Krishna's life, some unpleasantness occurred. In spite of his extensive travels and other pressing duties, he had made every effort to continue to keep the Samaj Sudhar Samiti on track from afar. Still, some critical rumors about the organization had been circulating since the previous year. In a reference to this criticism, Gopi Krishna wrote to one of his correspondents that this false prejudice against the organization was

> ...created by the false propaganda of equally false aspirants for political leadership or positions in the Government, who were envious of the selfless service done by Samiti and afraid of the criticism of the public for their own inability to achieve any tangible results, has vanished altogether.

According to Margaret, Gopi Krishna was also concerned that some laxity might have occurred among the volunteers during the periods when he had been unable to supervise Samiti as closely as he had in the past. Consequently, he had carried out some reorganization and redistribution of responsibilities to be sure any possible problems were resolved. With all this taken care of, he was able to contact his old friend H.N. Kunzru to let him know all was well with the organization. By 1973, Kunzru, in addition to his other accomplishments, was prominent in the national Indian welfare and reform society known as Servants of India. This was fortuitous because Gopi Krishna was in the process of applying for much-needed funding for the Samiti's Center for the Welfare of Destitute Women and Children, and there was no doubt Kunzru's support in attaining this financial aid would be invaluable. At the time, the center's ongoing efforts included three divisions, each headed by a qualified female instructor who trained the women and girls in general tailoring, in the use of knitting machines that could produce woolen socks and sweaters, and in the creation of traditional Kashmiri *gabba*—hand-hooked rugs made from recycled woolen blankets. In his application Gopi Krishna requested funding for the salaries for two additional qualified instructors to teach tailoring and gabba-making, for a clerk to do accounting, and for an attendant. He also requested aid in purchasing the necessary supplies of wool, yarn, thread, and cloth. Kunzru added his support to this application for financial aid, and when the funding was received, the important work of Samiti's Center for the Welfare of Destitute Women and Children was able to continue.

In order to put these efforts by Gopi Krishna to promote women's rights and abuse prevention in context, it can be noted that some five decades after she visited Kashmir, the noted Jungian author Robin van Löben Sels still vividly recalled how deeply impressed she was with the number of women whose lives had literally been saved by Gopi Krishna's work and how extraordinary it was to find that, under his auspices, this type of work had been going on in Kashmir for years before the rest of the world had begun to realize its importance. A fact, she emphasized, that was even more remarkable given that much of the world, including parts of India, still ignores the abuse of women.[112]

That Gopi Krishna managed to take care of matters with Samiti, make connections with so many important people, and still find time to write as much as he did in 1973 is quite amazing. He continued writing the lengthy introductions for both the *Vijnana Bhairava* and *Panchastavi* and the commentaries on each individual verse that would make the deeper meaning more accessible to Westerners. He also finished a version of the small book *From Human to Transhuman Consciousness* and wrote a nearly fifty-page paper to be handed out at the Council Grove Conference in lieu of his attendance. He also worked on an essay he had been requested to write for Lorin Loverde. A close associate of Margaret Mead and Joseph Campbell, Loverde was putting together a book of essays on consciousness. Another project was a lengthy essay that would eventually be widely published as "The Case of Alan Watts."[113] Perhaps his most extraordinary accomplishment, however, was that in addition to all the other writing done during 1973, by the end of December he had managed to complete a draft of *The Riddle of Consciousness*, a 150-page book of inspired verse.

It seems evident that Gopi Krishna's decision to remain in India in 1973 in order to write as much as possible was a good one. It was certainly justified by the role his previous publications were having that year in getting his message out. *The Biological Basis*, *The Secret of Yoga*, and *Kundalini: The Evolutionary Energy in Man* were continuing to make waves, and more editions of these books were being published. Alfred Scherz Verlag came out with a Swiss edition of *The Biological Basis*, and Turnstone Press had now published a British edition of *The Secret of Yoga*. In the United States, the hardcover Shambhala edition of *Kundalini: The Evolutionary Energy in Man* had been doing so well that the company decided to produce a paperback edition. Only the book tentatively titled *Questions and Answers* had not yet found a home with a major publisher. By the end of the year, however, it was making the rounds and being considered for publication.

Chapter Seventeen

Research Begins—The All India Institute
for Medical Science

After staying longer than usual in Kashmir at the end of 1973, Gopi Krishna arrived in Delhi on the third day of January, and the rest of that month found him at the house in Sarvodaya Enclave hoping to continue writing as much as possible. He poignantly explains this desire in a letter to his dear friend Evelyn Ferrantini, who had written at the beginning of the new year asking when he might be able to visit Europe again:

> To tell the truth I myself would like to come to Europe now. Only I would like to complete at least one more book before doing so. The moment we come into the glare of publicity, which has practically started to happen, it would be very difficult for me to then devote as much time to my writing work. Therefore I wish to complete one or two more books before there are other demands on my time. This is a sacred duty I must perform to be true to myself...

These demands on his time were already becoming apparent. The influx of visitors that had begun with the arrival of Gay Luce and Eric Peper had continued in varying waves, and it is safe to say that Gopi Krishna was now beginning to have to set boundaries to, in a sense, protect himself—or, perhaps better said, to protect his ability to write as well as the time and level of health he needed to do it allowed him. In the letter to Evelyn, he went on:

> There are already many letters from people seeking to meet me, but I do not wish my writing work to be disturbed. I have offers to address audiences in Calcutta, Bombay, Madras, and even in Delhi and big gatherings are assured, but so far I have declined. I am even averse to publicity at the moment, because once wide publicity is given to our work there will be no stopping the people from coming to meet me. I am very glad however if an affectionate friend is near to help, and in this also God has been gracious to me.

Surely the last line was added to assure Evelyn, who was hoping to visit India again, that she would be welcome. Another welcome visitor during that period was Tom Kieffer, Gene's son. A budding cameraman and cinematographer, Tom had been traveling in India for a few months working on a film with Elmer Green and his wife. Green, encouraged and enthused by the results he had obtained with using his biofeedback equipment on Swami Rama, had come to India hoping to find a number of yogis who could corroborate those earlier results.

Although Gopi Krishna was somewhat willing to meet with Green if the American wanted to come to Delhi, he maintained his stance that altered states of consciousness were not indicative of higher states of consciousness and that the biofeedback research being done on phenomena such as the ability to alter brain waves and body temperature was a distraction both from yoga's true goal of union with the Divine and from the research on higher states that he hoped to see done. He did not, however, denigrate the use of biofeedback in terms of health. What's more, during Luce and Peper's earlier visit he had, after evident cajoling by the two scientists, allowed himself to be hooked up to the biofeedback equipment they had brought with them. The result was that the pair were clearly amazed at the speed with which he was able to alter brain waves. True to his stated attitudes about this type of research, he quickly brushed aside the importance of any such ability.[114]

For whatever reason, Green did not come to Delhi—and Tom's visit was one that Gopi Krishna and his family were able to simply enjoy. Gopi Krishna also got his wish to focus mainly on his writing through much of that month. He was able to revise and make some additions to *The Riddle of Consciousness* and to continue overseeing the work being done in Kashmir on the *Vijnana Bhairava* and *Panchastavi*. He was also once again revising the edition of *The Shape of Events to Come* with the prose introduction which was being typed to prepare it for eventual publication in India.

This work proceeded well until the end of January, when a major turning point would mark Gopi Krishna's life. After it, despite his hopes, he would never again have as much time to focus solely on his writing. One of the factors behind this dramatic change was presaged by a letter he received on January 30 from Dr. B.K. Anand, dean and head of physiology at the All India Institute of Medical Sciences. AIIMS was one of the premier hospitals and research centers in India. It remains so even today, and recognition by the institute carried great weight. The letter briefly described research on the effects of yoga that Anand's department was hoping to carry out. Anand made it clear he was hoping to meet with Gopi Krishna as soon as possible. The meeting was arranged almost immediately, and on February 1, 1974, representatives from AIIMS met with Gopi Krishna in Sarvodaya Enclave to discuss research. In the next few days Gopi Krishna arranged for Dr. Anand to be sent *The Secret of Yoga*, a number of articles he had written, and a succinct summary of his ideas on research. Anand's focus was on physiology and, accordingly, the précis stressed organic structure and the brain:

> The papers I am sending will perhaps give some insight into the type of research I have in view. In a nut-shell what I aim at is that mystical or any kind of epiphanous experience, which is the basis of every great religion in the world, should become [recognized as demonstrable] of empirical verification on the basis of the biological transformations effected to make the experience possible. Can we ever take it for granted that there is no difference in the organic structure of an extraordinary man of genius and a common man even if, at the present moment, we are not able to

identify the variation, probably because our knowledge of the brain is still very incomplete and there can be biological differences which are beyond the probe of our instruments and methods of observation[?]

The same applies to religious genius. The research I have in mind is therefore aimed at the investigation of a baffling phenomenon of which science has no explanation at present....

With our cultural heritage India provides the most promising venue for the investigation, and it would be a source of great happiness to me if dedicated scientists, well grounded in the Indian tradition, were to take up the investigation in [the] spirit of science, man and God.

Soon, a detailed research proposal was being developed at AIIMS. The project, however, was put on hold for several months while Anand and his department concentrated on plans to host a major international conference in October. The focus of this conference was to be on possibilities inherent in researching the physiological effects of yoga and was, thus, directly related to the research AIIMS hoped to pursue. With over 2,000 physiologists from around the world expected, it would raise international awareness concerning yoga's validity in general and its viability as a valid field for scientific exploration. As such, the conference would be a catalyst in furthering the possibility that the research Gopi Krishna so ardently sought would, in fact, someday come to pass. In the meantime, this pause in AIIMS's efforts would give him the opportunity to continue writing and to meet with other people who could be helpful in spreading his message.

One of these individuals was Amaury de Riencourt, who had contacted Gopi Krishna in 1973 regarding his desire to meet with the yogi. After serving in the French army during World War II, de Riencourt had gone to Tibet. Spending five months there in 1947, he met with the Dalai Lama. When he returned to Europe, eventually settling in Geneva, he wrote his first book, *Roof of the World: Tibet, Key to Asia*. By the time he met with Gopi Krishna at Sarvodaya Enclave in February 1974, he had become widely acclaimed as an authority on India and China and was well-known to world leaders such as Jawaharlal Nehru. As a noted author, de Riencourt also had several highly commended books to his credit. A 1957 review of his book *The Coming Caesars* in the *New York Times* states, "If he is right—a few decades or a century from now—some later historian may dig out his book and call him a prophet."[115] Certainly he was a prophet, or at least a visionary of sorts, when it came to Gopi Krishna's ideas. After meeting with the yogi in February at Sarvodaya Enclave, he went on to promote the Pandit's work in France and to write *The Eye of Shiva*, a book that describes Gopi Krishna's ideas and could be said to be heavily influenced by them.[116]

During this period, Gopi Krishna had been suffering from excruciating pains in his thighs, an unexplained medical issue that would plague him on and off for the rest of his life. In spite of this, he continued through the rest of February to oversee the work on the Kashmiri texts, adding the *Shiva Sutras* to his earlier efforts. He also kept up his revisions on *The Riddle of Consciousness*, assiduously sending corrected pages to Margaret in Zürich for typing and in many cases retyping due to edits and changes.

Two of the visitors who came together in February were Dr. Baldoon Dhingra and Dr. G.S. Melkot. Baldoon Dhingra was a poet, scholar, and translator who was well-known in India and Europe. Author-editor of *Asia through Asian Eyes* and several other books, he lived in France. Along with his wife, he would come to do much to promote Gopi Krishna's work there until his untimely death a few years later. Dr. Melkot was an imminent physician as well as a member of parliament. Extremely interested in research, he headed the Gopal Clinic in Hyderabad and a number of yoga centers. During this visit Melkot mentioned that Dr. Green had dropped in at the Gopal Clinic during his tour of India. This comment instigated an illuminating discussion on research and the true purpose of yoga that Gopi Krishna later recounted.

[Dr. Melkot] said that the Centre he was running was making research on the healing and curative aspects of Yoga. I said that this is the misconception of the West. They label Yoga as merely a curative system with some possibilities of metabolic control, which completely eclipses its real purpose of mental transformation and spiritual unfoldment. He at once understood what I meant and said that the ideas I was expressing

completely tallied with his own views, but emphasis on the curative and health aspects was also necessary to interest the Western scientist....
He agreed that by showing Yoga as merely a curative system it becomes merely one of the manifold unconventional systems of treatment, like Acupuncture, Naturopathy, psychic healing and the rest and loses its unique value as the ladder to a higher dimension of consciousness.

Melkot, who had been invited to the Menninger Foundation, was preparing for a trip that would take him to Europe and the United States, where he said he would make sure Gopi Krishna's views on research were brought forward during his lectures and meetings.

Several other important visitors came to Sarvodaya Enclave during February of 1974. One, brought by Professor Dhingra, was Kamaladevi Chattopadhyay. A spirited activist and social reformer, she was one of the most famous women in India at the time. Another individual visiting that month was R.S.C. Iengar, a quiet Indian businessman with ties to the book industry who divided his time between India and England. Iengar was a man who shunned personal recognition but would go on for many years to be one of the most ardent promoters of Gopi Krishna's books.

It was becoming evident that Gopi Krishna's concern that "there would be no stopping the people" coming to meet him was already coming to pass to some extent. In spite of this, he accomplished a good deal during February, continuing to send revisions on *The Riddle of Consciousness* to Margaret. Although given his predilection for meticulous revision the work on this book would no doubt continue until it was published, by the end of that month Gopi Krishna was able to think of the work as finished. In a letter to Margaret he wrote, "Personally speaking, it is of the greatest solace and joy to me as I feel that it is only now that I have been able to present what I wished to say in an appropriate way." He could do this, he emphasized, only because the original work and the additional material had come to him while he was in a virtually trancelike state of inspired creativity. Nonetheless, in terms of his creative process, it is interesting to note that making corrections and revisions was a very conscious, intellectually involved activity.

For some time he had been saying that once this work in verse was completed, his goal was to write another book in prose. Accordingly, he started on this project in March while still in Kashmir. Although he missed the family members who lived in Delhi when he was there, he had come to realize that the water in Delhi did not agree with him. Hoping to spend as much time as possible in the north where his overall health tended to be so much better, he made the trip to Srinagar at the end of March and by the end of the month was ready to move back to Kashmir, where his overall health tended to be much better.

Once settled there, he again had visitors. Among them were two Chinese men currently living in British Columbia, Mr. Tan and Mr. Fung, who would eventually become instrumental in spreading Gopi Krishna's work in China.[117] Gopi Krishna again found himself trying to balance the necessity of meeting individuals such as these two men who would promote his ideas with the need to keep writing. Evidence that his writings were indeed becoming increasingly effective in this regard came in letters such as the one he received in May from a professor at Colorado University:

> I am using *The Biological Basis of Religion and Genius* as a text in a course I am teaching in the honors department of Colorado University, entitled "Creative Potential." Basically, we are studying "what's right with people." Your viewpoints concerning human potential are extremely vital and important, not only for the academic community, but also, for the whole world.[118]

Fortunately during these beautiful spring months in Kashmir, Gopi Krishna was able to continue to both write to and meet with people. The volume of prose he had begun in March proceeded to rapidly unfold, and he was able to work on it diligently through the rest of the spring. In June, he again met with Dr. Karan Singh, who had by this time attained his influential position in the family planning cabinet. Since renewing his contact with Gopi Krishna the previous year, Dr. Singh had become increasingly interested in the possibilities of research into phenomena related to yoga and other Indian traditions, and it is evident that he wanted the Indian government to be at the forefront. In June he arranged to have dinner with Gopi Krishna. At that time he also toured the Central Institute for Kundalini Research in Nishat. Having foreseen the growing need for a well-established center with available visitor accommodation, Gopi Krishna had been putting a good deal of effort into improving the property.

Throughout June he also maintained his usual heavy correspondence. One particularly important letter was from Dr. Surendra Kumar Manchanda, who was by then head of the physiology department at AIIMS. Although the plans for the physiology research had slowed since the first of the year due to the focus on the upcoming conference, Manchanda was now in charge of the project. In the letter he explained that he hoped to send a final draft of the research proposal and send it in the next few weeks. In spite of his exceptionally busy schedule, he met this goal. The proposal, entitled "Yogic Techniques in the Development of Higher Nervous Function," reached Gopi Krishna for his comments in July. In hindsight it is not surprising that Manchanda managed to fulfill his promise. An extremely efficient man, he held doctoral degrees in both physiology and medicine and would go on to make several major scientific contributions in neurophysiology. That Manchanda recognized the importance of Gopi Krishna's input on yoga research is evinced by his inclusion of all five of his then-published books in the bibliography of the proposal.

Although Gopi Krishna had been receiving letters from around the world from people who were experiencing varying degrees of kundalini awakening since his first book was published, the number of these types of letters was also increasing. Although he never failed to stress the fact that he was not a guru and as such did not take disciples, he answered each letter with careful attention to the symptoms described. Giving what practical advice he could, he frequently offered up gems of wisdom. In a letter written that June, he stated that the purpose of his writing was to make both the scientist and the average human being aware of

> ...this priceless endowment with which nature has gifted them and which can make their lives sublime. All our efforts at meditation, prayer and worship, all striving for a healthy temperate life and all our wishes to do good to others ultimately impinge on this divine instrument...[thus

bringing about] the beatific states of consciousness that crowned the lives of all great spiritual luminaries of the past. This potential in us is not of the nature of a mere organic machine which we can manipulate at our choice, but a profound, super intelligent source of life-energy which we cannot master but have to obey with deep faith, trusting in its omniscience to cause necessary transformations in our whole organic being until we touch the sublime heights to which we aspire.

Late June also saw a visit from George Tompkins. George, who had been involved in both film and video production, had been thinking for some time about how a film might be used to promote Gopi Krishna's ideas—a possibility that had also intrigued Gene Kieffer. Seriously considering the concept, George stayed in Kashmir into July. That month Gopi Krishna also received a visit from Dr. Stanley Krippner, the noted American psychologist who was becoming increasingly known for his research into paranormal phenomena. Krippner had recently co-authored *Galaxies of Life: The Human Aura in Acupuncture and Kirlian Photography*, a book that would have remarkably wide influence. Interested in these early speculations about the potential research value of Kirlian photography, Gopi Krishna was glad to have an opportunity to discuss the topic with Krippner. Although no serious scientific research using Kirlian photography to validate kundalini awakening ever came about, the yogi made a deep impression on Krippner. Even several decades later, the psychologist would write about his meetings with Gopi Krishna in his book *Broken Images, Broken Selves* in detail.

One reason psychologists such as Krippner and representatives from the various associations for humanistic and transpersonal psychology were interested in Gopi Krishna's ideas was related to a growing awareness of a phenomenon that would come to be widely known as *spiritual emergency*. Although this term wouldn't become more widely used until the late 1980s, when Christina and Stanislav Grof wrote about it, avant-garde psychologists had been aware for some time that individuals who were involved in a spiritual practice sometimes experienced crises. According to the Grofs' eventual definition, these individuals were "experiencing episodes of nonordinary states of consciousness accompanied by various emotional, perceptual, and psychosomatic manifestations [and were]...undergoing an evolutionary crisis rather than suffering from a mental disease."[119]

By the time the humanistic and transcendental psychologists had begun to visit Gopi Krishna in the early 1970s, his published works had made the relationship that he saw between the awakening of kundalini and the challenges he faced in the early years evident. Over the years, Gopi Krishna's thinking on the relationship between kundalini and mental disturbances would become further clarified. When the kundalini hypothesis was eventually formalized, it would include certain classes of mental illness along with the attributes of mystical experience, inspired creativity and genius, and paranormal phenomena. It was Gopi Krishna's contention that these classes of mental illness were associated with awakenings that had somehow gone awry and not with healthy awakenings, particularly those that were the result of a gradual, natural, ongoing evolutionary process.

The person Gopi Krishna discussed this aspect of kundalini with in the most detail was no doubt Dr. Elizabeth Hoch. A Swiss psychiatrist, Dr. Hoch arrived in Srinagar determined to practice there, eventually becoming head of the psychiatric studies at the Government Medical College and superintendent of the psychiatric hospital there.[120] Not long after her arrival in 1972 she met Gopi Krishna, and by 1974 the two were in close communication. Over the years she not only discussed many psychiatric cases with him, she successfully applied his suggestions for treatment. Dr. Hoch also provided him with detailed case histories (of course minus identifying information) on patients whose condition she believed was related to kundalini awakening. It seems evident from this that, although it would be years before the kundalini hypothesis was formalized, Gopi Krishna was exploring this aspect of awakenings.

According to Dr. Hoch, there was one area where they disagreed. In her opinion it was Gopi Krishna's contention that all mental illness was the result of some form of aberrant kundalini awakening. Whether her opinion in this was correct may well be debated by those intimately familiar with his writings. Regardless, she firmly believed some cases of mental illness she dealt with were indeed related to kundalini awakening and expressed gratitude for his insights into the treatment of those cases. A more contemporary view of the aspects of the kundalini hypothesis that deals with mental disturbances postulates that kundalini awakening, when unable to proceed in a healthy, natural manner, might eventually be found to be responsible for some forms of mental illness or be mistaken for mental illness. Beyond this, it is worth noting that for Gopi Krishna, Shakti in her manifestation in the body as kundalini-shakti and prāna-shakti was the energy of consciousness, of mind itself. In this sense, anything at all to do with the mind was perforce related to kundalini.

Regardless of how Gopi Krishna's view on this is interpreted, it is important to reiterate that, from his earliest pleas for research onward, he repeatedly insisted that no premise he proposed should be left unexamined: it should instead be subjected to the most rigorous scientific study possible.

Although he had made this point in his earlier works, he stressed it once again in the book that was in production in the United States that summer, *Higher Consciousness: The Evolutionary Thrust of Kundalini*. When he received the final galley proofs in July, he examined them carefully but quickly. He was able to send the galleys back to Julian Press by the end of the month so that the book could come out in the fall. In spite of all this activity during these summer months, Gopi Krishna also continued to work assiduously on the prose volume he had begun in March. Then, during the first weeks of August, he was suddenly gripped by the idea for a new book. Although this would also be a work in prose, it would be completely different. In describing the project, he noted that, with the exception of *Kundalini: The Evolutionary Energy in Man*, his books had all been philosophical or abstract in nature. In contrast this book would

...be able to maintain the interest of the reader throughout, for it is interspersed with narratives, anecdotes and stories. A large part of the scriptural lore of India will come in its range and it will solve some of the riddles over which eminent scholars, both of the East and West, have laboured in vain.

Astonishingly, this entire book, which would become the 260-page *The Dawn of a New Science*, was written between August 10, when he said the idea grabbed him, and the end of September. During this period he was in what he called one of his creative moods. These were often so intense he would only remember to eat when Bhabi, Margaret, one of his daughters-in-law, or one of his grandchildren reminded him to do so. This one was particularly intense, causing him to work even when he should have been sleeping.

This accomplishment was made more noteworthy by the fact that he was not only writing but also reading and researching a great many books. Many of these were classics by authors such as Evelyn Underhill and William James, but others were contemporary books, unavailable in Kashmir, that he was having friends send him from abroad. He was adamant about using material from these books so that his ideas could be supported by the latest, most up-to-date research. While this was effective then, some of the best-selling, widely respected books of the day, such as Ostrander and Schroeder's *Psychic Discoveries behind the Iron Curtain* and even Krippner's book on auras, are no longer seen in the same light. Other works on science that he referenced are now, decades later, also out-of-date. So while using these contemporary books was an effective strategy at the time, it now has the unfortunate effect of making some of the references seem dated. In spite of this, *The Dawn of a New Science*—a book accomplished in an astoundingly short time—remains a powerfully informative, in-depth exploration of stories, myths, and legends from the world's spiritual traditions. More importantly, this exploration comes from a state that can only be called revelation.

It is not surprising that when he finished this at the end of September he was in a state of exhaustion that lasted through October and into November. But it wasn't just the writing of *The Dawn of a New Science* that had drained him. In the twelve months since the late fall of 1973, he had also written, edited, and revised *The Riddle of Consciousness*, written a third of a book that was discarded, and corrected the galley proofs for *Higher Consciousness*, all while carrying on an extensive correspondence, meeting with visitors from around the world, and overseeing the work Samiti was continuing to do. Fortunately, Margaret arrived from Switzerland on October 7 to be of assistance for several months.

While Gopi Krishna was recuperating during those last few months of 1974, several highly significant events were taking place outside Kashmir. The 26th International Congress of Physiological Sciences took place in New Delhi in October, with Dr. Karan Singh giving the keynote address. Over 2,000 physiologists attended, with over 1,800 of them being from abroad. In spite of his department's heavy involvement, Dr. Manchanda continued his efforts to get the AIIMS research project off the ground. It was apparent that worldwide interest in yoga research was growing, and it seemed obvious to interested parties in India that their country's scientists should be leading the way. As minister of health and family planning, Karan Singh had become increasingly involved in this research, both in what was planned at AIIMS and in how his government could expand these efforts. Related to this burgeoning interest in the investigation of yoga, plans were being laid for a conference open to the public to be held in March 1975. Entitled "Seminar on Yoga, Science, and Man," the conference was to feature prominent scientists, thinkers, and yogis who would range from the Maharishi Mahesh Yogi, of Beatles fame, to Gopi Krishna.

In the United States, Gene Kieffer felt Julian Press had not put enough money into their promotion budget for *Higher Consciousness*. Making Herculean efforts to promote the book himself, he paid for ads he had created in not only the *New York Times* but a number of other publications. He had also been working hard to find a publisher for the *Meditation and Kundalini* manuscript, eventually securing a contract from the well-known publisher E.P. Dutton for the book that they would name *The Awakening of Kundalini.* The book consisted of a number of pieces that had been published previously. One chapter had originally been published in 1974 in the journal *Fields within Fields* as "Understanding the Transformation of Consciousness." Other chapters were "The True Aim of Yoga," which had come out in the magazine *Psychic* the previous year, and an essay, "Meditation: Is It Always Beneficial?" These works were yet another indication of both the extraordinary amount of writing Gopi Krishna had accomplished in the early 1970s and the astounding effort Gene Kieffer was making to get the yogi's work in print.

Gene did not, however, have the same success with his attempts to find a home for *The Riddle of Consciousness*. After continuing to find US publishers unwilling to put out full-length works of verse, he took on the project himself, determined to create a beautiful book that was worthy of the content.

As events in the larger world continued to swirl around him, Gopi Krishna remained in Kashmir, continuing to work with Margaret's help on catching up with correspondence and overseeing the Kashmiri text translations. At the beginning of December he returned to Delhi for the rest of the winter months. The cold in Kashmir was more bitter than usual that year, but he would have had to return in any case as Professor Baldoon had arranged for him to be interviewed by a prominent Delhi television station on December 3. The interview was televised the next week. While it no doubt added to the growing number of people wanting to be in contact with him, Gopi Krishna was able with Margaret's assistance to spend the final days of 1974 resting up in preparation for the year to come.

Chapter Eighteen

Yoga, Science, and Man—Gopi Krishna vs the Maharishi

At the beginning of 1975 Gopi Krishna was continuing to work on his correspondence and the Kashmir translation projects he'd been focused on at the end of the previous year. In addition to typing the letters dictated to her, Margaret was typing copies of *The Dawn of a New Science* so that the manuscript could be sent out. As she was planning to leave Delhi by the middle of February, it is easy to imagine that the two were working diligently to get as much done as possible. Gopi Krishna was hampered in this by concerns not only for his own health but for that of his family. He was still plagued by the ill health he had experienced in the autumn. Bhabi had not felt particularly well since December, and now neither his daughter, Ragya, nor her husband were in good health.

By this time Mr. Kaul had risen to a very important position in the High Court of Delhi. As such he had been a great support to his father-in-law for several years—involved in everything from cutting through India's thick bureaucratic red tape to arrange visas for foreign travel to promoting his books. Gopi Krishna was very fond of him and thankful that his only daughter's marriage—arranged as it had been long before his awakening had stabilized—had turned out so well. Knowing what a salubrious effect Kashmir always had on his health, Gopi Krishna was hoping to convince Mr. Kaul and Ragya to spend time there as soon as the weather warmed. It's possible that he would have considered leaving Delhi for Kashmir for the sake of Bhabi's and his own health too, but he had made a commitment to speak at the Seminar on Yoga, Science, and Man beginning on March 14.

Over the next few weeks he worked on preparing his talk for the conference. Sponsored by not only AIIMS but the Ministry of Health and Family Planning and the Central Council for Research in Indian Medicine and Homeopathy, it was going to be a highly important gathering. During the science portion of the conference, a number of prominent doctors and physiologists were scheduled to speak. The sessions related to yoga were to include not only Gopi Krishna and the Maharishi but also Prime Minister Indira Gandhi's personal guru, Dhirendra Brahmachari.

Although Gopi Krishna was not as well-known as the gurus of the Beatles and Indira Gandhi, his renown was continuing to grow. On March 3, an article on him had appeared in *The India Express*. Known as India's largest-circulation newspaper, it was published in Bombay, Calcutta, and Delhi. While the headline "Instant Genius through Yoga" seemed sensationalistic, the article itself expressed Gopi Krishna's ideas fairly well. At the same time an article, "New Light on Yoga Causes Stir," appeared in *The Free Press Journal* of Bombay, as did an article in *Nav Bharat*, a Hindu-language daily. In spite of their being hampered by the brief nature of newspaper articles, Gopi Krishna mentioned in a letter that he was pleased with how they represented "an introduction of our work before the Indian public."

During this period the plans for the March seminar were going ahead. Having the sponsorship of Ministry of Health and Family Planning was a tremendous boost to the credibility of the event. Being an official federal ministry, it had even more authority than AIIMS. There is no doubt that this involvement was due to a large extent to the influence of the minister himself, Dr. Karan Singh, who not only helped plan and promote the seminar but also gave the opening address, in which he described the AIIMS research project, stating that it revolved "particularly around the books on kundalini by Pandit Gopi Krishna, who is happily among us today."

The conference was in every sense a huge success. Prior to it, many people had assumed that the Maharishi, with all the current attention being heaped on him, would dominate the event. In advance of the seminar, adherents of his world-famous organization had gone to great expense to publicize both his participation in it and TM's claims to provide personalized mantras that would lead not only to transcendental states but also eventually to siddhis. In spite of his adherents' efforts at advance promotion, elements of the Maharishi's talk were challenged outright by Dhirendra Brahmachari, a swami vastly more respected by the Indian people, and the Maharishi's dominance of neither the seminar itself nor the publicity afterward came to pass.[121]

In contrast, the seminar was a great success for Gopi Krishna. Even the organizers seemed to be aware that this might be the case. After cautioning all the speakers on the topic of kundalini in advance that they might have only a very short time to speak, they told Gopi Krishna to take as much time as he wanted. In the end he spoke for an hour and a quarter to what was later described as a rapt audience.

There is no doubt that Gopi Krishna made a potent impression on the attendees, particularly in a comment that was made during a question-and-answer session when someone asked him how one could tell if a higher state of consciousness had actually been reached. After a pause Gopi Krishna replied, "Silence." Then gesturing to his eyes, he added, "And tears."[122] After all the clamor of words and ideas tossed about over the two days of the seminar, the sincere simplicity of his words caused a profound hush to fall over the room.

The ideas he expressed during his talk also made an impact on the scientific community. Over the next few weeks, several scientists asked to meet with him. They included Dr. Manchananda, Dr. Kurup, who was director of the Central Council for Research on Indian Medicine and Homeopathy, and Dr. Daulat Singh Kothari. A renowned scientist, Kothari had been president of the Indian National Science Academy in 1973. Currently he was head of a standing committee on yoga research. After the seminar, Gopi Krishna was also invited to a meeting of scientists at the National Science Academy, where his talk instigated an in-depth discussion of his ideas. Among the other invitations he received directly after the seminar was one to speak at the University of Delhi. The talk there was moderated by Dr. Kothari and was received with as much interest as the one at the academy. During this period Gopi Krishna was also visited by Swami Vishwananda, a nationally revered guru known for his social-justice work who had served as secretary of the Gandhi Smarak Nidhi, the memorial organization created by the Indian government to further Gandhi's social work and, as such, was the guide for Martin Luther King, Jr.'s 1959 tour of India.[123]

For some time Gopi Krishna had been thinking about the need for some type of center, or at least an office, in Delhi. The post-seminar flurry of activity made him more aware than ever of how beneficial this would be. It was also becoming evident there was a pressing need to have his books, now being translated and published in so many other countries, printed at a reasonable cost in India. After his talk at the seminar, many people had asked for his books, but his only book published by a major Indian publisher at that time was *The Secret of Yoga*, and the cover price was considered too high for the average person.

That the Maharishi had not been able to dominate the seminar was considered a good sign by Gopi Krishna as he had been continuing to hear disturbing news about TM. In the US, Gene Kieffer had become increasingly frustrated by the Maharishi's mass appeal. Since his first encounter with Gopi Krishna's ideas, Gene had worked tirelessly to find publishers for the books and gone to tremendous personal expense to promote them. Disheartened by the fact that the public hadn't taken to Gopi Krishna's ideas as they had the Maharishi's, he and other concerned supporters sent Gopi Krishna copious amounts of information on the spread of groups such as TM and of similar so-called gurus who were amassing fortunes by promising enlightenment with a mere touch or other methods that required little or no effort by the initiate.

No doubt concerned with the information he was receiving, Gopi Krishna took a fairly hard-line stance against organizations such as TM and their leaders. One of his objections was that the initiates were being charged for the mantras. It is obvious, from the current perspective, that mantras abound in a number of Hindu traditions and that it should have been evident even then that they could be found for free by anyone who searched for them in any library.

Beyond Gopi Krishna's concern that these young people were being taken advantage of financially was his firm belief that solely chanting a mantra—while making none of the efforts described in the *Bhagavad Gītā*, the *Yoga Sutras*, and other texts—would not bring about the higher states of consciousness leading to union with the Divine that was the ultimate goal of yoga. Mantra chanting on its own would not even bring about siddhis, especially not ones such as the power to levitate, which the TM organization was widely touting.

Of course, one reason TM was spreading was that many of the practitioners said they generally felt better and more relaxed when they practiced their mantra meditation. Over the decades a number of studies have supported this. As one contemporary Buddhist meditator suggested, such positive effects weren't particularly surprising. Common sense suggested that "if we're not engaged in our normal unhelpful (anxious, angry, craving) thinking, then the mind is going to quiet down."[124] During the period described in Chapter Sixteen when John White was suggesting that Gopi Krishna was being perhaps too cautionary about programs such as biofeedback, John also suggested that, given the many positive effects TM practitioners were reporting, Gopi Krishna might take a more tolerant view of the program, especially since he, John, had himself experienced some benefits after trying out the practice. In spite of this, a fact-facing journalist to the core, he passed on the results of a study done at Michigan State University that concluded that TM's benefits were basically due to the placebo effect.[125] The year-long study, conducted by Jonathan C. Smith, followed rigorous protocols. In the letter John quotes Smith's conclusions that, while TM did indeed have "psychotherapeutic" effects, "TM was no more therapeutic than a placebo treatment involving sitting down twice daily."

It is interesting to observe that when Gopi Krishna wrote about mantras in his correspondence or in his book *Higher Consciousness*, the discussion is invariably in the context of the types of amulets, charms, and spells being sold in India and elsewhere by pseudohealers and the like:

> The purveyors of Mantras, talismans, spells, and charms, belonging to different countries and faiths, claim equal efficacy for their favourite products. This shows that the real efficacy does not lie in the words or

formulas of these products but in the mental attitude of expectation and faith of those to whom they are applied.[126]

Although it falls into the realm of speculation on the part of this biographer, it seems highly probable that when Gopi Krishna was writing about mantras he was doing so in the context of TM and of the mantras that were being sold by supposed healers and false gurus along with other charms and amulets. At no place in the vast correspondence and writings reviewed for this book were any negative opinions found concerning the traditional sacred mantras that are still today used as a form of prayer. However, it is possible that even in this case Gopi Krishna would have attributed some of the efficacy of the mantras to "this mysterious power of mind over body"—keeping in mind, of course, that for him the individual mind was a mere drop in the all-pervasive, cosmic, divine mind. So, while Gopi Krishna never seems to have denied or denigrated mantras as one facet of a sincere spiritual practice, it is fair to say that he did not believe the many claims that repeating a mantra could bring about wondrous or near-miraculous results, such as bestowing riches or instantaneously curing a dread disease.

Regardless of all this, a main issue for him was that all the foofaraw around the claims of the false gurus was yet another distraction from yoga's true goal of bringing the meditator to the higher states of consciousness. These states, he firmly believed, were the goals not just for individual transformation but for the ongoing evolution of humankind. The stakes for humanity were, in short, huge. As stated earlier, a moderate lifestyle in tune with the tenets of the great spiritual teachings was absolutely essential for this evolution to proceed in a healthy manner. Another concern he had in regard to TM, along with other practices being called meditation, was that they were passive. In other words, they did not involve the single-pointed focus, *dhyāna*, that was meditation as described in the classical yoga of Patanjali as the seventh step in his eightfold path. Meditation, or dhyāna, flowed naturally out of *dhāranā*, the focused concentration of the sixth step after it had been mastered.[127]

The so-called meditations, on the other hand, produced what he described as the relaxed and somnolent states of mind indicated by the alpha and theta rhythms that were registered by biofeedback equipment. In this sense, there was nothing inherently wrong with them, they were simply variations on Emile Coué's famous affirmation "Every day, in every way, I am getting better and better" being repeated in the quiet state before falling asleep. Another potential problem with these types of meditation was that these somnolent states could produce vivid imaginative experiences that could be mistaken for true states of higher consciousness by the meditator who had little knowledge about what these states, attained as they were by the great saints and mystics, truly entailed.

One aspect of all this that definitely did not concern him was the fact that the so-called gurus were gaining such huge followings in the United States and Europe. He remained steadfast in his attitude that his efforts would proceed as decreed by the Divine. In a letter, he wrote:

Please keep your faith firmly pinned in Heaven. Great empires fell and crumbled to dust when the Power that had built them failed. Every meteoric rise, not grounded on Truth, must have a fall. It is for this reason that, though our progress is slow and no fanfare attends our movements, I am absolutely certain of our success.

The great Truths he often alluded to were those that were in accordance with the spiritual laws taught by the great teachers of all the spiritual traditions:

None of the three great luminaries of India, during recent times, namely Rama Krishna Paramahamsa, Maharishi Ramana [more commonly known in the West as Ramana Maharishi] and Shri Aurobindo, ever moved to great distances out of their Ashrams. Their teachings are still fresh and inspiring and their memory is still honoured by millions. We have yet to see what will be the verdict of posterity on the Gurus and Godmen, now touring in the West and drawing millions of followers round them.

We should not, therefore, be influenced by the thought that rapid movement from place to place or new-fangled methods of meditation or claims to supernatural powers in any way denote enlightenment or that an illuminated person would behave in the same way as they are doing. The one and only clinching test of real illumination is knowledge of the normally unfathomable spiritual laws which rule the destiny of mankind.... [Those who] belong to the category of the professionals who delve into the occult or use their inherent supernormal gifts to purvey for name, fame, wealth or other considerations...do not possess the prophetic vision to guide mankind on the tortuous path of evolution. This is the prerogative of the illuminati alone.

In contrast to the spreading, undiscerning acceptance in the West of the claims of so-called gurus, the interest in serious scientific research into yoga, consciousness, and "real illumination" spurred by his talk at the Seminar on Yoga, Science, and Man must have been a balm to Gopi Krishna. It was, however, also exhausting. Bhabi, too, was still not feeling completely well, and after the flurry of activity the two of them finally managed to leave Delhi for the more salubrious living conditions in Kashmir on April 12. Once there, Gopi Krishna began to reclaim his health. During the rest of the spring he was able to complete four chapters of what he hoped to be volume two of *Dawn of a New Science*. He also worked on finalizing the corrections to *Panchastavi* so that the Indian version could come out before the end of the year. Another project was to revisit the lengthy verse he had originally composed for Julian Huxley, working on an introduction that would turn it into a book relevant to the public at large. Around this time he also started to think about how valuable having a magazine or journal dedicated to accurate and intriguing information on kundalini might be. Like so many of his projects that began as merely a wisp of an idea, this would come to fruition over the next few years in the form of the quarterly journal called *Spiritual India & Kundalini*.

As a result of the interest generated by his talk at the seminar, he began to receive more letters from strangers than ever before. Fortunately, the secretary he had hired previously, Mr. S.N. Razdan, was handling much of the correspondence so that Gopi Krishna was not interrupted so much in his important work. It is evident, however, that the Pandit gave Razdan careful guidance in how these letters should be answered and which ones should be handed to him for personal attention.

The letters inviting him back to Europe were also increasingin number. Margaret had invited him to come in June and had gone so far as to send a ticket. Gopi Krishna had concluded, however, that several months in Kashmir would be more beneficial, and he decided to postpone the trip until November so that he could spend the winter months in Zürich. Although Switzerland would be cold, the water and air would be better for his health there than in Delhi.

The time he spent in Kashmir from April to November 1975 was as fruitful as he had hoped. Not only was he able to generate many ideas and a great deal of writing, he was able to receive a number of important visitors and make progress on his books being republished in India at prices affordable to the public. In addition, he was able to turn some of his attention back to Samiti and the centers for training widows and other women in skills they could use to lift them out of abject poverty.

During these seven months in Kashmir he also received a considerable amount of good news. Most significant, perhaps, was that *The Awakening of Kundalini* had been successfully launched in the United States in May. He heard, too, that the AIIMS project was progressing and that Manchanda had done a rewrite and update on the original proposal. In Bombay, an Indian publisher made a firm offer to publish an Indian edition of *Higher Consciousness*, and an editor, Sukhlal Mehta, had become very serious about starting a branch of the Kundalini Research Foundation there. In England, Iengar was busy promoting Gopi Krishna's books, and Dhingra and his wife were doing the same in France. All of these individuals were buoyed and optimistic about their efforts. Another enthusiastic visitor that summer was R.K. Karanjia. A dedicated journalist, Karanjia had in 1941 founded *Blitz*, a hugely successful weekly tabloid focused on investigative journalism. After meeting with Gopi Krishna in Kashmir, the newspaperman went on to promise the Pandit that his paper would spread the word on kundalini research. As you will see in the next chapter, this came to pass the following year. Well acquainted with Prime Minister Indira Gandhi, Karanjia also helped promote kundalini research by sending her copies of a number of Gopi Krishna's books. After receiving a very positive thank-you from her, he sent a copy of the letter to Kashmir. In it she wrote, "It is surprising that no, or so little, research has been attempted on such a vital subject..."

Karanjia's efforts on Gopi Krishna's behalf might well have been the impetus for Indira Gandhi's mentioning Gopi Krishna's name to Karan Singh, whose enthusiastic response to this opening was to stress the importance of the Pandit's work while emphasizing the reasons India should be the world leader in consciousness research.[128]

Before Gopi Krishna left for Zürich in November he received even more good news. His desire to have affordable editions of his work available in India was moving forward. A Bombay publisher had agreed to take on *The Awakening of Kundalini*. In Europe, the Swiss publisher Aurum Verlag had decided to bring out a German translation of *Higher Consciousness* and was considering doing the same with *The Awakening of Kundalini*.

In the US, Gene Kieffer had been continuing his tireless efforts. Over the past several years he had spent so much of his personal income purchasing the Pandit's books to mail to potentially interested parties that he had promised himself he would never do it again. In spite of this oath, he was so thrilled with *The Awakening of Kundalini* that he bought 700 copies from E.P. Dutton to send out. Perhaps Gene was encouraged to do this by one of his most significant coups. After being in contact with the *New York Times* for years, paying for numerous ads in the paper, and trying unsuccessfully to get them to publish articles, late in the previous year he convinced them to run a full-page article by Gopi Krishna on the op-ed page. He also had the manuscript of *The Dawn of a New Science* retyped and cerlox-bound so that it could be sent out to prospective publishers.

In the midst of these significant developments, Gene received a letter, and later a visit that summer, from a Canadian named Joseph Dippong who had been born and raised in Hungary. Although the Canadian's direct contact with Gopi Krishna would be severed in less than five years, his promotion of Gopi Krishna's ideas would have a more far-reaching effect than those of anyone except perhaps Gene Kieffer himself. Known as Joe, he was a controversial figure who had made a name for himself in Canada teaching self-improvement courses similar to the hugely popular seminars being offered by Silva Mind Control, EST, and Psi Mind Development in the United States. In fact, Joe frequently stated he had been a participant in a week-long encounter group in which the heads of those three organizations—respectively, José Silva, Werner Erhard, and Tom Willhite—had all participated. Encounter groups were a form of psychotherapy popular in the day, often carried out over a weekend or a week, that involved facing one's psychological issues with head-on truth-telling. By their very nature, encounter groups were confrontational, and extreme ones had been known to become physical. According to Joe, this happened during the course he took, and his air was accidentally cut off, causing him to have a near-death experience, including a vision of white light that he claimed changed his life, after which he started teaching courses in Canada that contained elements similar to the ones run by Silva, Erhard, and Willhite.

By the time he visited Gene, Joe was having considerable success with his courses in Canada. With his typical flamboyance, before leaving Gene's home he bought seventy copies of *Higher Consciousness* and ordered 1,000 copies of *The Awakening of Kundalini*. Over the next few months he continued to correspond with Gene. By the fall he not only had corresponded directly with Gopi Krishna but also had plans for promoting the Pandit's research in Canada well underway. When he learned that Gene planned to visit Gopi Krishna in Zürich, he insisted on coming along.

After meeting the Pandit in person, Joe returned home with his enthusiasm ignited. Without hesitation he formed two nonprofit organizations aimed at supporting kundalini research, the Kundalini Research Institute of Canada and the Canadian Psychic Research Institute.[129] As you will see in the following chapters, over the next four years, the organizations he developed and the people he enlisted would help Gopi Krishna in innumerable ways. By the end of 1979, however, Joe Dippong would cause Gopi Krishna a great deal of heartache.

Looking back on all this, the question arises of how an enlightened human being such as Gopi Krishna could have become involved with such a controversial figure. Part of the answer may lie in the fact that he was indeed an enlightened human being, but he was also a very human enlightened being. Beyond that, however, Gopi Krishna himself provided the answer to that question long before the Canadian would come on the scene, in a letter written to a supporter who was being highly critical of others. In this context, it is worth noting that in the thousands of pages of correspondence read in researching this book, not one instance was found of Gopi Krishna ever giving harsh or accusatory criticism. Even in cases where some form of rebuke was absolutely necessary, it was given in the mildest, most supportive manner possible. The excerpt below goes a long way to explain not only this attitude but also how controversial figures could have been involved in his life:

> We are dedicated to a holy mission and our aim is to spread a sublime message all over the earth. Success in such a mission is only possible when Providence is on our side, and our efforts can only count when they are backed by Divine forces. I cannot say how long the struggle would last but it would be a steep uphill task for many years to come. We do not know how many people would join hands with us in the sacred mission, and how many would help us with their advice, bodily labour or resources. They may number thousands and even tens of thousands. But one thing is sure that they will be a mixture of good and bad, saints and sinners, dedicated souls or exploiters, wise men and fools and so on. Our wisdom lies in taking help from all and, even where no help is possible, at least to make friends with all of them.

Chapter Nineteen

Dr. Karan Singh, the Indian Government, and Project Consciousness

G opi Krishna's arrival in Zürich on November 14, 1975, would be the beginning of his longest stay away from home; it would be a full year before he returned to India. After meeting with Gene Kieffer and Joe Dippong that month, he began working on various books as soon as he was able. For that writing to go well he needed to be not only well rested and in good health but also in what he often referred to as a *"creative mood" or a "writing mood."* In reference to these moods, he once told Margaret,

> I can never be certain about the creative moods. Only I know that I must honour them to give all that I can to mankind. I am now in a good creative mood, writing the next work in prose. I do not know how long the book will take or to what day the mood will last....

Looking back over the many written references he made to these moods, and taking into consideration what Margaret and his family had to say about them, it seems he experienced two distinct types. One was the almost trancelike condition in which he received the lines of verse that flooded into his mind; these were written down as if he were being dictated to. The other was the one in which he both wrote his prose and made revisions to any of his writings.

This state might be described as being perhaps less exalted or transcendent, but nonetheless one that involved to some degree a state of inspiration. Gopi Krishna never failed to make a point of this and, reflecting his deep-seated humility, never gave the credit for his extraordinary accomplishments to his own limited human intellect.

However, this human intellect—limited though it might have been in the cosmic sense—was prodigiously active in the painstaking revisions he made to his work. One reason these corrections and additions were necessary was the fact that the words came so quickly to him when he was in a transcendent state that he could not get them down before they vanished. As they had that day on the Tawi Bridge, the words came floating into his consciousness like crystalline specks of snow, melting before they could be grasped just as snowflakes do. Thus, when he later went over what he had written in a trancelike state, he would sometimes have to struggle to recall exactly what the missing words had been.

The first work he began once he was settled in Zürich was of the type where his conscious intellect was decidedly involved: he was doing yet another revision of *Panchastavi*. Although the Indian edition of the book had come out in that country before he had left, he had decided further improvements could be made on his exposition of the text for the next edition. When he finished this in February, he then began to work on another new book of inspired verse entitled *On War*. Unfortunately, little is known of this book as it was never published. While it sounds as if this manuscript might have dealt with some of the same issues as *The Shape of Events to Come*, this is not certain as no complete version of the manuscript has to date been found.

As the months went on he had to deal with an ever-increasing amount of correspondence, especially coming from India. Even though he was not in that country, the enthusiasm for his ideas generated by the seminar combined with the burgeoning interest in India-led scientific research continued. By the late spring of 1976, the steady stream of correspondence that had been coming to him in Kashmir from other parts of India had turned into a flood. Razdan, working in the office in the Central Institute for Kundalini Research office in

Srinagar, handled what he could of it; however, he had to refer much of it to Zürich for the Pandit's direct involvement.

In addition to the growing recognition sparked by the seminar, two separate events contributed to this onslaught of letters from India. One was the April 10 appearance of the first article in *Blitz* of the series promised by R.K. Karanjia the preceding summer. Although it is not clear whether an actual series ever appeared, the newspaper's influence was such that the impact on Gopi Krishna's renown in India from even one article was tremendous. While the thrust of the article was definitely on kundalini research, the letters it generated were mostly unrelated to scientific inquiry, just as most of his correspondence from his general readership had been since his work was first published. These letters fell into two categories. One was from people who wanted him to teach them how to awaken their kundalini; these ranged from sincere seekers wanting to make progress on their spiritual path to those who hoped to gain the siddhis described in the Tantric texts for their personal gain. The other type of inquiry was from individuals who were experiencing symptoms related in some way to those described in his accounts of kundalini awakening. These two types of inquiries were handled at this time much as they would be throughout his life. Those individuals who wanted him to awaken their kundalini were informed kindly but firmly, generally by office staff, that Gopi Krishna was not a spiritual teacher and that they could refer to his books for more information. Individuals who believed they were experiencing symptoms related to kundalini awakening were, however, handled quite differently. Gopi Krishna made every attempt to answer these inquiries personally. Paying careful attention to the experiences described, he responded with individualized advice whenever it was possible (see Chapter Twenty).

The second cause of the inundation of mail from around India was the initiative of Mr. Iengar. Using his influence in the publishing world of India, he had accelerated the goal of having affordable reprints of Gopi Krishna's book published there. By the spring of 1976, Indian editions of *Higher Consciousness, The Awakening of Kundalini*, and *Kundalini: Path to Higher Consciousness*—a pocketbook of the original autobiography without the Hillman commentary—were all readily available. To further publicize Gopi

Krishna's ideas, he spearheaded the creation of a promotional leaflet that effectively summarized these difficult concepts. After assisting in the production of the leaflet, he had hundreds of them printed. He then purchased scores of the Pandit's books, had them shipped to the Central Institute for Kundalini Research in Kashmir, and instructed Razdan to begin sending them out along with the leaflet.

One plan for distribution was for packets including as many as three of the books to be sent to every legitimate ashram or yoga center in India. A list of such groups and other influential individuals had been compiled earlier, so Razdan was able to begin sending out the packets as soon as the books were received. By late spring the responses were pouring in. One particularly positive response was from the Bihar School of Yoga in Munger, Bihar. Founded in 1963 by Satyananda Saraswati, a disciple of Shivananda's, the school evinced from its very beginnings an interest in scientific research into consciousness. Delighted to receive Gopi Krishna's books, they maintained contact with him until his death, issuing invitations for him to speak at their conferences and discussing how research based on his ideas might be done.

While Razdan continued to handle as much of this correspondence on his own as he could, a good deal of it had to be forwarded on to Gopi Krishna in Zürich for his personal attention. There is no doubt this took up a great deal of his time. Regrettably, little else is known of his time there. The reason for this relates to the archive mentioned in the introduction to this book. While this archive contains many hundreds, possibly even thousands, of letters, certain major gaps exist. One of them is the period from November 1975 to November 1976 when he was in Zürich. Thus there is little record of the people he may have met with or the talks he may have given during those months. Given a well-established pattern of his visits to Europe both prior to 1976 and after it, a good deal about his time there can be surmised. He must have been meeting people and giving lectures at times. He was simply too well-known by this stage of his life for those activities not to have taken place.

Perhaps the most frustrating fact about this dearth of archival material is that there is no record of his meetings with von Weizsäcker, Basedow, or any of the other individuals associated with the Research Foundation for Eastern

Wisdom and Western Science in Germany. It is simply incomprehensible that these meetings did not take place. Some small evidence that they must have is confirmed by a short letter written to Gopi Krishna by Basedow less than two months after the Pandit had returned to India. In it Basedow wrote that he, along with a number of other scientists, had recently been at a New Year's celebration at von Weizsäcker's home. In addition to indicating that Gopi Krishna's presence was missed at the gathering, the letter related one of the scientists' enthusiastic description of a research project he was going to begin as soon as he received some promised material from the Pandit. Basedow's wording in the note is plainly that of someone who has recently seen the person to whom he is writing.

Another obvious lack in the records is that there is no prior correspondence regarding an extensive video production featuring Gopi Krishna that was made in Zürich in the late fall of 1976. Considering all the complications involved in a major undertaking such as this, it is unthinkable that correspondence between the organizers, George Tompkins and Gene Kieffer, and Gopi Krishna or Margaret did not occur. In spite of this vacuum in the archival material, interviews with the principals have provided a good deal of information. The project began as an offshoot of the full-length film that George and Gene had both long hoped to make.

With his ongoing work in video production, George was aware how the quality of videotaping had been advancing. Given current standards, he knew that a videotape could be produced of a high-enough quality that it could be used in a variety of ways to promote Gopi Krishna's vision. The concept for the production was a simple one: a journalist was to interview Gopi Krishna asking a series of questions that would elicit his main ideas. Eight interviews were planned, two to be done daily over a four-day period. The obvious choice for the interviewer was John White, whose credibility as an author and journalist had continued to grow through the early seventies. When approached, John readily agreed to go to Zürich to do the interviews.

Making a professional production involved a good deal of equipment, and combined with the travel costs involved, it became a fairly expensive proposition. Along with the BioEnergy Research Foundation—a nonprofit organization that George had founded in California—the Kundalini Research Institute in Canada became a cofinancer of the project. Once this was established, Joe insisted on conducting three of the eight interviews.

Once the whole crew and equipment arrived, a room was set up in the house on Gemsenstrasse where the interviews could be done. Under George's direction, the taping proceeded as planned, resulting in eight half-hour, good-quality videos. Over the years, the videos have been shown in a wide variety of venues. Segments of them have been made available online, and a transcript of the John White interviews has been made into an ebook.[130]

John White also wrote more extensively about Gopi Krishna. Insights into the impression he made on White are found in an article he wrote entitled "Sex and Human Evolution." After expressing in a few words the pervasive fear of the day that the world was on the very brink of destruction, he wrote:

> With such an awesome prospect before us, the work of one man seems especially important. That man is Pandit Gopi Krishna...but don't think of him as a contemporary guru. He's not. When I met with him recently in Zürich, he made it clear to me that he seeks no followers, accepts no disciples and makes no demands for asceticism. Rather, his mission is to arouse interest in the nature of evolution and enlightenment, and to do this he wants coworkers in scientific and scholarly research, not devotees....
>
> All day long for the entire time I questioned him intensively, probing, scrutinizing, testing his position for holes. By the end of our intensive discussion, my reason, research and experience had led me to the conviction that what Gopi Krishna has to offer is of paramount importance to science and society. I was also impressed with the man's character—his humility, forbearance, patience, compassion and courage—as much as his intellect....[131]

Following these four days of intensive interviewing, Gopi Krishna remained in Zürich for some time before flying back to Delhi and then on to Kashmir. By around the third week of November he was settled there. Having been away so long, he found he had a great many matters to take care of, including Samiti's training centers for women. He was also receiving what he described as a continued rush of visitors. Some of the visits were from Kashmir TV personnel who were planning to do a profile on him featuring both his ideas and his social work. He was also in discussion with Dr. Karan Singh regarding research. While the minister had been actively involved in the proposed AIIMS research project since its inception, he had also begun to consider the possibility of a research project that would be focused more directly on consciousness itself than on physiology. He was now eliciting Gopi Krishna's input and was in the process of developing an official advisory committee for a research project that would be separate from but complementary to the one at AIIMS.

On December 11 the Kashmir TV crew arrived. After filming Gopi Krishna for the entire day, they returned three days later to take more footage. Once the filming was over, Gopi Krishna was able to plan his move to the warmer climate of New Delhi for the rest of the winter. All the while his supporters in North America had been busy. Having finally finished the high-quality production of *The Riddle of Consciousness*, Gene was able to send Gopi Krishna a copy of the book in December. In terms of other publishing efforts, 1976 had been a good year. *Kundalini: The Evolutionary Energy in Man* had remained popular. Shambhala was so happy with their hardcover sales in North America that they decided to come out with a more affordable paperback edition. They had also sold rights to the book in the United Kingdom. Sales of the book had also been going so well in Holland and Italy that second editions were coming out in those countries.

Confident that his ideas were spreading through both his books and interviews such as those done in Zürich and by Kashmir TV, Gopi Krishna returned to Delhi on December 19. By that time, however, Srinagar was having an exceptional cold spell. This, combined with what must have been the strain of traveling and doing so many intensive interviews, caused him to fall ill. He arrived in Delhi with a fever that lasted for several days. Fortunately the warmth of the city helped him recuperate fairly rapidly, for he was not given much time to rest. He was shortly contacted by Karan Singh, who had continued his efforts to set up his ministry's own research project. On January 8, 1977, he sent a telegram to Gopi Krishna officially inviting him to be a member of the advisory committee for his project, which would include a number of top scientists. This scientific study was to be known as Project Consciousness. While the original research project that Dr. Singh had been interested in was based at the All India Institute for Medical Sciences in Delhi, primarily in the physiology department, this project was to be run out of the National Institute for Mental Health and Neurosciences in Bangalore. Known as NIMHANS, the institute was, as it continues to be, internationally known for its work in neurology, and it must have seemed eminently logical that a study on yoga that would emphasize consciousness should be located there.

As Dr. Singh had been actively laying the groundwork for Project Consciousness for some time, efforts proceeded rapidly. The first meeting of the advisory committee occurred on January 14 at Karan Singh's official residence. The launch of the project generated a great deal of media coverage. As interest in research spread around India, the Bihar School of Yoga in Munger supported the work by forming its own committee for research into kundalini and altered states of consciousness.

At the end of January, Gene arrived for a short visit at the start of a world tour he was making for business connections. By early February, Gopi Krishna had been made aware that, in Canada, Joe had begun plans to bring 300 or more Canadians who had taken his courses to India to meet with Gopi Krishna in Kashmir. Although this plan might have seemed pretentious, it became evident over the next while that Joe was serious. Soon, an August date for the World Conference on Kundalini—a series of lectures by Gopi Krishna over two weeks—was set. While the plans for overcoming the obstacles involved in arranging a conference of this magnitude in Kashmir would necessarily become a major focus from that time on, important events were occurring in a number of other areas of Gopi Krishna's life.

Even though he was in Delhi, he continued to make sure the craft-training centers for women were being properly overseen in Kashmir—where two of the three active centers had had to shut down for the winter months due to the extreme cold. Much of the other work he did during those months leading up to the conference was related to various aspects of publishing. Urged by Iengar and others for some time, Gopi Krishna had come to the conclusion that it would be beneficial to take more direct control of his writings by publishing them under the auspices of various Kundalini research centers rather than outside publishers. To this end, the Kundalini Research and Publication Trust was formed. Due to the intricacies of the Indian legal system, this was an involved, time-consuming endeavor. One of the first benefits coming out of this was the implementation of the idea for a high-quality magazine that he had had two years previously. By the spring, serious work on this project had begun with the goal of producing a publication featuring well-written, thought-provoking articles on kundalini's role in evolution and spiritual transformation.

Understandably, his writing during these exceptionally busy months was not as prolific as it sometimes was. Still, he managed to write out his lectures for the seven discourses he was to give during the conference. Although he would, as usual, end up giving the talks extemporaneously, the final material would eventually become a 124-page book.[132] Enthusiastic as he was for the forthcoming magazine, he also managed to write an article for it entitled "Kundalini: The Guardian of Human Evolution." A lengthy piece, it would be spread over the first three issues of the magazine.[133]

Even though the Central Institute for Kundalini Research now planned to be more directly involved in publishing these and other of Gopi Krishna's writings, established publishers were not being disregarded. Interest in translating *Kundalini: The Evolutionary Energy in Man* had been generated in France, Spain, and Japan. In 1977, work on the book in those countries was already in progress or in the process of being contracted. In India, a larger publisher was involved in the completion of a Gujarati translation, and one was being done in Hindi.

Writings about him were also increasing. In England, the magazine *Yoga Today* came out with a piece on his ideas. In India, articles appeared in *The Indian Express* newspaper and in *Pondicherry Yoga Life*. Located in the same city as that magazine, Sri Aurobindo's organization published John White's piece "Evolution and the Future of Humanity" in their publication *World Union* in October. Interest in research was also spreading with a group of PhDs in

Madras forming a Kundalini Research Foundation there, while another group was laying plans to start one in Tamil Nadu.

In contrast to all this positivity, one serious blow did occur in 1977. In March, a snap national election was called. When Indira Gandhi's party lost, her government fell. Although Karan Singh won his own election in his district, and thus remained a member of the parliament, he was no longer an official minister, leaving him with no more power or access to funding for projects than any other member of the losing parties. His dream of having the government's backing for a research project at NIMHANS largely based on Gopi Krishna's ideas was no longer feasible. In spite of this, it is interesting to note that Project Consciousness remained on the NIMHANS's agenda for some time.[134] One of the founders of the original project, the widely acclaimed neurologist Dr. Turaga Desiraju, continued research on theories of consciousness and on the study of neuron physiology in yoga and remained in contact with Gopi Krishna until close to the end of the Pandit's life, even inviting him—and, in fact, urging him—to lecture at a national conference on "Yoga, Brain, and Consciousness," sponsored by NIMHANS in 1982.[135]

With progress on so many fronts, it is evident that, even with the setback to Project Consciousness, 1977 was a very encouraging year. Undoubtedly, however, the most significant event of the year was the attendance of the 234 Canadians at the World Conference on Kundalini. The majority of the Canadians were young people in their twenties to early thirties. Few, if any, thought about what a massive undertaking their visit was going to be for Gopi Krishna, his family, and his supporters. Even with the technologies and expediencies of the modern world today, organizing a conference of this magnitude in a rural area is a time-consuming, labor-intensive project. Carrying the event off in Nishat, a rural, virtually undeveloped village in 1977 in the Himalayan foothills, was a massive feat. Although Nishat is today considered to be on the outskirts of Srinagar, in those days the village was some miles from the city proper. Just how little development there was in that area at the time is revealed by the fact that Gopi Krishna, in spite of being influential, was still struggling to get a phone installed in the Central Institute for Kundalini Research.

Arriving by May to help, Margaret threw herself into the task with Swiss efficiency. The additions and renovations on the buildings that had been going so slowly for so long were put into high gear. A tent that could accommodate up to 400 was located for rental. Chairs were rented, bleachers erected, and toilet facilities—long before the availability of handy blue portables—were arranged. Plans were made to serve snacks and chai to the attendees, who were expected to include more than 100 people in addition to the Canadians. Many were Indian dignitaries whose attendance had to be prepared for. Volunteers were recruited, other workers were hired, and Gene, George, and Tontyn all made arrangements to arrive early to help.

Beyond the arrangements for the conference itself, other aspects of the Canadians' trip had to be seen to. The planes flying from Delhi to Srinagar were not large enough to take the entire group at once, so the flights had to be carefully planned. Srinagar was not a main destination for foreign travelers, and there were challenges in finding appropriate accommodation for such a large group. Gopi Krishna was determined to look after the welfare of this group just as he had always done for any individual who had come to visit him. Knowing he would need breaks between the days he gave his lengthy lectures, he wanted to make sure the Canadians would be able to take in as much of the beauty of Kashmir as possible during his rest periods. Accordingly, arrangements were made for the group to visit nearby gardens, forests, and waterfalls and to take boat rides on the famed lotus-strewn Dal Lake.

Perhaps presaging grief he was to cause in the future, Joe did not make these preparations any easier, at times changing well-laid plans and occasionally insisting on taking control from Canada concerning arrangements in Kashmir, a land he patently knew nothing about. Another slight complication created by Joe was his insistence on bringing along a cinematographer to video the Canadians' journey so that a film could be made of the trip. While having the conference filmed caused additional problems, the cinematographer was a thorough professional named Robert Rouveroy. A Dutch-Canadian, Rouveroy would go on to become internationally recognized for his work on a number of well-known films.

In spite of the many obstacles, all the intricate planning was finalized in time, and on August 16, the Canadians marched en masse up the steep hill from the village of Nishat to the Central Institute for Kundalini Research. Wearing shorts or jeans with their matching white T-shirts emblazoned with a red kundalini symbol, they made a sight the villagers could not resist coming out to see. When the group finally reached the top of the hill the institute's buildings were perched on, they were awestruck. The broad, green, and grassy hill they stood on sloped away, and beyond that the sacred Himalayan peaks rose. Jagged, snowcapped, and majestic, the mountains took their collective breath away.

The lectures given were just as awe-inspiring. Gopi Krishna discoursed on the characteristics of enlightenment, the meaning of illumination, and karma and meditation. Perhaps most significantly, abandoning his long-held hesitancy to give instruction on how to awaken kundalini, he gave his advice on "How to Win to Cosmic Consciousness." Before going on to explain how a moderate, ethical lifestyle determined the success or failure of this process, he set down a concise, comprehensive summary of the basic premise that motivated his call for research:

> The idea underlying most of the religions is that God has created this universe, that God has created man, say in His image, and that man has to live a certain way of life, and to worship and meditate in a certain prescribed manner to win his favor, to win His grace, and to win liberation for the soul. But we are now presenting a different view to the world for the first time in history, and that view is that we do not dispute that there is a divine Power, a mighty intelligence behind the universe. But that divine Power is not exercising its authority to demand that people should worship Him, that people should exert themselves in any way, or take to penance or asceticism to please Him. We do not assert anything of this kind.
>
> What we say is that there is an almighty Power behind the universe, and He has framed certain laws which govern life as well as matter. And

one of the laws is that the human race should evolve till it reaches a state of consciousness where, in addition to the physical world, which it is perceiving through its senses, it can perceive the subtle mental or spiritual world also. And that this law is acting on the brain, that the brain of every human being is evolving to manifest a higher state of consciousness, which will bring every individual a close approach to Divinity; which will raise every individual above the fear of death and dissolution. But that it is not God directly who, as a tyrannical ruler, wishes us to take to asceticism or to hard penances to achieve this end, but it is the law of evolution, which we have not been able to unfold completely, that requires that we should observe a certain way of life and behavior to accelerate and to help this ever-active process of evolution, and not to impede or retard it.

Leaving the conference in Kashmir as awestruck as they had been when they arrived, the attendees returned to Canada. Gopi Krishna, Margaret, Tontyn, the family, and the local supporters were left to catch up on all the work for the institute that had been set aside during this enormous undertaking. Production resumed on the magazine, and by the fall the first issue of *Spiritual India and Kundalini* came out. They also had to deal with the new opportunities media attention on the conference had generated. Correspondence, including invitations to speak at prestigious organizations, such as the Gandhi Peace Foundation, rose yet again. It became obvious that the institute in Nishat needed to be expanded further to accommodate future visitors. Margaret remained for five more months to help with the office. Tontyn helped in this regard too but also set his architectural skills to work designing two buildings. A concerted effort on everyone's part resulted in two new guesthouses being ready for Western visitors by the end of 1977.

Back in Canada, Joe was coming up with what was another seemingly impossible plan. It had become very obvious that Gopi Krishna was badly in need of more assistance. Seeing this, Joe became determined that KRI Canada would find volunteers who were willing to go to live in India under its sponsorship. Much to many people's amazement, on December 14, 1977—just four months after they had been to Kashmir—four Canadian volunteers arrived in Delhi, eager to dedicate themselves full-time to furthering kundalini research.

Chapter Twenty

Advice for Spiritual Seekers and Kundalini Experiencers

Preparations for the volunteers were underway well before they arrived. As always regarding visitors, Gopi Krishna was concerned that every aspect of their well-being be looked after. In this case, even more care had to be taken as this was not simply a short visit; they were planning to stay for several months, with another set of volunteers coming to replace them when they left. Aware of how adversely the North American constitution could be affected by the food, water, and climate of India, Gopi Krishna was determined that volunteers be as happy and healthy as possible. By the time four Canadians, Mike, Winifred, Paul, and David, arrived in mid-December, safe, clean living quarters had been found for them near the house in Sarvodaya Enclave, and they were soon being coached on how to shop for and prepare food that would keep them healthy.

For Gopi Krishna these people were a gift from heaven that answered his long-held hope for more assistance: with their help, the Central Institute for Kundalini Research would be able to bring many of its planned projects to fruition. To say that the four volunteers hit the ground running to accomplish this would be no exaggeration. By the beginning of 1978—just a few weeks after their arrival—they had begun production on the second issue of the magazine and started on the transcriptions of Gopi Krishna's latest writings. Once again, in record time, he had completed another prose manuscript. This one, *Yoga: A Vision of Its Future*, was finished in February. By the end of that month, the manuscript was being proofread so that the publishing arm could get an Indian edition of the book out as soon as possible. Other efforts included works that had not been previously published, including *The Dawn of a New Science* and the revised *Panchastavi*. The *Vijnana Bhairava* with its translation and commentary still needed to be published, and reprints of *The Secret of Yoga* and *The Biological Basis of Religion and Genius* were in the works. The Canadians, Tontyn, and Iengar were all involved in these efforts. In April of 1978, three more Canadians, Jim, Ed, and Ricarda, came to help. Over the next two years, some of these seven would remain, while others would be replaced when they needed to return permanently to Canada. Other replacements were young men known as Chuck, Jimmy, and J. Norman. This pattern of alternation would continue, so that while there were fluctuations in the numbers over the years, Gopi Krishna would never be without at least some Canadian volunteers for the rest of his life.

Having this help allowed Gopi Krishna to launch one of his most significant research projects. Although both Karan Singh and AIIMS continued to be interested in physiologically based research on the biological aspects of kundalini awakening, impediments existed that would undoubtedly result in it being a long time until the results of such research were known. One problem was that the development of equipment that could measure any type of bioenergy was only in its infancy; another was that technology capable of actually measuring energies as subtle as prāna was undoubtedly far in the future. Gopi Krishna had, however, envisioned a type of research that could be launched immediately. Based on the lives of the great mystics of the world's various spiritual traditions, one aspect of this study would be a comparison between the specific characteristics of their mystical experience with the way these experiences had been described in the age-old yogic texts. Another aspect would be a comparison between these mystics' personal characteristics and those of the enlightened yogis, especially those traits that were apparent after the transformation engendered by enlightenment had occurred.

Gopi Krishna believed that the revelation of the extraordinary parallels between these mystics' experiences and those of the awakened yogis would clearly indicate that the transformative, spiritual force they credited their experience with—be it known as *holy spirit*, *ruach hakodesh*, *tummo fire*, *jing-chi-shen*, or any of its other names—was one and the same.[136] A revelation of this nature could have, he believed, profound implications for validating not only kundalini's existence but also its role in the transformation and evolution of consciousness. Entitled *The Anthology of Expanded Consciousness Experience*, the project attracted the attention of Dr. Indu Prakash Singh, a highly placed Indian statesman, who took on overseeing the project as president of the project committee. A loyal supporter of Gopi Krishna's ideas, Dr. Singh would go on in his career to become the deputy high commissioner of India in England and eventually the Indian ambassador to Nepal.

Dr. Singh was clearly aware of the profound implications inherent in a project of this nature. As Gopi Krishna stated in a letter to one scientist who questioned the value of anything but actual physiological research,

> All revealed religious scriptures of the world and all great compilations of mystics extant today, one and all, depict the subjective experiences of an awakened Kundalini. There is no class of human beings in which Kundalini has bloomed so well as in the great mystics of the world, and, next in order, the great geniuses of mankind....
>
> If we wish to compare the experiences of individuals in whom Kundalini was awake in the most benign healthy manner then the only arena for our search is provided by the great mystics and geniuses born from the earliest times to our day....
>
> We need a thorough investigation of both these areas of the Kundalini phenomenon, vis the subjective experiences embodied in the writings of the great mystics and the inspired compositions of great geniuses and also the biological activities which attend the awakening of the power.

In addition to becoming directly involved in major projects such as the anthology, the Canadians assisted with other activities such as the still-increasing amount of correspondence. As had been the case since the publication of his first book, many of these letters were from individuals who fell into two categories—those who wanted to become disciples so that they could awaken kundalini, and those who were experiencing possible kundalini awakening. While the answers to this latter group may have been written by Tontyn, Margaret, staff at the Central Institute for Kundalini Research (CIKR), or the Canadian volunteers, their content was personally directed by Gopi Krishna himself. The diligent, compassionate care with which he answered these letters reveals his profound concern for every individual who was undergoing an awakening. While his books often emphasize the importance of kundalini research in terms of the evolution of consciousness of the human race as a whole, these letters underscore his belief that this research was also necessary to provide science and medicine with the knowledge that would help the increasing number of individuals experiencing varying degrees of kundalini activity have awakenings that proceeded smoothly.

As mentioned earlier, the answers to the letters from would-be followers were generally answered with a short, kind note explaining that Gopi Krishna did not take disciples, recommending his books, sending copies of articles, and sometimes sending a book for free. Letters from people who were having profound mystical experiences or experiencing other characteristics of kundalini awakening were, on the other hand, almost always answered individually.

Some of these letter-writers simply requested information; when this was the case, it was given in a straightforward, easy-to-understand manner such as in the response to this correspondent who had written with very specific questions:

The enquiries in your letter are replied to as follows:

1. The flow of the vital current to the brain will be automatically reduced if you stop meditation, intensive reading or even thinking on religious and transcendental matters. It is wholesome in such a state to keep yourself occupied with light manual work, such as

gardening or household work which do not need concentrated application of the mind. Walking for an hour or two daily is also a good way of keeping [the] mind relaxed, provided the walk is taken away from traffic, in a calm secluded countryside or a park.

2. The brain becomes gradually accustomed to the currents if a moderate, regular life is led, giving as much as possible rest to the brain with sufficient sleep, light exercise and regulation in meals.

3. When the brain is adjusted, retirement from ordinary life does not become inevitable but from the very beginning, self-control, moderation, purity of heart, kindness, regard for fellow human beings and the cultivation of other noble traits of character are necessary. A well-balanced, wholesome mode of life is always necessary.

Other letter-writers seemed to need a bit of what might be called correction to set them on a healthier path. For instance, those wanting to follow the tradition of becoming spiritual mendicants and leaving their families were gently admonished:

In view of the fact that you have a family to support, it would not be in accordance with the principles of Karma Yoga to abandon them to their Fate. But the attempt should be made to shoulder the full responsibility of the household and, at the same time, to use the available time after this is done, in the service of the Lord and fellow human beings both.

A man whose goal was to awaken his kundalini in order to gain paranormal siddhis that he could then use in a widespread effort to help others was reminded that the great religious traditions considered psychic or miraculous powers to be an impediment to Self-Realization:

You can help the poor, the sick and the helpless, even without awakening your Kundalini first by diverting your efforts to this end. In fact, success in Yoga, resulting in the awakening of Kundalini, depends not only on meditation and other exercises, but also on ones good and benevolent actions, which include selfless service.

Therefore, instead of setting your mind on the awakening of the Power, as a prelude to selfless service, the better course would be to act the other way round and start the mission of service to merit the Grace of Heaven which is essential for success in spiritual unfolding.

Another correspondent who needed guidance, a young woman living in the Australian bush with her two children 150 miles from the closest town, is an interesting example of this. She wrote to Gopi Krishna describing a life-altering experience she had had when she was twenty-eight years old. The mother of a six-year-old girl at the time, she was living in Beirut, working as a so-called bar girl, drinking too much, and surrounded by untrustworthy people. At a point of bleak despair and heartbreak, she had an epiphany:

In an instant I was completely transformed. My whole body became full of life and light. I felt complete.... It felt like and looked like I was in heaven, except everything was here and now and alive. I could really see, hear, smell, taste and feel for the first time and there was a big light outside and I knew then that God was light... The love I felt showered the complete earth.

During this intense mystical period she also experienced spontaneous creativity and a sudden ability to understand French. It was not surprising that with her unsettled, unhealthy lifestyle, the euphoric aspects of the experience did not last, leading her to a period of several years when she wandered, lived in poverty, searched for answers in other religions, and had another child. When she wrote Gopi Krishna, her daughter was thirteen and her son three years of age, and she was slowly recovering from a serious illness. She was thinking of making a trip through Indonesia and Asia and making her way to see Gopi Krishna in India. "God is my only real goal," she writes. "To reach him again and to help this planet is my only desire apart from making a home somewhere for my children...."

In his response, Gopi Krishna guides her gently off the extreme aspects of this path and onto one that will see her caring for herself and, especially, her children:

> I have read of your experiences and your sufferings and my heart has been deeply touched by what you have undergone. The divine Power in us does not work in the same way in all human beings and the manner of its arousal and the experiences it brings in its wake are varied with different individuals.
>
> There are differences in constitution, temperament, culture, upbringing, ideas and the environment of different people and the power also works according to the sum total of our bodily and mental characteristics under laws which are still unknown to Mankind.
>
> The suffering can be mitigated and peace and harmony attained if we submit ourselves to the ordeals and trials of life with a spirit of surrender and faith in God. The Universe from the atom to gigantic suns is ruled by immutable laws and frail human beings are no exception to this rule. When our whole solar system in which our earth is but a small-sized planet obeys these eternal laws and revolves night and day in obedience to them, how can we puny human beings whose total number occupies but a fraction of the vast space provided by Earth ever hope to rebel and live outside the laws that rule the Universe[?]
>
> I am sure that keeping in view this fact and the ephemeral nature of human life you will resign yourself to the Divine Will while taking all possible care of the physical needs of your own body and mind, and in this way fulfill your duty towards God, who has brought you into existence and your children who depend on you till they can stand on their own legs....

Just as correspondence increased in 1978, so did the invitations to speak. Accordingly, that year he gave a number of lectures. One very successful series was held at the Yogi Centre at the University of Delhi. However, the one with possibly the most far-reaching consequences was one sponsored by the Brahma

Kumaris in Delhi. Rather than being a religious branch of Hinduism, the Brahma Kumaris thought—and still think— of themselves as an organization that provides spiritual education. From its origins in the 1930s, the group has stood strongly for the rights of women and the equality of all, regardless of caste. At the seminar held early February 1978, Gopi Krishna's talk was greeted with enthusiasm. When it was over he was surrounded by people who wanted to speak with him. One of them, evidently another one of the other speakers, was Pir Vilayat Inayat Khan, the son of the man who had founded the Sufi Order of London in 1916. After fighting with the British forces in World War II, Pir Vilayat had become active in his father's movement. Taking it over after his death, he developed the movement into the Sufi Order of the West, a spiritual organization that became established in many countries, perhaps most notably the United States. Three years prior to meeting Gopi Krishna, Pir Vilayat had purchased land there and founded the Abode. By 1978 the Abode had become a focal point for retreats, conferences, and seminars related to the alternative spiritual movement that had been sweeping the United States.[137]

Even though the two men met only briefly at that February 1978 seminar, Pir Vilayat was undoubtedly impressed: shortly afterward, he issued a formal invitation for the Pandit to make a presentation at a conference in New York that the Sufi Order of the West was planning. To be held in November of that year, the conference was expected to have well over 2,000 attendees.

At about this time an invitation to speak at a summer holistic conference in Montana also arrived, as did one to speak at a conference in California. Given all this North American interest in his work, it was agreed that Gopi Krishna should finally make a major trip there. Having learned a great deal from previous travel experiences, Gopi Krishna planned to first land in Zürich, where he could spend time from late spring to early summer preparing the material he would need for his talks.

Just prior to leaving for Zürich in April he wrote to Margaret discussing the invitations to speak at the holistic conference in Montana and the Sufi conference in New York, saying,

It seems to me that by the Grace of Heaven, this would be a very busy time for me in the West. Who knows what other invitations will be received and what developments would occur.

It seems evident that Gopi Krishna was looking forward to these opportunities to spread his message by speaking to larger numbers of people. It is interesting to note that this seems to represent a marked change in attitude from the one he once held. In the days of the publication of his early books, he wanted those who were arranging his talks to organize meetings with small groups of scientists, academics, and/or highly interested individuals. The same is true about any conversation he had about possible trips to the United States when his early books came out there. Even though there was certainly more than one reason for doing so, he also turned down invitations to speak at big conferences such as the one in 1971 mentioned in Chapter Fourteen for the World Congress for Enlightenment backed by Kripalu Yoga founder Amrit Desai that had been expected to attract literally hundreds of thousands of participants.

As stated earlier, Gopi Krishna believed that a deep, widespread knowledge of kundalini was one of the first steps in making the kind of kundalini research he envisioned come to fruition. With the publication of his books by major publishers in so many countries, it seemed that the message should be spreading rapidly. However, the reality in the publishing world was then, as it is now, that for books to be sold, they needed to be promoted. Certainly publishers in the United States at the time considered having an author appear as a featured speaker at a large conference was possibly the most effective method of both selling books directly and spreading word of mouth about a book.

Of course, it might not have been a growing awareness of the harsh realities of the publishing world that caused this change in Gopi Krishna's attitude. Any number of factors might have influenced him. For instance, experiences such as speaking to all those who had gathered for the conference in Nishat in 1977 might have revealed what a profound personal connection could be made with a large group of people, and further, that individuals touched in this way might then be motivated to gain a more in-depth understanding by reading his books.

Regardless of why his attitude altered so radically, it did. From the fall of 1978 when he spoke at the Sufi conference in New York to the end of his life, traveling to and making presentations at important conferences would occupy a great deal of his time and energy.

In one sense, what is important about this change in attitude is that it provides a good example of how he could and did change over time. In his conversations over the years with people close to him, he often referred to a visceral awareness that the kundalini energy, now active for so many decades, had never stopped its ongoing process of transformation in either his body or his consciousness. In response he was continually having to adapt his eating habits along with other aspects of his lifestyle.[138]

He also made very significant adaptations in the way he expressed his undying conviction that kundalini—regardless of what it was called in different traditions—was the evolutionary energy that was propelling humanity as a whole to higher states of consciousness and that our living the way the great spiritual teachers had urged us to live was the key to its success. Striving for greater clarity, he was continually finding simpler, less complicated ways of conveying his complex concepts. A wonderfully concise example of this is found in a response he gave to a question during a meeting with a small group in 1978. After citing many cases of true mystics from various traditions who were living examples of the transformation of consciousness, he added:

So what I am saying has been said in another language by all the illuminated and by all the prophets and saviors of the past. I am not saying anything new. The only thing that I add is that it is a process of evolution and our brain is evolving, and that if research is directed on this phenomenon of mystical illumination and the brain is subjected to investigation on certain lines, what I say will be empirically proved.

And the urgency for this investigation lies in the fact that our brain is now evolving very fast, but our social, political and educational systems are not in harmony with it. Therefore, either we will have to adjust them voluntarily to the demands of evolution or Nature will force us to make this adjustment by her own methods which can be drastic also.[139]

Not only did he strive to find ever-better ways to communicate his ideas, he also prepared material specifically tailored to every group he spoke to. Faced with three upcoming conferences in the United States as well as a number of smaller gatherings by then arranged by Gene, he was aware he would have a large amount of material to turn out during the few months of preparation time he had planned in Zürich. When the difficulty of producing all this material while still keeping pace with the many demands on his time became evident to Joe, he offered to have KRI sponsor a volunteer who would come to Switzerland to help.

Before leaving India, Gopi Krishna had been somewhat concerned whether the young woman who had volunteered would be able to handle all the work he was about to give her, for it now included much more. In the few months before leaving for Europe, he had not only written a draft of one of the conference talks, he had completed *Yoga: A Vision of Its Future*, a work he said would be a small book of about ten or eleven chapters. He had also finished a draft of a book entitled *Kundalini: The Guardian of Human Evolution*. The first two chapters were polished for publication in the first two issues of *Spiritual India and Kundalini*, but the rest of the work was still in handwritten form. "This and the other book," he wrote to Margaret, "will take a good deal of my time and energy before they are suitable for the press."

In addition to the handwritten material needing to be typed—and no doubt typed again for revisions—there were other tasks:

I would definitely need clerical assistance in Zürich for the completion of this work. A number of books have to be looked up and their summaries prepared, also many references have to be filled in both these books. It is because I had good literary assistance available here that I have been able to compose three books in this period of four months, besides attending to numerous other tasks.

Fortunately Monika, the volunteer, was more than up to the task. She was not only fluent in German, which made Margaret's life easier, she was also a very bright, well-educated woman who had excellent clerical skills.[140] By the end of April, she was settled in Gemsenstrasse helping the Pandit with his work. Over the next several weeks, it became apparent that the summer conferences in Montana and California might not happen, and by June they were both canceled. This allowed Gopi Krishna to postpone his trip to North America until the fall so that he could keep making progress on his many projects.

During this period, his efforts to promote kundalini research in Europe received a blow. In March, Karl Basedow, the director of the Research Foundation for Eastern Wisdom and Western Science, had suddenly died. From this point onward, little is known of the foundation in relation to Gopi Krishna's goals for research. Fortunately, efforts in other parts of Europe were continuing. Both Amaury de Riencourt and Baldoon Dhingra were promoting Gopi Krishna's ideas in France. The two had spoken at a seminar along with Pir Vilayat there that spring. Another ongoing effort in France was the publication of a French edition of *Kundalini: The Evolutionary Energy in Man*. Widely noted author on yoga and Hinduism and Sanskrit scholar Dr. Tara Michaël had agreed to take on the project. She did so with such efficiency that her translation, *Koundalinî, l'énérgie évolutrice en l'homme*, came out in France before the end of the year.[141]

After his time in Zürich, Gopi Krishna traveled in the autumn to North America, where he conducted the small-group discourses that Gene arranged at the home he now had in Connecticut before making his way to New York City for the conference being sponsored by the Sufi Order of the West, entitled the New Dimensions Conference. Attended as expected by over 2,000 people, it was opened with an address by Pir Vilayat on November 17.

Gopi Krishna's talk was heralded as a success. Although he gave it extemporaneously, he had given a copy of his prepared material to Gene shortly before the conference. Gene was so impressed by the content, he somehow managed to get over 2,000 copies of the speech printed up so that it could be handed out to the conference attendees. This version of the talk eventually became the small book known as *The Real Nature of Mystical Experience*.

Tens of thousands of copies of the booklet would eventually be printed by the kundalini research foundations in North America.

The event garnered extensive media attention. This, combined with the success of the Pandit's presentation, resulted in even more people coming to the postconference discourses at Gene's home. Among them was Edward Kelly, a scientist from Duke University.[142] Other visitors included Paul and Pat Fenske, a couple who were actively involved in the Spiritual Frontiers Fellowship, an organization that had been begun early in the 1900s by Christian ministers to promote interfaith dialogue along with a deeper understanding of the mystical aspects of faith.

Paul, a Protestant minister, and Pat, a clinical psychologist, had spent three years in Hong Kong working at Chung Chi College, an educational institution that was both Chinese and Protestant. Paul had once written that

> [my] seminary experience taught me that traditional theology has few answers. The years in Hong Kong taught me that all true sacred traditions are based on eternal truths. The following years have given me insights and bases for knowing that healing and holistic living are realities.

The Fenskes found much in Gopi Krishna's worldview that resonated with their own. After spending a considerable amount of time with him before he left, they invited him to return to the United States the following year to speak at the annual Spiritual Frontiers Fellowship Conference that would be held in Philadelphia in May of 1979. Gopi Krishna accepted their invitation, in effect committing himself to another trip to North America. From this time onward, the Fenskes would remain active promoters of Gopi Krishna's vision, even after his death.

During the small-group discourses they attended, Gopi Krishna was asked yet again for his advice on how to attain enlightenment. After discussing the evolution of consciousness in terms that ranged from Christianity's tenet that the kingdom of heaven is within to Buddhism's notion of the state of awakening to the bodiless existence, he reiterated that he did not take disciples. If any guidance was indeed given by a guru to his disciples, it needed to be completely individualized. Traditionally this involved the guru living with the sādhaka in an ashram, where the seeker could be observed, often for years, so that this individualized supervision could be properly given. He went on to describe the slow, safe way to reach self-realization that needed only the guidance from within:

> The slow way every one of you can adopt. And that slow way is in all religions, but I would just like to mention it. It is, in the first place, to have a healthy body and a healthy mind. Slowly to develop yourself in human attributes. The first attribute is love—universal love, love of the family, love of friends, love of the universe, even love of...enemies.
>
> Then to develop compassion. When we are seriously ill or in some terrible difficulty, we wish that others would empathize with us and we are happy, we feel consoled if someone comes to us and expresses his sympathy for ourselves. We feel very much soothed. We should understand that the others need the same thing. So an attitude of compassion and of love. It is essential.
>
> Then, devotion, truth, honesty, patience, perseverance. I do not say that they can be cultivated in one day, but the attempt should be there. And Nature is forgiving. But the attempt that has to be made first is to develop ourselves because these are the characteristics of illuminated consciousness. The man is purified and all these attributes develop in him so that if we consciously develop them, we are coming nearer and nearer to the higher state.
>
> This is one, and the second is regular prayer and worship. And if we meditate, that meditation, too, should be a prayer. Mechanical meditation is a hindrance rather than a help. To do meditation because it is a routine, it is of no help. Here, in all these disciplines, we are trying to seek audience of the Lord of the Universe. Our ego must be melted first. And all we do must be in a spirit of prayer, of a humble solicitation to grant us the interview. We can never force ourselves into the presence of the Almighty. No drop can become an ocean. We have to seek it with submission, with humility, to be like children. This sophistication has

to be given up. Our hearts are to be purged of all impurities and we have to mingle our ego with dust.

With such an attitude and regular prayer, meditation as a prayer, I think success is sure. It is a very tough journey. But if one has a deep urge inside and very little...ego, if one is true and honest, loving and sympathetic, charitable and compassionate, he is sure to win success. He is sure to awaken one day to his own glory, even if for a moment, even if for a few minutes he awakes to it, his life is transformed. He knows that he has won.

Chapter Twenty-One

Saints and Sinners, Wise Men and Fools

Gopi Krishna remained in the New York area until mid-December of 1978. In addition to his meeting with the Fenskes, two other encounters made an especially poignant impression on him. One was with a group of African Americans and the other with a Hopi leader. These encounters represented new cultural experiences for him and left him with a feeling of deep affinity for both groups. The African Americans invited him to a gathering in Harlem where he spoke with them for about three hours; he shared later how wonderful the experience had been with these affectionate, loving people who had showered him with embraces and kisses before he left. The second deeply moving meeting was with Thomas Banyacya, a renowned Hopi Elder who wanted to discuss the relationship between Gopi Krishna's prophetic writings and the Hopi prophecies. According to an almost-thousand-year-old tradition, the Hopis had been given a series of prophecies on the potential destruction of the earth and were entrusted with preserving the natural balance so that the earth might be saved. Until 1948, these prophecies were passed down as a secret oral tradition. At that time, a group of Hopi spiritual leaders—motivated in part by the probable relationship between the atomic bomb's mushroom cloud and a massively destructive gourd of ashes described in the prophecies—chose four individuals to impart the prophecies to the world in hopes that it might be saved.

Thomas Banyacya was one of the four, and from that time on he dedicated his entire life to saving the earth from "the ravages of modern materialism and greed." It is no wonder Gopi Krishna's meeting with this extraordinary man was so meaningful.[143]

In spite of how successful this visit had been, it left him so exhausted that instead of spending a few days recuperating there before flying to Delhi as he had planned, he was not well enough to go until mid-January. Even then his health was still in question. Deeply concerned, his family insisted on his having medical tests, which resulted in a recommendation to have his gall bladder removed. Deciding to postpone the surgery, he began to pay meticulous attention to his diet. This, combined with the beneficial effects of Delhi's warmth, helped him improve. Even though he did not feel fully recovered until mid-February, he spent the rest of January hard at work. His first task was overseeing the Canadians. While he had been gone, they had made excellent progress on future editions of the journal as well as the production of Indian editions of the books. To build on this momentum, he now picked four of the volunteers to travel across India to major cities, where they would speak to supporters, promote the newly available books, and watch over book distribution.

He also had to attend to the requests for personal meetings and public talks that awaited him. One important visitor, José Hermógenes, arrived in Delhi only a few days after the Pandit. Remembered today as the father of yoga in Brazil and one of the great yoga teachers of all time, Professor José Hermógenes de Andrade Filho had founded the Hermógenes Institute in Rio de Janeiro in 1962. By the time Hermógenes met Gopi Krishna in 1979 he was already widely renowned. Deeply impressed by Gopi Krishna's ideas, he made a commitment to see that a translation of *Kundalini: The Evolutionary Energy in Man* would be published in Portuguese.

Another significant event in January was a request for Gopi Krishna to give the inaugural address and to moderate the first session of the Delhi celebration of The Mother's Birth Centenary. This anniversary of the birth of Mirra Alfassa was being celebrated all around India, with a national commemorative postage stamp even being designed in her honor. Mirra was the woman to whom Sri Aurobindo had given the title The Mother. He considered her to be his equal in yogic stature, and over the years she became the moving force behind the growth of the Sri Aurobindo ashram in Puducherry, his international following, and school and the creation of Auroville, the still-extant spiritual township near Puducherry that was designed with the goal of creating a place on earth where human unity could be realized. That Gopi Krishna had been asked to give the inaugural address for the celebration being held at the University of Delhi was evidence of what high regard he was held in by the Sri Aurobindo organization. The letter confirming his participation notes Gopi Krishna's "keen interest in human values." It goes on to regret the contemporary loss of human values that has occurred in spite of unprecedented gains in science and technology and to reach out to Gopi Krishna as someone who could speak on how the education system could be restructured to better foster "humility, simplicity, nonviolence, straightforwardness, integrity, honesty, self-respect, love for fellow beings and other creatures." Clearly, the importance of the values Gopi Krishna stood for was becoming more widely known.

The fast pace begun in January continued into the next month. Even though Gopi Krishna stayed in Delhi, continuing progress on the Central Institute's property in Nishat had to be monitored, and the welfare centers in Kashmir sponsored by Samiti had to be overseen. Again this year the centers had had to be closed during the coldest winter months, but once the worst weather was over they were running again, continuing to teach gabba-making and other potentially income-producing skills for the women attending. Of the four centers that had been operating successfully, the three in Nishat, Shalimar, and Harvan were still flourishing, while changes needed to be made to the one in the village of Chandpura in order to keep it functioning.

Through much of February and early March, four of the Canadian volunteers continued to travel throughout India, while the others remained in Delhi to work on various publishing projects. Because *The Real Nature of Mystical Experience* had by then already been printed successfully in North America, they were eager to get the Indian version into production. The Publication Trust was also considering a new edition of *The Shape of Events to Come*, including revisions to the prose introduction that Gopi Krishna had finally declared in mid-March to be finished.

With so much to take care of on so many fronts, those first months of 1979 must have flown by. This was especially so because no sooner than Gopi Krishna had become settled in India than he had to start making plans to return to North America, as he had made a firm commitment to the Fenskes to speak at the Spiritual Frontiers Fellowship Conference to be held in Philadelphia in May. In the meantime, he had agreed—possibly after being pressured somewhat—to take part in two summer gatherings in Ontario sponsored by KRI Canada. As the only featured speaker at both, he was slated to give lengthy discourses over a number of days.

Since he had learned that breaking the long journey to North America with a spell in Zürich was the best way to maintain his health, by March he had made plans to leave for Switzerland in April. This break in Europe might also give him a chance to meet with von Weizsäcker. When Gopi Krishna had been in Zürich on his return from New York the prior year, von Weizsäcker had been able to speak with him by phone but not meet him. Both men were hoping they would be able to meet face to face this time.

It was finally decided he would fly to Zürich on April 16. In spite of the number of activities demanding his time leading up to his departure, he found time to write another small book that would eventually be titled *Kundalini in Time and Space*. About seventy pages long, it was begun on April 6 and completed on April 13. Discussing this speed, he once explained that although these books were written so quickly, he took extreme care to make sure "no wrong statement" appeared in them:

> I am very cautious and very careful.... I only write what will be proved to be true even after a hundred years. I weigh every word just to see that I have not written anything that is against fact. And sometimes I revise the book twice, thrice, four times, and it is retyped again and again and again... I am not very fond that people will say of me that he is a very great literary figure, or a great philosopher, or a great writer, or a great poet. I am concerned that they should tell me that this man spoke the truth. That is what I want. And all my books are oriented with that object....

Arriving in Zürich with his draft of *Kundalini in Time and Space* in hand, he was soon able to begin perfecting it with this level of exacting care. While there he was also able to meet with von Weizsäcker, who drove to Zürich from Germany to spend six hours conferring with the Pandit.

His productive time in Zürich over, Gopi Krishna left in May for the Spiritual Frontiers Conference in Philadelphia. This would, however, only be the beginning of a full North American schedule that had been laid out for him. When he had been on his 1978 New York trip, he had not added a visit to Canada, and this had been a source of disappointment for the Canadians who had been at Nishat in 1977. At Joe Dippong's urging, however, he did promise to make a lengthy visit to Canada on his next North American trip. Upon learning that Gopi Krishna would be in Pennsylvania in May, Joe began to make plans for what he hoped would be a huge conference featuring Gopi Krishna in Toronto in June. He also began to plan a course that Gopi Krishna would teach after the conference. The plan was for this course to be held for several days on a beautiful, pristine Northern Ontario lake where Joe enjoyed camping on holidays, often encouraging those who had taken his more advanced courses to join him. The plan for the course featuring Gopi Krishna's presentations was for the course participants—for the most part, those who had gone to India—to camp on the lake, while Gopi Krishna and Margaret would be accommodated in a cabin in a nearby resort. This course would be the first and only time any direct interface would occur between Gopi Krishna, who was being sponsored by the registered nonprofit organization KRI, and the courses Joe offered through the organization PSI, known by this time as People Searching Inside.

While Gopi Krishna was certainly aware and supportive of the Kundalini Research Institute, he had been given only the very vaguest idea about these courses. When Gene had first written to Gopi Krishna to pass on the information about Joe, he had mentioned the courses. Gene, however, had no direct knowledge of them as he had repeatedly refused Joe's offers for him to come to Canada and participate in them. As time passed and KRI's extraordinary endeavors rolled on, it seems probable that it did not seem particularly significant to anyone in Switzerland or India that the individuals who were promoting

KRI had for the most part been participants in one or more of these courses. For his part, Gopi Krishna's only real experience of these course participants was in the truly lovely group who had come to Nishat and, more recently, the Canadian volunteers whose resolute dedication was helping spread the concept of kundalini research throughout India. These courses did not attract young people who were lost or in despair, as some of the New Age groups were said to do. The vast majority of individuals who participated were bright, well-educated, and well-employed. The 234 who had made the trip to Nishat presented such a healthy, happy demeanor that not only Gopi Krishna but his family and all the supporters could not help but be impressed. The same was true for the impact made by the Canadian volunteers.

If anyone in India asked about the courses—and there is no record in the archives of anyone having done so—it is likely they would have been told about the benefits of learning to meditate and the mind-development aspects of the course related to improving memory, stopping smoking, and learning about the tremendous potential power of a positive mental attitude. Course participants were also exposed to the idea that there were universal laws, that commonplace concepts such as the Golden Rule had far more profound implications than they previously might have believed, and that helping others was to be a primary goal. Another important aspect of the course that would undoubtedly have been shared was the importance of necessity of living a balanced, moderate life. It is less likely, however, that anyone asking about the courses would have been told about the EST-style encounter-group and confrontation techniques, widespread in the 1970s, that were part of the one advanced course that was offered. Not only did Gopi Krishna have no idea about this element of the advanced course, there is absolutely no doubt that he had no idea that Joe carried these confrontational practices into his daily interactions, using them—always with the ostensible goal of helping the individual being confronted be a better, happier person—to manipulate and take control of every situation.

Although Gopi Krishna was not aware of this before his 1979 visit, it was not long after his arrival in Canada that he began to hear hints of these negative aspects of Joe's interactions with people. While most of Gopi Krishna's time leading up to the June conference was to be spent, as usual in such circumstances, preparing material for his talk and various other writing, time had been set aside for him to meet with small groups and individuals who had questions for him. During some of the individual sessions, he began to hear more about what was in fact behind KRI's—and thus Joe's—tremendous success in taking the huge group to Nishat, in providing the Canadian volunteers in India, in the creation of the film of the Canadians' 1977 trip to India, and in the publication of Gopi Krishna's books in Canada. He began to learn that none of this could have been accomplished without the blood, sweat, and tears of the PSI course participants. For many of them—particularly for those who were now employed by the organizations—their involvement in these activities had basically taken over their lives, with much time being dedicated to promoting the PSI courses. Granted, Joe was somehow funneling money from these legitimate for-profit courses into the registered nonprofit KRI. These funds, in turn, were unequivocally being used to promote knowledge about kundalini and kundalini research. Regardless, Gopi Krishna's concern from the moment he heard about any of this was for how the lives of these individuals were being negatively impacted. They were not living the moderate, balanced lifestyle that was promoted by the courses. Given Gopi Krishna's view that a moderate lifestyle was a fundamental key to the gradual, healthful awakening of the evolutionary, transformative energy, it is easy to imagine that his distress at this discovery was immense.

In spite of undoubted deliberation on how to best handle this situation, he also managed to spend time as he usually did prior to conferences. He worked on revising *Kundalini in Time and Space* and on another book of prophecies. This book had originally been intended as a small one that could be published for the conference, but—as he laughingly told a group of listeners—this had not been working out as planned, because the book kept growing:

> But as I just now said, it is Heaven that is granting all this knowledge, so the book is now growing towards a bulky book of about two hundred and fifty pages.... So I am in a bit of a dilemma...

His solution was to begin a small book that could be printed up for the conference. This became the booklet *Reason and Revelation*, while the longer book became *Biblical Prophecy for the Twentieth Century*, a volume that would be published later. While writing these pieces, he was also, as usual, writing the talks he would give to the public at the June conference. However, it can be speculated that he was also beginning to plan a frank, open lecture to give to his loyal KRI followers at the northern lake.

The June conference was held at the University of Toronto's Convocation Hall, an auditorium that seats 1,700. Joe's hopes of filling it up were not even close to being realized. Still the conference had about 400 attendees, attracted some media attention, and was not by any means a total failure. In terms of Gopi Krishna's life, however, the talks held lakeside a few weeks later had a far greater impact. Throughout this book, it has been shown that from the earliest days of his enlightenment, kindness and compassion were two of his greatest guiding principles. Nowhere was this shown more than when he had to offer criticism of any kind, and so, in the kindest way possible, in his talks at the lake he expressed the changes that needed to be made. He wanted it to be absolutely clear that there was no connection between the PSI courses and KRI. But even more importantly, any volunteers doing any work for KRI had to be living balanced, healthful lives that included plenty of rest, recreation, and freedom from harsh criticism or the fear of it. This, of course, went hand in hand with Joe having to relinquish his autocratic control, to begin to listen to others, and to deal with the precious souls around him with unerring love, compassion, and kindness.

Regardless of how subtle Gopi Krishna tried to be in this general rebuke, the upshot was that many of the young people who had been actively involved with the PSI courses decided to break off any association with Joe. As this meant they were no longer involved in KRI, Joe's army of volunteers was cut virtually in half. The immediate fallout of this exodus was that the funding coming from the courses that had been supporting KRI's printing of Gopi Krishna's books and the volunteers in India was decimated. After his first violently angry reaction at what he saw as a betrayal, Joe appeared to come to his senses, apologizing profusely and promising to right any wrongs he had committed. On the group's return to Toronto he spent time each day begging Gopi Krishna for forgiveness. Over the next several months, it appeared to the

KRI members who had remained that Joe had indeed listened to Gopi Krishna's admonishments, and a number of fundamental changes were made. Although many of these improvements lasted for the next year and a half, they gradually dissipated. By the end of the second year, virtually all of the volunteers and employees of the various organizations had broken off all contact with anything associated with Joe.

All this was, however, still in the future. At the time of Gopi Krishna's departure from Canada in the late summer of 1979, the fate of KRI Canada and the question of whether Joe could redeem himself enough for Gopi Krishna to be able to ethically maintain any kind of association with him were uncertain. This ambiguity combined with the immense stress caused by the upheaval in Toronto had been extremely hard on Gopi Krishna. When he arrived at the next stage of his North American trip, a visit with Gene at his home outside New York, he was in an exhausted state. Nevertheless, he made an effort to see some people who were eager to meet with him. While he was able to recuperate at Gene's to some extent, it wasn't until he was under Margaret's dedicated care in Zürich that he was well enough to fly home.

When he arrived in Delhi at the beginning of October, more medical tests revealed that he was suffering from an unspecified imbalance or infection in his liver. With treatment he slowly began to improve. In spite of his not being in full health, the next few months were busy. Determined to remain detached from the upheaval in Toronto, the Canadian volunteers had proceeded with the assignments Gopi Krishna had given them before his departure. *The Shape of Events to Come* with the final version of the introduction had finally been published in India. Once it was out, Gene had begun ordering copies to distribute. To support the sales, he ran a series of promotional ads in *New Age Magazine*, the leading alternative spiritual/holistic publication of the day in North America. Combined with his other efforts, these ads met with some success, but not as much as Gene had hoped for.

Since Gopi Krishna had only arrived in Delhi in October, it was not practical for him to return to Kashmir, especially since his health was in question. Regardless, he had to oversee matters including the ongoing social work and the continuing improvements to the center in Nishat. As usual, correspondence had built up during his absence there and in Delhi. One welcome letter in October was from Nicole Dhingra, Baldoon's wife. Gopi Krishna had been struck with the tragic news earlier that year that the renowned literary figure who had been such an ardent supporter of his ideas in both India and France had died. The shock of his early, unexpected death had left Nicole in a state of deep grief for many months, but this letter indicated she had begun to recover. Not only was she now able to begin to take part in her normal life, she was eager to carry on the work she and her husband had done promoting kundalini research in France. As both the Dhingras had been dear to Gopi Krishna, he was relieved to hear that she was doing so much better.

Another significant letter in October was from organizers for the First Global Conference on the Future being scheduled for July of 1980. This huge international conference, coincidentally in Toronto (i.e., with no connection whatsoever to KRI or its associates), was to feature scientists, environmentalists, and luminaries such as David Suzuki, and Gopi Krishna was invited to speak. This invitation, along with one he had received from Edward Kelly at Duke University, caused Gopi Krishna to begin considering another North American trip, especially since the invitation from Duke—a university famed for its hardcore research in the realm of the paranormal—represented a feasible venue for launching authentic kundalini research.

> Dear Sir:
>
> I am writing you on behalf of our research group here at Duke. Over the past several years we have developed a sophisticated computer-based facility for psychophysiological research with human beings. Our main interests are in the areas of consciousness change and, secondarily, parapsychology. These interests are both professional and personal, as we are also all with varying intensity involved in meditation and related personal growth activities.
>
> Several of us have read one or more of your earlier books, and several of our group were in the audience at the recent weekend meeting in New York. We have all been deeply impressed both by your extraordinary experiences and by the scientific attitude that you express toward

them. Consequently, we would like to explore the possibility of your coming to Durham to work with us in our laboratory, preferably for a substantial period of time.

I stress that you would not be treated here as an object of hostile "scientific" scrutiny. Rather you would be our colleague in studies of various phenomena whose reality we all accept and which we simply want to understand better. Our function would be to provide a congenial though technically rigorous environment for whatever research lines you and we jointly decide to pursue. I have no doubt such a collaboration could prove outstandingly productive in numerous ways.

Is this proposal of interest to you? If so, kindly advise me as soon as possible so that we can begin to work on details.

Sincerely,

Edward F. Kelly, PhD

As this correspondence progressed, it was suggested Gopi Krishna visit Duke in the spring of 1980. This resulted in the Pandit asking researchers at Duke if his visit could be put off for several months. He also decided to forgo attendance at the Global Conference on the Future. The original invitation included the alternative of sending a paper to be read during the sessions, and the Pandit decided to take this option.

In spite of having had so much to oversee in October, by the end of the month he was feeling well enough to begin writing as long as he was careful not to overstrain his system. Over the next few weeks he was well into writing not one but two new books in prose. Both major projects, one was to be called *The Magic of Mind*; the other was another volume of his autobiography. His plan was for this volume to deal with the years from approximately 1939 to 1953 while yet another volume would deal with the period from 1953 to 1968. This material would cover what he referred to as the eventful period when he was involved in social work. It was also, he said in a letter, "the crucial period of my inner transformation."

By the end of December 1979, he wrote to a friend saying that great progress had been made on these two projects since he had begun seriously working on them in November.[144] Given that his writing was going so well, he preferred to spend the next several months, if not the entire next year, in India to avoid being uprooted by travel.

Chapter Twenty-Two

Upheaval and Controversy Take a Toll

In spite of his intention to spend 1980 immersed in writing, the year was fraught with adversity that not only thwarted his plans but took a terrible toll on his health. One of the first difficulties concerned the Canadian volunteers. When it had appeared that the during months after he had left Canada in 1979 his concerns were being addressed, Gopi Krishna retained some contact with KRI Canada in the hope that the organization could come to fulfill its tremendous potential. In spite of this continuing, if guarded, contact, the funding for the volunteers in India was slowly drying up. Whether out of necessity, spite, or a combination of both, Joe eventually insisted that the volunteers return to Canada, even writing to the Indian government to say that KRI was revoking its support of their stay in India. While this had no effect on their status, the lack of funding did.

Because the Canadian volunteers ardently desired to stay in India to help Gopi Krishna, the process of compelling them to return home was drawn out and acrimonious, causing Gopi Krishna great distress. When it ultimately became evident that the situation in Canada had not substantially changed, all contact between kundalini foundations elsewhere and the Canadian organization were severed. Eventually all but one of the volunteers were obliged to return to Canada. This was a terrible blow to the Pandit. Not only had he become exceptionally fond of them, their work had become essential to many projects that had been launched since their arrival.

Another major upheaval in Gopi Krishna's life that year was related to the property in Nishat where so much time, effort, and money had been invested in expansion. One of the most important transactions in this ongoing enhancement had been the purchase of an adjacent piece of property. Although he held the fully paid legal deed to the property, he would have to spend many months trying to prove it. To some extent the background for this dispute lay in the animosity between Hindu and Muslim factions in Kashmir that had been flaring up, particularly since the partition of India. Ultimately this dispute would result in virtually all the property owned by Kashmiri Brahmins being confiscated. Although this illegal confiscation of Hindu-owned assets did not culminate until the early 1990s, when virtually all Kashmiri Brahmins were forced out of their homeland, it had been going on to some extent for decades. It was not uncommon for brigands simply to take over land either by force or through the use of false documents that were created with the collusion of corrupt government officials. This happened in the case of the property in Nishat, with a man claiming to hold the deed to the land and, thus, the guesthouse that Gopi Krishna had had constructed on it. In spite of the fact that it quite obviously appeared to be a forged document, the corruption among government officials made it possible for the man and his son to instigate a drawn-out battle in court. Even worse than the legal dispute, however, was the violence that ensued. A common tactic in these kinds of land grabs was the hiring of thugs to damage the property or to threaten or even attack current occupants and workers in an attempt to frighten the owners into dropping the legal battle. While these tactics did not deter Gopi Krishna or his family, they were terrifying and, in this case, caused considerable damage to the buildings on the Nishat property. To put the seriousness of these difficulties into context, it must be noted that after Gopi Krishna's death, but prior to the Kashmiri Brahmin exodus of the 1990s, two men who were guarding the Nishat property were shot to death, and the entire property, including all the houses, was taken over.

This calculated harassment took an immense toll on Gopi Krishna. Sometime after making his usual seasonal move to Kashmir in the spring he became ill.

Following several bouts of varying degrees of illness, he was hit with the worst attack of sickness he had undergone in decades. This serious illness, along with the period he needed for slow recovery, lasted for over four months. Not until well into November did he begin to improve. Unfortunately, this improvement did not last long as the difficulties with the property forced him to stay in Kashmir until the end of December where yet another exceptionally bitter cold spell combined with the lack of indoor heating set back his recovery.

While the adversities of 1980 did prevent Gopi Krishna from making the progress he had envisioned at the beginning of the year on the next volume of his autobiography and on *The Magic of Mind*, he still managed to write a surprising amount. One project involved two pieces dealing with life after death. Written in response to a reader who had mistakenly interpreted his emphasis on the biological aspects of kundalini to mean there was no soul or spiritual essence that survived physical death, one was entitled "Do We Survive Death?" The other was a piece that would eventually be published as "Life Is Everlasting."[145] However, the most remarkable writing done during 1980 occurred when, for the first time, he received lengthy amounts of inspired verse in Kashmiri. Up until this point, except for the few verses that had come to him in other languages during his earliest experience of inspired creativity, verse had only ever come to him in English. Another first was that at times this inspired verse came to him even when he was not physically well. Intermittently throughout 1980, hundreds of lines of this verse flowed into him. It seemed to him to be the most lyrically beautiful verse he had ever written. Struck by the power of the words, he envisioned them being set to music so that they could be performed throughout Kashmir, even by troupes that would sing, dance, and play instruments in the streets. This dream was never realized, no doubt at least in part because of the many adversities he faced during the year.

During this challenging period of his later life, Gopi Krishna started to more seriously consider an idea he had had for quite a while: finding a location in India with a consistently moderate climate where property could be purchased for the creation of another institute for kundalini research. With their temperature extremes, neither Delhi nor Srinagar was suitable for year-round residency. How much his decision to accelerate this search was influenced by his personal experiences with his Kashmiri property or what he might have seen as an escalating deterioration of the sociopolitical situation in that area is not known. What is known, however, is that at some point during 1980 he came to concentrate on the town of Dehra Dun in the province of what is now Uttarakhand as a likely spot for a permanent branch of the institute for kundalini research. Although still near the beauty of the Himalayan foothills, this city was considerably south of Srinagar; thus, it was much easier to access from Delhi. Once Gopi Krishna became certain that Dehra Dun was the ideal location, his son began to seriously explore the area. By the end of December 1980 he had found a very promising property located in what was then an almost rural area on the outskirts of the city.

One reason so much was accomplished during this difficult year was that Margaret spent a good deal of time in India, and the one Canadian volunteer who had managed to stay was joined by another. In spite of the obstacles, the young woman who had volunteered to assist Gopi Krishna in Zürich before his trip to North America in 1978 decided to go to India to help any way she could.

There were also positive developments on other fronts. That his message was continuing to spread at home was evinced by an ever-increasing number of inquiries from Indians concerning kundalini experiences. In other parts of the world, Gene was continuing his tireless efforts to promote the already-published books in the US, while supporters in Europe, such as the Naims at the Yoga Centro in Florence and Evelyn Ferrantini in Berlin, were writing to inform him of the ways they were promoting his work. In Brazil the Portuguese edition of *Kundalini: a energia evolutiva no homem* spearheaded by José Hermógenes was published at the end of the year. In France, Amoury de Riencourt's book in French as *L'oeil de Siva: la convergence du mysticisme oriental et de la science occidentale* was published, soon coming out in England as *The Eye of Shiva: Eastern Mysticism and Science.* Heavily influenced throughout by Gopi Krishna's thought, an extensive amount of material in the book explored his views on the convergence of Western science, mystical experience, and kundalini.

Another influential thinker who met with Gopi Krishna in 1980 was Claes Nobel. A descendant of Alfred Nobel, Claes was an internationally known humanitarian in his own right. Motivated by a deep concern for the well-being of the earth, he was also a passionate environmentalist. In an effort to awaken the world to the potentially disastrous effects of the loss of human values and of environmental degradation, he created a 1972 manifesto called "The Nobel Laureates Declaration on the Survival of Mankind." Reiterating Alfred Nobel's desire to improve the human condition, the document pointed out that, unless the earth's environment was preserved, this goal could not be achieved. Due to Claes's efforts, the declaration was signed by seventy-eight Nobel laureates who pledged "to conserve our natural heritage and to achieve a dynamic balance between Mankind and Nature in a world in which Man can live in Dignity, Peace and Brotherhood."[146] Still dedicated to this ideal eight years later when he traveled to India to meet with Gopi Krishna, he spent several hours interviewing the Pandit, soliciting his advice on whether the Nobel laureates' statement could be achieved.[147]

Even though 1980 had been blessed with positive moments such as Claes Nobel's visit, Gopi Krishna was undoubtedly glad to put the year behind him when he finally arrived in Delhi a few days before Christmas. He was also still ill. So weak, in fact, that during the first days of January in Sarvodaya Enclave he was sometimes sleeping as much as twenty hours a day. In this state he began to sense that he needed to make changes once again to his diet. Following this inner guidance, he did so. In a letter to Margaret, he reflected on this need to adapt:

> It is how our systems change and our bodies adjust themselves to this amount of age. In fact, through all this period from the time of the awakening there have occurred amazing changes in my diet. If I failed to grasp the need for the change intuitively or intellectually, the reaction caused in my system forced me to do it...

The dietary changes, the rest, and the warmth of Delhi soon had him showing improvement. By mid-January he was ready to receive visitors. One was José Hermógenes. Accompanied by a group of highly interested Brazilians, he proudly presented Gopi Krishna with copies of the recently published Portuguese *Kundalini: a energia evolutiva no homem.*

This uplifting visit was followed a few weeks later by the advent of yet another Canadian in mid-February. Michael had been one of the four original volunteers but had had to leave India earlier due to ill health. Since shortly after that time he had been working in Canada to save enough money to return to India. Fortunately, from the moment funds for the Canadian volunteers had first begun to dry up, concern for them among their friends at home had grown. The result was that an impromptu, informal means of donating money for their living expenses had come into being, and enough funds were regularly collected for these three volunteers to remain in India for the rest of Gopi Krishna's life. Over the next while, the group who wanted to continue supporting the work in India became a still informal, but officially registered, organization known as Friends in New Directions, or FIND.[148]

Michael's arrival could not have come at a better time. Gopi Krishna was ready not only to make the move to Dehra Dun but also to begin constructing a site for what would be called the Kundalini Yoga Experimental Project. In the first week of January, Nirmal wrote to his father describing a piece of property he had found in Dehra Dun that he felt would be perfect for their plans. These plans included what can be seen as a major shift in Gopi Krishna's focus. For decades, his efforts had been aimed at spreading interest in his theories among established scientists who could then develop and carry out the research he was proposing. During these years, he also described a research project that would involve selecting a number of potential candidates with whom he himself would work, teaching them techniques that could potentially awaken kundalini. In those who were successful, the attributes of kundalini awakening could then be studied. Establishing this project now became a main objective. In a letter to Evelyn Ferrantini written in mid-January, he briefly summarized it:

> During the past few years, I made a thorough search of a place which could suit our purpose, climatically and politically both, a place with a stable and peaceful atmosphere and a mild climate, without too much hot or cold....
>
> The purpose of the Experimental Centre is to invite volunteers for training in intensive forms of Yoga, which lead to the arousal of

Kundalini. Unless we are able to demonstrate the physiological aspects of an awakened personality, the views I am expressing will not receive the hallmark of a scientific discovery. It might take years of training for one to reach the state of maturity where a healthy arousal becomes possible. But there is absolutely no doubt that one day this demonstration will become possible with the result that the academic world will, for the first time, become aware of a cosmic law that rules the destiny of mankind.

In his conversation with Claes Nobel, he also spoke of the project, giving a few examples of the areas participating medical doctors and scientists might explore:

Physiological evidence in the blood; in the cerebro-spinal system; in the brain; in the nerves and even in the organs; in the tissues, differences between an illuminated human being and an average person....[149]

While it was clear that Gopi Krishna expected scientists to be involved in this project, it can be deduced that from this point onward his aim was to establish the research project himself rather than looking to the wider scientific community to do so.

During the first several months of 1981, various family members and volunteers spent time in Dehra Dun making preparations, from finalizing the purchase of the property to renting nearby accommodations that could be used until the buildings planned for the property could be constructed. With these arrangements completed, on May 10, 1981, a rented truck was loaded with personal belongings, office contents, and other necessities. Gopi Krishna, Margaret, Nirmal, and two of the volunteers followed the truck in a taxi, officially moving—or *shifting,* as it is said in India—the main center for kundalini research to Dehra Dun.

Once there, the volunteers immediately got to work on the property, planting fruit trees, flowers, and a vegetable garden. The first order of business, however, was to order materials for the construction of a fence. Fencing off newly purchased land, wrote Michael humorously in a letter to a friend in Canada, was necessary to "keep out the cows and goats and sundry people who wander through at all hours of the day." While little other actual construction was accomplished that summer due to the arrival of annual monsoons in July, architectural plans for the proposed buildings and the application for the necessary permits were in progress.

In order to avoid the deluge of rain, Gopi Krishna returned to Kashmir for a time. The Canadians alternated doing the same. By the time the monsoons were over, however, Michael was back in Dehra Dun overseeing matters there while the others remained in Kashmir. Although Gopi Krishna had every intention of returning shortly to Dehra Dun, he became caught up, as he often was in Kashmir, with issues related to Samiti and the property there and did not manage to leave there until the end of the year.

While the main focus of 1981 was undoubtedly on the plans for the experimental center in Dehra Dun, a number of other significant events occurred. Perhaps the most extraordinary was the creation of another book of inspired verse, *The Present Crisis*. Begun in mid-March when Gopi Krishna was still in Delhi, a complete draft of the 200-page book was written in less than three weeks—a period that included not just the writing but revisions as well. The work was remarkable not only for the speed of its creation but also because it represented a marked departure from Gopi Krishna's earlier verse in a number of ways. For one, it was written in blank, rather than rhyming, verse. This literary device was one that Leslie Shepard had recommended to Gopi Krishna years before as one that would make his verse more acceptable for contemporary readers. The Pandit had attempted to follow this advice, but until the inspiration that resulted in *The Present Crisis*, this poetic form would simply not come to him. For another, there were distinct differences in tone from his earlier works. Much to his own amazement, in addition to the deep spiritual teachings and profound messages for humankind that his revealed verse normally contained, these stanzas held instances of humor, even biting satire. When mentioning this volume in his letters, he often called it a "wonder book." In one letter, he makes a statement that only seems to be half-joking when he says that he would like to see a challenge offered up to anyone who thinks they could create a poetic work of this length and caliber in three weeks.

It is needless for me to say that the manner in which most profound problems of human life are discussed with brevity and precision is so amazing, at least for me, that I am lost in wonder when I recall that many of these paragraphs dealing so skillfully with abstruse problems have been written down as if I was copying from an invisible open book in front of me.... What is contained in this book is but a fragment of what is to come. As I have already indicated, I believe that a new chapter has opened in my life and a new phase has begun. What I now need is a quiet place with a calm environment to work in.

The reference to a new chapter, or a new phase, is also significant. In the few short years that remained of his life, he would make at least three other references to having achieved yet another level of higher consciousness. Certainly, he felt the Kashmiri verse he had begun writing the previous year represented evidence of a transformation in consciousness. Early in 1981 these exceptionally lyrical verses started to come to him again. By the third week of February he had written another 200 verses. Verses appeared in Urdu and Hindi, too, additional languages he had never written in using verse form before. Feeling strongly about their importance, he also translated over 100 of the earlier Kashmiri verses into English, planning to do all of them in the future.

Evidence that interest in his work was spreading came on a number of fronts in 1981. Invitations to speak were received that year from all across India. One was from a coalition of noted yoga schools that included the Bihar School of Yoga; another was an obviously repeated exhortation from Dr. Turaga Desiraju at NIMHANS urging Gopi Krishna to speak at their conference on "Yoga, Brain, and Consciousness" to be held at the beginning of 1982. Most, if not all, of these invitations appear to have been turned down, apparently due to a combination of factors that ranged from health issues and the demands of constructing the experimental center to the imperative he experienced to write when the mood of inspired creativity was upon him.

The year 1981 also gave Gopi Krishna an opportunity to honor his long association with von Weizsäcker. In preparation for the famous physicist's seventieth birthday the following year, admirers in Germany had planned the publication of a book commemorating his life, and the Pandit was asked to contribute a chapter. In it, he wrote that he was presenting von Weizsäcker in light of his image of what the scientist of the future would be like as the physicist "comes nearest to the picture I have in mind of one who presents a happy blend of the scientist, the philosopher, and the mystic in his personality."

In 1981, Gopi Krishna also received several important visitors. In February a large group came from Japan that consisted of doctors and scientists. Headed by Mr. Keijiro Fujikura, it marked a growing interest in Gopi Krishna's ideas in that country. Following their meeting, Fujikura made it known that he was determined to see that a version of *The Shape of Events to Come* was published in Japanese.

By October Fujikura had accomplished his goal, with a translation of the book having been completed and a publisher contracted. Other evidence that the Pandit's reputation was growing in that country came when he was contacted by Hiroshi Motoyama. Internationally known for his research on *chi* as a subtle energy that had parallels in other cultures, he asked Gopi Krishna to write the foreword for his book *Theories of the Chakras: Bridge to Higher Dimensions.*[150]

Another interesting visitor in 1981 was the Nobel Prize laureate George Wald. An ardent peace activist and environmentalist, Wald taught biochemical sciences at Harvard for many years. He was widely known for his passionate, outspoken commentary on the threat posed by pollution, overpopulation, and nuclear escalation. One of his most famous statements was made in conjunction with the first Earth Day in 1970. Quoted in the *New York Times* and a number of other sources, he predicted that civilization would destroy itself in less than thirty years if the human race did not take immediate action to deal with these threats. Motivated by these concerns, it is easy to see why the scientist wanted to meet with Gopi Krishna. He seized the opportunity to do so when he attended a seminar in Delhi that December on what was being called the *living state*—an examination of the human condition that included both biology and philosophy.

Following this meeting, Gopi Krishna left Delhi on about December 21 to return to Dehra Dun. The new year of 1982 dawned with him settled there, determined to see the construction of the buildings that would house the

Kundalini Experimental Project. For those of us living in the developed world today, it might be hard to imagine just how difficult bringing a building project like this to completion would have been over forty years ago in an undeveloped area, especially one where education, training, and skill development were available to only a small percentage of the population. Once the construction of the buildings was begun, every aspect of the project had to be supervised every day. Workers with the proper skills often could simply not be found. The hiring of a man whose claim to be a skilled bricklayer was heralded as a gift from heaven, and his work on the entire project proved to be invaluable. This level of dedicated work was, however, often not the case as dishonest practices were rife on construction sites. When the bricks were brought, for instance, they were not stacked but dumped in a massive pile so that it was impossible to count them to determine whether the purchased number of bricks had been delivered. One of the Canadian volunteers related another example. He could not understand why Gopi Krishna adamantly insisted that he make a written note of exactly the number of workers the crew foreman brought with him every day, until the foreman handed in a bill that claimed daily pay for several more workers than he had ever brought to the site. When confronted with the volunteer's written record, he acquiesced with a shrug.

Even with the help of the volunteers, just attending to the countless details involved in the project took a heavy toll on Gopi Krishna's energy. Dealing with the corruption took an even greater toll. Since confronting dishonesty is difficult for even the average ethical person, it is easy to imagine how heartrending it would be for someone who lives in a state of higher consciousness, aware of the glorious, divine potential in each human being. For Gopi Krishna, whose preference was always to lift others up rather than to put them down, it could be a great strain and finding solutions often took a good deal of effort. Nevertheless, Gopi Krishna always strove to find a solution that would lift others up rather than to put them down. Michael tells how one day a worker who had been absent from the Dehra Dun site tried to collect wages for more days than he had worked. When confronted, the man said he needed the money for his sick mother. In spite of the man's legitimate need, Michael did not want to give in to his false claim for wages in front of the other workers.

When Gopi Krishna came upon the scene, he instructed Michael to give the worker precisely what he was owed and nothing more. He then spoke quietly to the man, telling him to come to him privately to receive some extra money. In this way, Michael did not lose his authority, and the man got the funds he needed for his mother. Regrettably such straightforward, one-on-one solutions to endemic fraud were not possible with so many different suppliers, foremen, and workers involved.

Additional help with the construction came in October in the form of Canadian volunteer Alf, who arrived to witness Gopi Krishna in the trancelike state of inspired creativity that was the fount of all his writing. For, as truly remarkable as it might seem, amid all the stressful demand on his time, Gopi Krishna had managed to write yet another book over the summer months. Throughout the summer he had been working on revisions. By the fall, he had finished a final draft that, having been retyped by one of the volunteers a number of times, was now ready to be proofread for publication. This book, *The Wonder of the Brain*, was his last prose work before his death.

At the time, however, all thoughts were to the future: the experimental center was coming very close to being a reality. Over the next two months, work on the main building was completed. In December, Gopi Krishna and the volunteers moved in. The structure consisted of independent living areas upstairs and down, each complete with kitchens and Western-style bathrooms. The central feature of the ground floor was a library, which was soon shelved wall-to-wall with books that would provide research material. The separate living quarters easily accommodated the four volunteers, Gopi Krishna and Bhabi, who came as soon as she could, and Margaret, who arrived in December to see what had been accomplished. Margaret had also come to India in order to accompany Bhabi to the betrothal ceremony for their beloved granddaughter Sunita. Known affectionately as Dolly, she had often been of help to her grandfather when Jagdish's family was with him, and Gopi Krishna deeply regretted not being able to attend.

In Dehra Dun, Margaret found that the lemon and peach trees, the flowering plants, and the vegetables that had been planted the year before were now flourishing on the grounds around the completed building. The center was well on the road to being the place of serenity and beauty conducive to the studying of the biological basis of mystical experience that Gopi Krishna had envisioned. As he wrote to a correspondent shortly before the building was completed:

> I am a humble person, a householder, who treats the experience I have as a gift from Heaven, which, I believe, I had not done anything special to merit. I believe that the time has come when the paramount importance of the mystical experience or Samadhi must be accepted as a demonstrable reality, indicating the summum bonum of human life. In the ultimate analysis, the material and the spiritual fuse into one, for Brahman is one. So long as we are confined in the body, methods have to be found to achieve our awakening from the dream of Maya. Kundalini Shakti is the key provided by nature to achieve this aim. What I am trying to say has, thus, both a spiritual, [and] also a physiological significance. Just as our own personality is a composite of two elements, the spiritual and the physical, in the same way, the instrument of liberation, as also the methods to achieve this end, as for instance Yoga, have also these two ingredients, namely a spiritual and a physical one. The disciplines are aimed for the mind and the body both and not only one of them.

Chapter Twenty-Three

International Talks—Sufis, Hopis, and Humanists

This year, 1983, was the penultimate of Gopi Krishna's life. January began with no thought—at least by his friends and family—that he would live just over eighteen more months. It was in many ways, perhaps ironically or perhaps not, the most productive year of his life. Although it was not the one in which he wrote the most, it was a year in which he reached the largest audiences, which, in turn, garnered tremendous enthusiasm for his ideas. To say the year was a whirlwind of activity is no exaggeration. Speaking at three internationally significant conferences, he traveled to Switzerland, Germany, Austria, Canada, and the United States. In addition to the major conferences, he made countless presentations to smaller groups that ranged from a handful of engrossed listeners to packed lecture halls. In spite of all this activity, he still supervised from afar the publication of the journal, the distribution of his books, the work of Samiti, and the ongoing construction in Dehra Dun. And even though he did not produce the extraordinary amount of writing he did in some other years, he wrote an astonishing amount given all else that he accomplished.

Was this tsunami of exertion the cause of the eventually fatal illness that would begin to plague him by the end of the year? Or was it the final valiant effort of a man with a mission who wanted to use the limited time he knew he had to the fullest advantage possible? These questions are, of course, impossible to answer. Regardless, this last full year of his life was a remarkable one. Its beginning found him comfortably ensconced in the main building at the experimental center with Margaret and all four Canadians still there to help him with everything from dictation to managing the ongoing construction of the buildings that would be needed for the completion of the complex.

With all this finally well in hand, Gopi Krishna was able to attend to the projects that had not received full attention over the last several months. The first order of business was to send two of the volunteers to Delhi to see to matters related to the Publication Trust that ranged from producing another issue of *Spiritual India & Kundalini* to fulfilling the backlog of orders for books.

As always there was correspondence to attend to, often with people from around the world who wanted his advice. One was from a supporter in Japan who found himself in a health crisis. Written just prior to New Year's 1983, Gopi Krishna's response described a means of accessing the power of meditation or prayer in healing. After expressing his compassion for the man's situation, he wrote:

> We live in a world strictly ruled by law, but, above all, by a compassionate Almighty Power, which listens to our prayers.
>
> The body has its own powers which come to our rescue in illness, but, above the body, the healing powers of the soul are unlimited. We should make use of the best treatment prescribed by medical science and, at the same time, seek the aid of healing powers of the soul. Our hope and faith in the Grace of Heaven should abide to the last.
>
> Please devote a few minutes every day in invoking the aid of the spirit in overcoming the illness. This you can do by sitting in a convenient posture on the floor or in a chair, for five to seven minutes, in a warm, comfortable room, protected from chill and wind, after sun-rise in the morning or before sun-set in the afternoon. The mind should be composed and free of other thoughts. After this is done in a positive, optimistic frame of mind the attention should be directed to the ailing part of the body and held there for a few minutes.

In this interval a silent prayer should be made to the spirit to heal the ailment, and it should be imagined as if a vivifying stream of spiritual force is pouring on it to effect the cure. This should be done without causing any strain in an entirely hopeful state of mind. You can do it once, in the morning or two times, in the morning and afternoon, as is convenient for you. If sitting is difficult you can even do it reclining on a sofa or bed. Please continue to have every trust in Heaven and maintain an optimistic frame of mind.

As correspondence from around the world arrived, so did visitors. Eager to see the progress that had been made at Dehra Dun by 1983, José Hermógenes came from Brazil, as did Mr. Fujikura from Japan. In the third week of February, Gene Kieffer arrived from New York planning to tape a series of interviews with Gopi Krishna that he could make available to the public as audiotapes and articles, some of which were eventually published in the book *Kundalini: Empowering Human Evolution*.[151]

Shortly after Gene arrived, Margaret returned to Switzerland. There was a good deal of work there to be done. When she had originally arrived she had brought with her an invitation that had come to Zürich from the International Transpersonal Association asking Gopi Krishna to speak at a large international conference planned for September in Davos, Switzerland. The ITA had been founded primarily by the psychiatrist Dr. Stanislav Grof in 1978 as an international adjunct to the Association for Transpersonal Psychology.[152] One of the ITA's main purposes was to sponsor international conferences. From the first one held in 1972 in Iceland, these conferences attracted the attention of many of the alternative psychologists, psychiatrists, scientists, authors, and spiritual teachers of the day.

Once Gopi Krishna accepted the invitation, detailed planning for the trip began. The stay was to be a lengthy one. In addition to the time that would be needed to renew contacts in Europe, an invitation to speak at a second international conference there was received. Sponsored by a German group known as Forum International, this one was to be held in the village of Alpbach in the Austrian Alps shortly after the Davos conference. Based in Freiburg,

Germany, Forum International was an organization that had been formed for the express purpose of putting on conferences, seminars, and presentations on topics related to the shifts in consciousness and the transformation processes that people experienced.

Gopi Krishna's acceptance of these invitations, when he had so often turned down requests to speak in the past, may have indicated what excellent opportunities to spread his message these conferences were thought to be—especially since he was still having health issues. In a letter written to Margaret shortly after she had returned to Zürich, he confessed that he had not felt truly well throughout the whole winter and that throughout his audiotaping sessions with Gene, he had suffered from painful swelling in his feet. This pain in his lower extremities had been a serious recurring problem for some time. During Margaret's and Gene's visits he had refrained from mentioning either the pain or the general feeling of ill health as he did not want to worry them. He did, however, see doctors and undergo a number of medical tests, which were apparently done in Dehra Dun. These tests indicated that neither his liver nor his kidneys were functioning as well as they should. His blood-sugar level was also very high. Even though these results were worrisome, he went ahead with his plans to travel.[153]

When word went out that he would be returning to Europe, von Weizsäcker and other German scientists expressed their desire to meet with him. In order to do this, to renew other acquaintances, and to have time to work on his talks for the two conferences, it was decided that he would fly to Zürich in May at the latest, and in April he traveled to Delhi to take care of matters before his flight. While there, he had the earlier medical tests redone, and he attended to increasing trouble he had been having with both his vision and the hearing aids he had been using. A solution that delighted him was the acquisition of new prescription eyeglasses that had a hearing aid in each stem. Moreover, these glasses had darkening lenses that he felt would provide a big comfort to his eyes, suggesting that light sensitivity may have been a problem for him.

While he awaited the results of his medical tests, the weather in Delhi became unusually warm for April. Even though this began to affect him adversely, he did not want to leave. This was especially so because Ragya had recently become so ill she had to be briefly hospitalized. Fortunately, by the end of the month she was much improved, and she had the great pleasure of announcing the engagement of her son Rakesh. On top of this good news, Gopi Krishna's test results came in with encouraging results. With all this in place, plans for him to fly to Zürich after the first week of May were finalized.

On his arrival Margaret entreated him to take a rest. He did rest, but not for long. Although he had written a draft of his Davos speech while still in Dehra Dun, he was soon working on revisions that he was very pleased with. Near the middle of the month Stanislav and Christina Grof came to visit, interviewing him for three hours. Christina, who Gopi Krishna later said had asked many of the questions, described the profound experiences with kundalini that had occurred during the births of her two sons. Discussion also centered on a kundalini project the Grofs planned to launch and on the forms of treatment for people undergoing crises. Around the same time in May, Gopi Krishna received an invitation to write a lengthy article on sexuality and spirituality for Da Free John's magazine *The Laughing Man*. Viewing the sample issue sent with the request left the Pandit in a quandary: the magazine seemed like it might be an effective forum for promoting his ideas; however, on reading an article by Da Free John in the issue, he realized he would have to flatly contradict the self-proclaimed guru's ideas in his own magazine, and this did not seem like the proper thing to do.[154] May continued to be busy, with the Pandit giving a lecture in Bern; just prior to the end of the month he gave another one at the University of Zürich, where the hall seating over 200 was filled to capacity. The next day he traveled to Basel to give a talk at Peter Oswald's yoga school, where he built on the good relations he had made there in his previous trips to Switzerland.

In June the steady stream of visitors that tended to occur when he was in residence in Gemsenstrasse continued, with a highlight being a visit from von Weizsäcker on June 20. By this time a number of sessions with scientists in Munich had been planned, and von Weizsäcker was looking forward to spending more time with the Pandit once he had arrived in southern Germany. The largest of these gatherings was held on June 30. Following these highly successful but exhausting meetings, Gopi Krishna was able to spend time in peaceful surroundings in Starnberg, where von Weizsäcker had now made his home.

After Gopi Krishna returned to Zürich, Margaret made plans to take him to the chalet in Engelberg. By this time, he had received repeated entreaties from Canada and the US to extend his trip to the West by coming to North America after the two big conferences were over in September. Once it was determined that he would come to Canada, members of FIND began planning a few informal lectures along with a number of opportunities for individual meetings. In New York, Gene was doing the same.

While these arrangements were proceeding in North America, Gopi Krishna was able to spend the last ten days of July and the first few weeks of August in the peaceful beauty of Engelberg writing and revising his talks for the upcoming September conferences. While he met with some visitors, such as his longtime French supporter Amaury de Riencourt, he was able to not only work on revising his talks but also produce a significant portion of a new book. Just prior to the last week of August he moved to the very pleasant apartment that Margaret had found for them in Davos, where he was able to continue to write. In a letter to Gene from Davos he mentioned the new book, saying he had already produced enough material to make up a small volume of about 100 to 150 pages. Regrettably, no record has yet been found of what this proposed book might have been. It seems fairly certain, however, that the material for the upcoming talks, which is available, would have made up part of the book.[155]

During this lead-up to the day of his speech, he also spent time being interviewed, both by the attending journalists and a Swiss-Italian television network. He also received a number of important visitors. One was Michel Random. Born Stefano Balossini, Random was a noted French filmmaker and author who had become famous for his works on the martial arts of the Far East. He was particularly known for his book *Les arts martiaux ou l'esprit des budo*, an exploration of the true spirit of budo, or Japanese martial arts. Both interested in science and spirituality, the two men formed an immediate bond.[156]

The Davos ITA conference began on September 1. As at previous ITA conferences, the speakers included some of the most widely recognized names of the time, many of whom have remained influential to this day, such as the

Grofs, the Vipassana meditation teacher Jack Kornfield, the psychiatrist Elizabeth Kübler-Ross, and the Jungian analyst Marie-Louise von Franz. Although not so widely known and revered then as he is today, the Fourteenth Dalai Lama, Tenzin Gyatso, was also a speaker. Dr. Karan Singh came from India; presented the day before Gopi Krishna's speech, his talk was extremely well-received.

The talk Gopi Krishna had written out for his presentation was a blunt one. Pulling no punches, he pointed out that, while some current gurus had even hundreds of thousands of followers, it was not proof that they were enlightened. Indeed, he emphasized, the "cases of spiritual illumination have been rare in history. Mystics like Kabir, Rama Krishna, Rumi, or Meister Eckhart have been few and far between." He went on to raise the question of why throughout history the great civilizations fell right when they were at the peak of their glory.

But the mystery is solved when we realize that the human brain is still in the process of evolution toward a more perfect state in which a still-superior pattern of consciousness is possible. A natural, frugal, healthy life, content only with the basic needs of the body and the mind, free of ego, immoderate ambition, lust and greed for wealth—more ready to serve [rather] than to rule; altruistic and compassionate—is the only life concordant with the principles of evolution.[157]

He noted that these principles were the very ones set forward by the founders of the world's great religions and pointed out—accompanied, it can be easily imagined, with a bit of an ironic smile—that it was interesting to note that not one of them had promoted greed, lust, or the hunger for power. In another somewhat ironic moment he referred to current scientific investigations into what were being called *"mystical experiences"*—ranging from the effects of hypnosis and the alpha and theta states induced by biofeedback to states triggered by drugs—without the scientists ever seeking the corroboration of a single great mystic.

Keeping in mind that Gopi Krishna saw kundalini as a universal force simply given different names in different traditions, he referred to this force as the guardian of this process of human evolution and recited one of his most beautiful descriptions of her. Citing references to her as the almighty power in great Tantric works such as the *Saṭ Cakra Nirūpaṇa*, *Panchastavi*, and the *Saundaryalaharī*, ascribed to the philosopher Śaṅkarācāryaḥ, he stated:

> Kundalini is the Gayatri in the Vedas, the supreme mantra that every twice-born Hindu must recite with his morning ablutions. The syllable *om* is the symbol of the same power. As Prana-Shakti, Kundalini is the architect of all forms of life in the universe. She is our thinking, our speech, our imagination, our creativeness, the energy that brings us to life, guides us in infancy, fills us with fire of love in adolescence, with ambition and the desire for adventure in youth, and then slowly withdraws the vigor she had bestowed unto the last breath, when a mortal ceases to be an actor in the drama of life.
>
> Kundalini will continue to remain a mystery till the end of time. Even when some secrets of this power and the methods to awaken it become a part of human knowledge, this marvelous element of creation will still continue to be beyond the reach of our intellect.[158]

This prepared speech went on to reiterate his often-stated point that, while the unimaginably colossal cosmic force of prāna-shakti would not now or at any time in the future yield to the mechanistic studies of mere human scientists, the physiological effects of the awakening of kundalini in individuals could indeed be studied.

Because the ITA was an offshoot of the Association for Transpersonal Psychology, Gopi Krishna gave careful attention to this guardian of human evolution—the cosmic essence of the intelligence and the mind itself—for, when aroused in "a body not attuned to it, without the help of various disciplines, or not genetically mature for it," it could result in unbalanced mental states. At the conclusion of his prepared speech he made his plea that his audience, intelligent and well-meaning as they were, look to teachings of the great spiritual teachers for guidance:

The aim of spiritual disciplines is not to make one insensitive to the environment or to the pain and suffering of fellow human beings. The one great lesson that the lives of all great spiritual teachers impart is that the greater the degree of illumination, the more sensitive does the illuminated mind become to the sorrows of fellow beings and more resolutely does it act to alleviate the condition. The lives of Zoroaster, Buddha, Mahavira, Lao-tzu, Moses, Socrates, Christ, Mohammed, Śaṅkarācāryaḥ, Guru Nanak, Saint Teresa of Avila, Ramakrishna, and Gandhi provide the models for what I say.

Selfish occupation with one's own salvation, when the world is burning, is not a sign of spiritual regeneration. The first effort of one who aspires to the vision of God is to purge his mind from egotistic thought and (as a Karma Yogi) set himself to the task of extinguishing the fire. It is for this reason that I am presenting the world situation in an objective way, to draw attention to the acute problems that need the effort of one and all of us to solve.[159]

The speech he had written for Davos was indeed powerful, but he set it aside to speak, as he often did, extemporaneously. With the sense of audience that always characterized his presentations, he tuned into their interest in yoga, elucidating the disciplines involved in Patanjali's eightfold path. Portraying yoga as an age-old science, he also gave a brief, particularly lucid description of individual prāna in relation to kundalini-shakti as the cosmic creative force.

In the Indian Shaiva philosophy, and even in Vedanta, the universe is one whole ocean of intelligence. And this intelligence works by its own power. That power is Shakti or prāna, and of this ocean of intelligence, which is eternal, all knowing, we all are drops. We are not the body, we are not the face, we are not of the earth, but every one of us is a drop from this ocean of Cosmic Intelligence.

The aim of Yoga is to bring back this drop of intelligence, which is imprisoned in the body, back to its glory and monarchy. And this is the aim of our life according to the Indian tradition. How it is achieved, as I said, by Yoga or meditation, what actually happens is that this prana in the body is altered. In the West it is known that the "solar force" builds a solar body around the soul. This solar body is lustrous, luminous, luminosity, luster. Light is a prominent feature of all mystical experience. Anybody who has the mystical experience experiences light, experiences Life. Which means that a new sheath is now working around the soul. In India it is known as *divya-deha*—the shining body—or *siddha-deha*—the perfect body.

When you see the picture of a saint or of Christ or a Buddha you see a halo of light around them. This halo of light is a symbol of the inner light which permeates the mind or the brain of the enlightened one.

Making it very clear that he was explaining these facts to them so that they would understand the true purpose of yoga, he went on to make a plea to them to turn their attention to the province of the spiritual and try to arouse its power in their own bodies. In that way, he said, they would be able to discern the true nature of the situation in the world; they would be able to see what needed to be done.

In conclusion, he thanked the audience for listening so patiently, adding one potent remark: "But mere saying and listening will not solve the problems of the world. It never did."

Chapter Twenty-Four

Dehra Dunn—The Experimental Centre for Kundalini Research

As soon as the conference in Switzerland ended on September 4, Gopi Krishna left for Alpbach, Austria, where the Forum International conference was scheduled to begin on the sixth. The Dalai Lama, who also traveled from Davos to Alpbach, was scheduled to give the opening address on that day. Like the ITA conference, this one had attracted not only these two great spiritual teachers but a number of leading scientists and philosophers, including Fritjof Capra and David Bohm. Even in this illustrious setting it was evident the Gopi Krishna's words stood out.

The Forum International's conference at Alpbach was called in English "Other Realities: The New Convergence of Natural Science and Representatives of Spiritual Disciplines" or, in German, "Andere Wirklichkeiten: Die neue Konvergenz von Naturwissenschaften und vertreter spirituellen Disziplinen." Looking at Gopi Krishna's efforts to make contact with scientists and encourage scientific research over the prior thirty-three years of his life, it is obvious he was very pro-science, always advocating the roles both the spiritual and the empirical had to play in getting humanity back onto its proper evolutionary path. At Alpbach, however, he gave the impression—at least, to some—that his talk came down hard on the side of the importance of the spiritual. In his introduction to Gopi Krishna's talk, editor Rainer Kakuska noted that the renowned physicist Fritjof Capra had made the comment that when he shut his eyes during the presentations, he could sometimes not tell if he was listening to a scientist or a spiritual teacher. Kakuska then went on to make the point that he did not think Fritjof would have said that about Gopi Krishna's talk. In Kakuska's opinion, he was the only one among all the speakers who clearly took the side of the superiority of religion. His talk, Kakuska said, was "an eloquent plea for us to recall to consciousness the millennia-old truths brought to mind by the founders of the religions of all time."[160]

Nevertheless, it goes without saying that Gopi Krishna did not fail in his presentation to make this lifelong plea to science to do the crucially needed research on kundalini. While his planned talk for the conference sponsored by the transpersonal psychologists in Davos focused to some degree on the brain, the evolution of consciousness, and the imperative of science to research the relationship between the two, his prepared presentation for Alpbach came at the same conclusion from a different angle. In this talk he emphasized the crucial need for a unifying principle for science and religion. Although he did, as Kakuska pointed out, emphasize ancient spiritual teachings and the spiritual laws governing nature and reality, he stressed that it was through studying kundalini—or *"Holy Spirit,"* as he referred to it in many places—that science could come to a real understanding of the laws that govern not just the cosmos but all reality as we know it and the pinnacle of evolution that humanity is meant to attain. In calling for the critical effort needed in developing this unifying principle, Gopi Krishna spoke not just of the division between science and religion but of the diverse and discordant factions that exist within each of them. "How," he asked, "can we change this world when there are so many differences, so many quarrels, so many contradictions? We must be able to find a unifying principle if we want to save mankind from disaster." The key to discovering this principle, he said, would be found in discovering the "cause behind the religious experience." He then added:

...Buddha, Krishna, Mohammed, Christ and all the great mystics or religious teachers of mankind, their experience has been the same. This is acknowledged by all great students of mysticism, including

Bertrand Russell, that the experience is the same. The experience is of a unifying principle in creation; of oneness; of one presence; of one God; of oneness with all living creatures. This is a fundamental feature of mystical experience. One finds that one is not an isolated being, but a part of a whole. And this whole is not dead. It is a living whole. It is an intelligent whole. And its intelligence is beyond anything we can conceive.[161]

One of the great differences between this talk and his previous pleas for kundalini research was that he called not just on science to take up the studies he was describing but for religions—and/or individual members of religion—to do so as well. In this context, however, it is essential to know what he meant by the word *religion*. As he said in a 1978 interview with Louis Rogers, after the professor asked him a question about the importance of religion,

Before we talk about the importance of religion, perhaps it would be better to say a few words, what is meant by the word *religion*. The reason is that people interpret the word *religion* differently. Therefore, it is better to clear this point first.

Religion means the impulse rooted deep in human nature to establish one's relationship with the universe—to know "Why I am here?" "Who am I?" "What is the cause behind the universe?" and "What relationship [do] I bear to that cause?" Religion also implies a sense of wonder, awe, and respect for the Creator who has brought us into being, with a longing to pray or worship Him. This tendency has been in evidence from as far back as the dawn of human culture.[162]

In making his call to the individuals gathered at the Alpbach conference, he said:

So if we wish our efforts to succeed, if we wish peace to come to the earth, and if we are earnest in this, if we are not inclined to be dogmatic or only to care for ourselves and we look at the issue from a broader angle, there is a great need at this time for all spiritual organizations to unite, to come closer to each other, to overlook the faults and to unite on good principles. And then not to wait for scientists—now, please, for Heaven's sake: prove that God is there—but to start their own investigation.

The time has come for that because the conditions of the world are such that every rational human being who has the good of mankind at heart must act for himself.

Another extraordinary moment in this talk was when he referred, as he did in his Davos speech, to the stirrings of kundalini awakening among those in the audience and elsewhere:

And all those who have this urge in you, who wish that religion should be revived, that something should be done to have a loving and a happy humanity, in them, this power is stirring; in everyone in whom there is an intense desire for spiritual experience; in them, this center is just stirring a bit. And if they live the life which is decreed, which is described in the religious scriptures of mankind, they will surely, in one form or the other, have an experience of this state. It may come in a dream, just for a few seconds, it may come during the day; it may just in a moment, when you are looking for some beautiful landscape, the idea might come to you. Your own self might reveal itself in that moment. It happens to thousands of people, millions of people all over the earth.

Although true enlightenment must have a much more enduring effect, these types of experiences were indicative that the center in the brain known in yoga as the *brahma randhra* was stirring. Studies on this activity, Gopi Krishna said, would produce the unifying principle for science and religions. This, in turn, would put humanity back on the evolutionary path, saving it from the imbalance caused by so much of humanity having developed a gigantic intellect while allowing its spiritual nature to become stunted.

After delivering this powerful speech, he left for a brief rest back in Zürich before making his way to Toronto, Canada, where many friends were awaiting his talks. He spent two weeks there and gave lengthy lectures on three days and spent much of the remaining time meeting with individuals who were interested in carrying on kundalini research. During this period in Canada, he was surrounded by enthusiastic individuals who were eager to carry out his work, in particular the research articles he hoped to publish in *Spiritual India & Kundalini* on the lives of mystics and geniuses, which would show how their spiritual experiences paralleled those of the yogis who had awakened kundalini.

The enthusiasm Gopi Krishna had met with in Toronto followed him to New York City. One of the purposes of his stay in the city was in response to an invitation to speak at the United Nations Organisation during Disarmament Week. Held on October 23 in the Great Entry Hall of the General Assembly Building, the evening seminar was arranged by the People's Assembly for the United Nations. The opening and closing remarks were given by Robert Muller to the approximately 1,000 people in attendance.[163] An assistant secretary general often called the Prophet of Hope, Muller was known for efforts within the UN to promote world peace and the importance of the spiritual. He often said that his position of being a top-level statesman gave him a vantage point that allowed him to see the connection between the political/cultural and the spiritual.

The seminar was obviously structured to reflect that view. The theme was "Forum for Survival: Moral Imperative and Political Commitments." In addition to Gopi Krishna, the presenters included Pir Vilayat Inayat Kahn from the Sufi Order, the Black activist Reverend Ambrose I. Lane, Sr., and Sister Blaise Loup, a Catholic nun concerned with social justice. Three Indigenous spokesmen were also present. Wallace Black Elk, who would go on to become famous for his book *Black Elk: The Sacred Ways of a Lakota*, performed a prayer ceremony for the gathering. The Hopi Elder David Monongye also spoke. Like Thomas Banyacya, Monongye was one of the four Hopi Elders given the task in 1948 of carrying the Hopi prophecies to the world in the hopes that Hopi wisdom would help prevent the potential future holocaust presaged by the use of nuclear weapons in World War II. The third Indigenous leader to speak was Leon Shenandoah, who was the tadodaho, or the spiritual and political spokesperson, for what was then known as the Six Nations Iroquois Confederacy but is now more properly called the Haudenosaunee Confederacy.

On the flyer for the event, Gopi Krishna was quoted as urging the UN to promote disarmament, adding "the race cannot survive the nuclear age, unless there occurs a complete change in our social and political structures, and spirituality, pruned of all superstition and falsehood, becomes the guiding star of our life." A quote from Robert Muller's book *The New Genesis: Shaping a Global Spirituality* also appeared on the flyer:

> This is why we must also be grateful to anyone who gives the work of the United Nations a spiritual interpretation...the march towards that transcendence has now started on a planetary scale, and we are privileged to be among its first witnesses and workers. We must cater to it, nurture it, love it, help it grow in beauty and in strength, so as to fulfill the prophecies of all spiritual leaders.[164]

Gopi Krishna continued his valiant lifelong efforts to further humanity's march toward this transcendence over the next few weeks in New York City. Following the meeting at the UN, he was flooded with even more visitors than usual, sometimes meeting with twenty or more a day. Enthusiasm for writing compelling articles and for creating a polished, competitive North American version of the journal was soon high, as it had been in Toronto. During this period Gopi Krishna also received invitations to speak in France, Spain, and Italy and needed to have Gene fly to Portugal in his stead to deliver a paper there. Buoyed by this cresting wave of dedication to the promotion of kundalini research, Gopi Krishna left New York City not only as hopeful about his work as he had ever been but also more eager than ever to get the experimental project underway.

Unfortunately, or perhaps even tragically, by the time he and Margaret made it back to Zürich by the tenth of November, his body had begun to feel the effects of the tremendous strain of the last several months of exertion. Although his original plans were to return to his family in India after resting for only a week or so, he developed a number of problems, including a blood pressure reading of 200/120. Ultimately becoming seriously ill, he was unable to leave his bed for three weeks. By mid-December he was beginning to feel a little better; however, he was still quite ill. Then suddenly on Christmas Day—a time of the year when so many events, significant and momentous had occurred in his life—he began to write. With inspiration flowing through him, in a matter of several days he had written in rhyming verse a draft of the final work of his life, *The Way to Self-Knowledge*. Like his other works in verse, the book contained entreaties for the changes that would prevent world catastrophe, but it was far more than that. Within its simple, melodic verses were secreted the steps to transform not only the world but each one of us into a being with self-knowledge, a being who, in knowing the Divine within, reached higher states of consciousness.

Early in January he was finally able to fly to Delhi, but even once there, he wasn't strong enough to go on to Dehra Dun. The next seven months, the final ones of his life, would be fraught with bouts of severe illness that contrasted abruptly with periods of recuperation and productive health. Decades later, observers are left wondering whether the Herculean effort he put into his travels, talks, and meetings in 1983 left him so depleted that his body could simply not recover. What is known, however, is that in India he was eventually diagnosed with an intestinal infection common to that country. Because his doctors there had somehow missed it earlier, it was suspected to have been draining his health for as long as two years. Once under the assiduous care of Bhabi and the rest of the family in the warmth of Delhi, he improved somewhat. He was able, even in his weak state, to work on revisions to *The Way to Self-Knowledge* but not strong enough to move to Dehra Dun. He had every intention of going there as soon as possible but had to be well enough to endure the long drive as there was still no air service to that city from Delhi.

While he was in Delhi, it became evident that his reputation in India had continued to grow just as it had in the West. Along with many invitations to speak, his correspondence included requests for his input that came from organizations such as Bharat Nirman, an all-India social-justice organization launched under the auspices of Indira Gandhi. One of the more out-of-the-ordinary communications came from U.A. Asrani, the author of *Yoga Unveiled: Through a Synthesis of Personal Mystic Experiences and Psychological and Psy-*

chosomatic Studies, who was urging Karan Singh to put forth a bill in parliament that would send a delegation of Indian yogis, headed by Gopi Krishna, to the United Nations Organisation to usher in an era of international peace.[165]

Over the next few months, his condition continued to ebb and flow until April when, the day after he handed in the final revisions to *The Way to Self-Knowledge*, he descended into another crisis. His condition became so ominous that the family called Margaret, telling her to come. She left Switzerland immediately, arriving on May 2 to join the family as they watched over their beloved Pandit, who, much to their joy and amazement, suddenly began to improve. When Margaret left several days later, they were all convinced he would continue to recover. By this time, however, the rising heat in Delhi was making it imperative he be moved to a cooler climate. As Srinagar could be reached by plane—and Bhabi would no doubt be more comfortable caring for her husband in their old familiar home—it was decided to take him there instead of Dehra Dun. Two of his grandchildren, Sunil and Anju, came along with Bhabi to help, and Nirmal was soon to follow.

By mid-June in Kashmir, he seemed to be nearly his old self. Catching up on correspondence over the next few weeks, he contacted many of his longtime supporters, such as Tontyn Hopman in Switzerland and Peter Hoffman, currently in India, who was already making inroads in having *The Way to Self-Knowledge* translated into a number of South Indian languages. Determined to build on the tremendous momentum begun on his travels, he also wrote to his North American supporters, encouraging work on the polished, Western version of the journal and the other ideas they had for expanding support for research. At the same time in India, he kept the Canadian volunteers busy. Although one of them had been forced by health issues to return home, the remaining three continued to be focused on producing the next edition of the journal, but especially on seeing the Kundalini Yoga Experimental Project in Dehra Dun completed.

As this focused activity on important matters in the outer world had been going on, transformations in his inner world had been occurring. With his descents into critical illness and surprising recoveries, particularly the recovery in mid-June, he was aware that a remarkable change was taking place in his consciousness. While his everyday thinking was not as effective as it normally was, he was aware of an unmistakable inner transformation. Mentioning this only to those closest to him, he stated unequivocally that he had reached a new level of consciousness. Exactly what this transformation in consciousness was or how it would manifest in his future writings was not yet evident to him. In a letter to Margaret on June 19 he wrote:

> I can now do a bit of mental work also, but not for long periods of time. I feel strongly that the gift of expression will be restored to me....
> I feel I might soon be in a position to devote myself to writing work, but what would be the ideas expressed and what direction my ideas on Kundalini will take in the future, I cannot say. It has to be kept in mind that the subject of Kundalini is as vast as the sky. The illuminati of the future, whose number will constantly increase from age to age, for as long as mankind is ordained to stay on earth, will continue to add to this knowledge in the same way as scholars, scientists and philosophers have been adding to our knowledge of the mundane world from the distant past to our day. In other words, there is no end to the science of Kundalini. It is possible the present painful experience might have been nature's way to change the direction of my restricted thought and to draw my attention to other aspects of the Divine Power, which I could not have grasped in my previous state.

One thing that was apparent to him was that he was, in a sense, a different person. On a few different occasions during these last weeks, he mentioned that all he had written in the past appeared to him like "figments of a dream." He would not have been able, he said, to make an addition to an earlier work or even recite a line from *The Way to Self-Knowledge* that he had been working on only weeks before. Still, he was keenly aware of how important this work was and, as always, gave credit to a higher power working its genius through him rather than crediting himself with being any sort of genius. While at the present time this new level of consciousness he was experiencing remained in a sense a mystery to him, he was hopeful that in a month or two he would come to a better understanding. In the meantime, he said simply:

> What kind of genius will now manifest itself I cannot say at this stage. It will all depend on the Will of Heaven and the mysterious Power to which I owe my life and ability.

Even when he was feeling his best during this period, he was not able to move as he had wished to Dehra Dun. His health was not the only consideration. Rising political strain in Kashmir had made the situation extremely tense. With the ongoing strikes, curfews, and animosities looming, travel was becoming more difficult. Gopi Krishna, along with two of the Canadian volunteers who were by then with him, was essentially stuck in Kashmir. This left Michael alone in Dehra Dun. Extremely concerned regarding how isolated he might be feeling there, Gopi Krishna was nonetheless convinced his presence was essential, stating repeatedly in his correspondence how reassuring it was to know that the Canadian was there to oversee all the issues related to the development of the experimental project.[166]

The critical importance of this project had not decreased in the slightest for Gopi Krishna, particularly with the way enthusiasm for his work was building. Even before the construction had reached its current stage, with the main building and three outbuildings for small residences completed, he had been communicating to others about how quickly the project might be launched. A key point was that he already had Indian scientists on board. One was the scientist Dr. Jamuna Prasad, who had already expressed his willingness to spend time in residence at the facility. Already well-known in India, Dr. Prasad would eventually become internationally famed for his work in parapsychology, particularly in the study of verifiable cases of reincarnation. After mentioning Prasad's interest and referring to interest by other researchers, Gopi Krishna wrote in a letter to a supporter:

> Instead of waiting till the construction for the whole project is completed, we can make a start by inviting case histories of those who have been

practicing meditation for a number of years and have started to notice significant changes in the areas of perception. All we have to do would be to publish an advertisement in a few magazines or papers, both here and in the States, saying that these histories are needed for the purpose of scientific study, as for instance, to evaluate the effect of meditation on the cerebrospinal system and the evolutionary processes of the brain. I shall make out and send you a questionnaire to which those interested in the study will have to respond. This will include enquiries about the system normally associated with the awakening of the Serpent Power. We need not mention the word *Kundalini*.

It will take a few months to advertise and to receive letters in response to the advertisements. There are many, many people who are experiencing peculiar sensations or symptoms as the result of yoga, meditation, or Zen, but are not able to account for them. Nor are their spiritual teachers able to give them a satisfactory explanation for their peculiar conditions. Hence, I feel we shall have plenty of material for starting the research....

As soon as the construction work is over, our Canadian friends will be free to attend to the classification and tabulation of the work. It would be an exciting field of study for them. We shall have others, too, to do the good work. At the same time an advertisement of this kind is likely to cause a stir....

We have two important cases of Kundalini Awakening, which correspond to the symptoms I have mentioned. One is that of a colonel in the Indian Army, stationed in Kashmir...the other is Head of the Department in Botany in the University of South India. We have other cases, too, some of them in Europe. Other well known scientists and scholars may also come forward, including those who were associated with our organization in West Germany.

If I were assured about the availability of funds, even a modest amount, I would have a nucleus of scientists ready here in Dehra Dun for the preliminary work in the research project. The expense will not be much, but it will have an electrifying effect on the media as also on the learned interested in this work, both in India and abroad....

When Gopi Krishna spoke at Alpbach in Austria, he made a strong point for members of spiritual movements to take up the research. Certainly, he never stopped urging the established scientific community in this direction, but his determination right up to the last days of his life to see the Kundalini Yoga Experimental Project fully operational in Dehra Dun showed that he had the courage of his convictions and was willing, as always, to follow up his words with actions.

What the world has lost in his coming so close to launching the experimental project and communicating from a yet-higher state of consciousness we will never know. Gopi Krishna would, however, tell us not to mourn for these losses and to look, as he unfailingly did, to the "will of heaven."

His last days were a testament to that. Through June and much of July, Gopi Krishna had seemed to steadily regain his health. Then, a few days before his death, he had attacks of pain that he assumed were his old troubles with his liver and kidneys. When remedies that had eased these conditions in the past failed to work and the pain increased, a doctor was called in. Diagnosing pneumonia, he prescribed antibiotics. As Gopi Krishna had said earlier in life, medication did not necessarily work in the body of someone who had gone through a profound transformative process in the same way it did in the average person. In this case, the prescription caused a negative reaction. Gopi Krishna's labored breathing became even more excruciating. By this point the doctor in Srinagar was insisting that he be taken by ambulance to be hospitalized. As the family's concern for him escalated, those who were still in Delhi tried to get to Srinagar. Unfortunately, because the steadily growing political tensions in Kashmir had spiraled to the point of virtual lockdown, neither the family members in Delhi nor Michael were able to get flights to Srinagar.

On the last day of Gopi Krishna's life, frantic phone calls flew between Srinagar and Delhi, but no one was able to convince the Pandit to go to the hospital. In spite of the agonizing pain, his mind was completely lucid; he was absolutely determined to remain at home. After a difficult night and a morning of labored breathing, he died in his beloved Bhabi's arms a few minutes after the hour of noon on Tuesday, July 31, 1984.

His final ceremony was carried out in front of the house in Karan Nagar according to Hindu custom. The rest of the family, who had finally been able to get to Kashmir, were in attendance, as were Margaret, the three Canadian volunteers, and many of his dear friends. Also present was Karan Singh, who paid great honor to Gopi Krishna by laying out twelve white lotuses[167] and saying, "In the 19th century India gave the world Ramakrishna. In the 20th Century she has given the world Gopi Krishna."[168] His body was cremated later that day and his ashes were sprinkled into a river flowing through his beloved Kashmir Valley.

In Toronto several months before his death, Gopi Krishna emphasized the absolutely pivotal role his social and charitable works had played in his awakening or, as he put it, "to whatever Grace was granted" to him. Certainly, the last breath of his life energy was given in that cause: two of the last few days before his death were spent in the role he had held all his life as a force at the forefront of social justice in his native land. Many hours during those precious final days were spent meeting with leaders of the Hindu community, devising ways to ensure that all those who so desperately needed social services would continue to receive them during the current political crisis.

Within this context, the last words of his talk in Davos—*Saying and listening will not change the world. It never did*—take on even deeper significance. During his last talk in Toronto, which would be the last public lecture he would ever give, he was asked what disciplines were the best to practice in the pursuit of higher consciousness. He replied that while many useful disciplines existed, what was far more important—indeed, what was essential—was love in action.

> What is essential is love, is good action, is service, is truth. That can keep you better from distractions than even meditation. Help. Help. Be an elder brother. That is not only on an individual basis, but on a racial basis also. The elder brother has to help. The stronger brother has to help the weaker. Wherefrom do we get our ideas? An elder brother, seven years old, who has a brother three years old, walking by his side,

when a stream comes, the elder brother at once sits down and puts the younger one on his back and carries him across that stream. Wherefrom? It comes from the Divine source. Our thoughts come from there. This is our heritage. We have to help, as I said, that all the resources of one whole planet are at our disposal. What life have we to lead? Our life has to be full of help.

The race is evolving. It cannot evolve if we all are selfish. It can only evolve if the strong help the weak, the wise the fool, and the healthy the ill, and the rich the poor. It can only evolve then. And that is the teaching of all religions of mankind.

We have not understood the importance of the teachings of Christianity or Hinduism or Buddhism. But this is the law. Since the race is evolving, it cannot evolve unless those who are first to move ahead bring their other fellow beings along with them.[169]

Epilogue

Although the experimental centre in Dehra Dun was never completed after Gopi Krishna's death, his ideas have continued to spread. Much of this work has been carried on by the Kundalini Research Foundation in New York and by the Institute for Consciousness Research in Canada. In Europe, Margaret Kobelt headed the Swiss Kundalini Research Foundation until her death in 1997.

Through the efforts of these and other organizations, Gopi Krishna's books have remained in print. ICR has created ebooks of all his published writings, several previously unpublished pieces, and many of his discourses, and they are now producing audiobooks. ICR also continues with the Anthology Project by furthering the cross-cultural literary research into the lives of saints, mystics, and inspired geniuses that provides evidence of kundalini's universal nature. For a list of all papers or to contact ICR, see www.icrcanada.org. The Emerging Sciences Foundation at www.emergingsciences.org in California is also working to further the research at www.emergingsciences.org.

Endnotes

Chapter One: The Roots of Rebirth

1   In Kashmir, Cong refers to saffron and Maal refers to the Sanskrit word mala, which can mean "garland" or "crown"; thus Gopi Krishna's mother had a particularly lovely name, "Garland of Saffron."

2   Gopi Krishna, *Living with Kundalini: The Autobiography of Gopi Krishna* (Boulder, CO: Shambhala 1992) 81–82. While it is widely accepted that this event occurred on Christmas Day, it is only certain that it happened on or near Christmas Day.

3   Many other forms of Shiva worship, or Shaivism, are found throughout India. Kashmiri Shaivism is a very specific form of Shiva worship that has a Tantric element. See Kamalakar Mishra, *Kashmiri Shaivism: The Central Philosophy of Tantrism* (Varanasi: Indica Books 2011). For Śakti/Śiva nondualism, see Boris Marjanovic, *Abhinavagupta's Commentary on the Bhagavad Gītā* (Varanasi: Indica Books , 2004), 177–179.

4   Krishna, Living with Kundalini, 41.

5   Krishna, Living with Kundalini, 10.

6   Krishna, Living with Kundalini, 80.

7   Gopi Krishna, *The Kashmir Discourses* (Amazon KDP Edition: ICR & KRF 2020).

8   Krishna, *Living with Kundalini*, 83.

9   Graham Schweig, *Bhagavad Gītā: The Beloved Lord's Secret Song of Love* (New York: Harper One 2007) 246.

10   Georg Feuerstein, *Encyclopedic Dictionary of Yoga* (New York: Paragon House 1990) 190–191.

Chapter Two: From Suffering to Finding Solace

11   This misconception about kundalini awakening is currently widely propagated by some teachers of what is purported to be kundalini yoga. It is, however, contradicted by the age-old Tantric texts related to kundalini. These texts offer repeated cautions but also extol it, describing the transcendental state of Divine Oneness that Gopi Krishna eventually reached.

12   Minor Shivratri festivals take place each month of the lunar calendar, but the Maha Shivratri or Great Shivratri festival takes place once a year, generally in what is February or March in the Julian calendar.

13   Krishna, *Living with Kundalini*, 162–163.

14   Krishna, Living with Kundalini, 112

15   *Bhagavad Gītā*, 16:2, quoted in Krishna,Living with Kundalini, 116. The "descendent of Bharata" to whom the god Krishna is speaking is Arjuna.

16   While kindness and compassion are traits lauded by Gopi Krishna, neither is specifically listed in the yamas and niyamas of Patanjali's classical yoga. The yama *ahimsa* is often translated as "nonharming"; compassion is included in some later lists of the yamas.

Chapter Three: Trial and Error—Learning to Live with Awakening

17   It is worth noting that in the many interviews with family members and people who knew Bhabi during her lifetime, there was never a negative word spoken: she was held in universal love, admiration, and esteem.

18   Hari Singh did not cede Jammu and Kashmir to British-controlled India until 1947 (see Chapter Four). His son, Karan Singh, became Maharaja for a short while and was a great supporter and friend to Gopi Krishna throughout his life.

19   Gopi Krishna sometimes describes this perceptual alteration as being like a "chalky coating."

20   Gopi Krishna, *The Kashmir Discourses* (Amazon KDP Edition: ICR & KRF 2020).

21   As will be seen, this need for rigid regularity in food intake remained with Gopi Krishna all his life.

22   Gopi Krishna, *Secrets of Kundalini in Panchastavi, Canto II:12* and *Canto II:2* (Darien, CT: Bethel Publishers 2010).

23   Krishna, *Living with Kundalini*, 260.

24   Gopi Krishna, *Kundalini: The Evolutionary Energy in Man* (Boulder, CO: Shambhala 1971) 185–186 and *Living with Kundalini*, 265–267. Both these sections contain detailed descriptions of this experience.

25   Due to a discrepancy in the autobiographies, it is unclear whether Jagdish also accompanied Bhabi, although it seems likely that he did. Nirmal, by his own recollection, was certainly there.

26   Not all Hindus are vegetarians. Like some Hindus, particularly those living in the colder climates, Gopi Krishna's family consumed eggs, fish, mutton, and chicken.

Chapter Four: Fighting for Women's Rights in the 1940s

27 In 1958, Gopi Krishna also became secretary of Bharat Sevak Samaj, a national social organization that today promotes literacy, skill development, and retraining for those in need in India. He remained in this position until 1970.

28 Conflict reached one crisis point in 1980 when the land in Nishat where the Central Institute for Kundalini Research was originally located and the 1977 World Conference on Kundalini was held was attacked by brigands, property was damaged, and, tragically, two guards were killed.

29 Krishna, *Living with Kundalini*, 284.

30 Krishna, *Living with Kundalini*, 284.

31 A shalwar kameez is the traditional outfit made up of leggings and tunic.

Chapter Five: War, Poverty, and Emerging Cosmic Consciousness

32 *Pathan* is also spelled *Pashtun* and *Pushtuns*. The common language is Pashtu or Pushtu, which is from an Eastern Iranian language group.

33 This conflict is often referred to as either the Indo–Pakistani War of 1947 or as the First Kashmir War.

34 M. Ilyas Khan, "Partition 70 Years On: When Tribal Warriors Invaded Kashmir," BBC News, October 22, 2017, www.bbc.com/news/world-asia-41662588.

35 The history of Muslim–Hindu relations in Kashmir is an extremely long, complex one. For a compelling account of its roots, see Rakesh Kaul, *The Last Queen of Kashmir* (New Delhi: HarperCollins 2016). Written by Gopi Krishna's eldest grandson, it takes a fascinating look not just at Kashmiri history but also at ancient reverence found in Kashmir for kundalini-shakti.

36 Krishna, *Living with Kundalini*, 286.

37 Krishna, Living with Kundalini, 288–289 makes it sound like these attempts at poetry in Jammu in 1949 were his first. However, during an interview with Ragya, she indicated that even before she left home there were periods of this extreme absorption during which he could be seen, in an apparently transcendent state, counting out rhythms on his fingers. It was assumed by the family that he was at these times composing verse in his head. Note: Ragya was definitely not certain of the years when these states occurred.

38 This original bridge has since been replaced.

39 Gopi Krishna, *The Kashmir Discourses* (Amazon KDP Edition: ICR & KRN 2020).

40 Krishna, *Living with Kundalini*, 289.

41 Krishna, Living with Kundalini, 290–304. For a detailed description of Gopi Krishna's experiences during the period when his awakening began to stabilize in Jammu beginning in December 1948, see the chapter "Stretching Out Immeasurably in All Directions."

Chapter Six: When Poetry Drips like Honey from the Pen

42   Georg Feuerstein, *Encyclopedic Dictionary of Yoga* (New York: Paragon House 1990) 156–157, 297.

43   Gopi Krishna, *The Kashmir Discourses* (Amazon KDP Edition ICR & KRF 2020).

44   Max Müller, trans., The Chandogya Upanishad, Third Prapathaka, Khanda 13:8, www.hinduwebsite.com/sacredscripts/hinduism/upanishads/chandogya.asp.

45   Feuerstein, 197–198. These verses have been translated in many ways, e.g., in *English translation of Chandogya Upanishad* by Swami Nikhilananda: "Now, the light which shines above this heaven, above all the worlds, above everything, in the highest worlds not excelled by any other worlds, that is the same light which is within man. There is this visible of this light: when we thus perceive by touch the warmth in the body. And of it we have this audible proof: when we thus hear, by covering the ears, what is like the rumbling of a carriage, or the bellowing of an ox, or the sound of a blazing fire. One should worship as Brahman that inner light which is seen and heard. He who knows becomes conspicuous and celebrated, yea, he becomes celebrated" (Part 3:13, verses 7–8. www.consciouslivingfoundation.org/ebooks/13/CLF-chhandogya_upanishad.pdf).

46   *Saundaryalaharī of Śankarācārya, V.K. Subramanian, trans. and commentary (Delhi: Motilal Banarsidass 2006) 9–10. Whether Gopi Krisha was familiar with the text at this point is not certain, but it seems unlikely that he would not have been. Note on editing: The apostrophe after the word poets was added.*

47   Krishna, *Living with Kundalini*, 237.

48   It is irresistible to speculate on the "coincidence" of these two crises occurring around the Christmas holiday. Although Gopi Krishna would not have celebrated this holiday, it appears that, at least in 1943, he was expecting the extended holiday that would likely have been celebrated in the government offices of Jammu and Kashmir. Even though it was still a princely state and not technically part of British-ruled India, it may well have been influenced by British customs.

49   Lilian Silburn, *Kundalini: The Energy of the Depths, trans. Jacques Gontier* (New York: SUNY P 1988) xiii.

50   Gopi Krishna, *Gopi Krishna Discourses: Zurich, Nishat, New York* (ICR and KRF 2010) 173–174. Note: It is likely Gopi Krishna translated this verse by Lalleshwari directly from the Kashmiri. The following is a translation found in a book Gopi Krishna's personal library, Jayalal Kaul, *Lal Ded* (New Delhi: Sahita Akadmi) 98.

   In life I sought neither wealth nor power,

   Nor ran after pleasure sense,

   Moderate in food and drink, I lived a controlled life,

   Patiently bore my lot, my pain and poverty,

   And loved my God.

Chapter Seven: Social Justice—Amid the Ravages of War

51   The story of how the Hindu troops were captured at Bunji and Gilget is interesting and extremely controversial as the leader of the conquering troops, Major William A. Brown, who "declared" Bunji for Pakistan, was a British officer ostensibly fighting for the British and thus Indian—rather than Pakistani—cause in the war. He later claimed he followed his heart as he felt most of the people in the area were Muslim and that this is what they wanted. Non-Muslims were taken prisoner and held captive. The author is not sure if Bhabi's brother was a soldier or if he was just caught up in the melee. See www.quora.com/Why-did-Major-William-A-Brown-help-Pakistan-with-the-Gilgit-issue.

52   Krishna, *Living with Kundalini*, 327.

53   Krishna, *Living with Kundalini*, 327.

54   Krishna, *Living with Kundalini*, 328.

55   Krishna, *Living with Kundalini*, 328.

56   Exactly when these buildings were constructed or exactly what was there when Samiti first obtained the property is not known.

57   See Krishna, *Living with Kundalini*, 305–311 for more detail.

Chapter Eight: Radical Acts, Writing, and Rejection

58   Bethen Bell, "Erin Pizzey: The Woman Who Looked beyond the Bruises", BBC News, November 10, 2021, www.bbc.com/news/uk-england-london-59064064.

59   Sunil Raina Rajanak, "The Goddess of Kashmir," *Speaking Tree* (May 2017), www.speakingtree.in/article/goddess-of-kashmir.

60   Gopi Krishna and James Hillman, commentary, *Kundalini: The Evolutionary Energy in Man* (Boulder, CO: Shambhala, 1967) 38–39.

61   Krishna, *Kundalini: The Evolutionary Energy*, 39.

62   Dick Russell, *The Life and Ideas of James Hillman* (New York: Helios Press 2013) 410.

63   Russell, 409–422.

Chapter Nine: How to Call for Research into Kundalini

64   It is possible another, later letter from Rider & Company was received, but no record of it has been found.

65   This is evidently Gerald Joseph Yorke (1901–1983), who traveled in the East, wrote a number of articles on Eastern religions, and became heavily involved with Aleister Crowley.

66   See www.bsscommunitycollege.in/objectives.asp.

Chapter Ten: James Hillman and *Kundalini: The Evolutionary Energy in Man*

67 Clara Hopman, a.k.a. Clara Quien, is perhaps most well-known for her statue *Gandhi Spinning*, which is in the Gandhi Memorial Center near Washington, DC, and has been exhibited at the Smithsonian.

68 Rhea Quien Hopman, *Tontyn Hopman's Autobiography on Kundalini*. Unpublished manuscript, © Rhea Quien Hopman.

69 Personal interview, Teri Degler with Tontyn Hopman, Switzerland, 1990.

70 It is not clear from the letters exchanged in this section whether Gopi Krishna was working on the third volume of the work or if there was now a fourth volume, nor is it certain what of this material had been completed when he wrote his first response to Hopman.

71 Kamalakar Mishra, *Kashmir Śaivism: The Central Philosophy of Tantrism* (Varanasi: Indica Books, 2011) 179.

72 As of this writing, no copy of this booklet printed in India has been located.

73 Gopi Krishna, *Kundalini: The Evolutionary Energy in Man* (Boulder, CO: Shambhala, 1971) 233–234.

74 Krishna, Kundalini: The Evolutionary Energy,241.

75 Krishna, Kundalini: The Evolutionary Energy,240.

76 Boris Marjanovic, trans., *Abhinavagupta's Commentary on the Bhagavad Gītā* (Varanasi: Indica Books 2004) 26. Gopi Krishna quoted various translations of this passages from the *Bhagavad Gītā*. This one is from eighth-century polymath Abhinavagupta, perhaps the greatest philosopher of Kashmiri Shaivism.

Chapter Eleven: Jailed! Leading the Hindu Resistance in Kashmir

77 Volker Kluger, "The 'Peace Angel of Helsinki' Wanted to Save the World," *Journal of Olympic History 25*(1), 2017, International Society of Olympic History, http://isoh.org/wp-content/uploads/2019/02/314.pdf.

78 Kluger.

79 There is extensive speculation that her primary supporters were Reinhard Gehlen and the Jesuit Father Robert Leiber. Both have controversial histories beyond the scope of this book to explore. In brief, Gehlen was a Nazi lieutenant general who deserted to the Americans, later joining them in their fight against communism, becoming spymaster of Germany's federal intelligence service, the BND. He was forced out in 1968. Father Leiber was a secretary to Pope Pius XII and died in 1967. By 1968 Sinai apparently had no financial backing. For more see Kluger and "Der gekaufte Engel des BND," Süddeutsche Zeitung, February 9, 2018, www.sueddeutsche.de/politik/barbara-rotraut-pleyer-dergekaufte-engel-des-bnd-1.3803656.

80 Kluger, 13.

81 Krishna, *Living with Kundalini*, 304.

82 Triloki Nath Ganjoo, "Sri Sheetal Nath: Abode of Sheetleshwar Bhairava," https://kashmirdairy.wordpress.com/me-sheetlesvara-the-sheetalnath.

Chapter Twelve: Finally Published—Acclaim in the West

83   "The Göttingen Manifesto," www.uni-goettingen.de/en/54319.html.

84   "Carl Friedrich von Weizsäcker," www.atomicheritage.org/profile/
carl-friedrich-von-weizs%C3%A4cker.

85   Gopi Krishna, *The Biological Basis of Religion and Genius* (New York: Harper and
Row 1972) 2.

86   Personal interviews, Teri Degler with Margaret Kobelt, 1989, 1990. All direct and
indirect quotes and references to Margaret come from these interviews unless otherwise stated.

87   Gopi Krishna, *The Coming War, unpublished* manuscript, 1968. Any further references
to *The Coming War* refer to this version unless otherwise stated.

88   Gopi Krishna, *The Shape of Events to Come* (Nishat: Central Institute for Kundalini
Research 1968). Second and third editions of *The Shape of Events to Come* were
published by the Kundalini Research & Publication Trust, New Delhi, in 1979 and
1980, and contained a ninety-page introduction in prose.

89   William James, *The Varieties of Religious Experience*, ed. Matthew Bradley (Oxford:
Oxford University Press 2012) 290.

90   Krishna, *Living with Kundalini*, 292.

91   Gopi Krishna, *Kundalini Empowering Human Evolution: Selected Writings of Gopi
Krishna*, ed. Gene Kieffer (New York: Paragon House 1996) 59.

92   Gopi Krishna, *Gopi Krishna Discourses: Zurich, Nishat, New York* (ICR and KRF 2010)
61–62 and author recollections. Note: Gopi Krishna's reference here to beginning to
write fifteen years after his awakening, rather than the twelve years generally referred to,
can be assumed to refer to around 1964, when his poverty was lessened to the degree
that he could concentrate more seriously on writing.

Chapter Thirteen: Von Weizsäcker—A Renowned Physicist Takes Up the Call

93   For more on Mother Giovanna Francesca see https://catholicsaints.info/
venerable-luisa-ferrari/.

94   Interview of Gene Kieffer by the author, in May 2016.

95   Story related by Margaret Kobelt, who noted that she accompanied him on most of his
later travels so that he was looked after properly.

Chapter Fourteen: Exploring the Biological Basis of Religion and Genius

96   The languages translated from the original include German, Dutch, Italian, Portuguese,
French, Spanish, Gujarati, and Japanese. In the 1990s, Leslie Shepard took the
autobiographical material from *Kundalini: The Evolutionary Energy in Man* and
integrated it with material from two other autobiographical manuscripts that Gopi
Krishna had written during his lifetime. This work, entitled *Living with Kundalini*, has
become a second Shambhala Gopi Krishna autobiography. Many of his seminal
thoughts on kundalini and its awakening are woven throughout his life story.

97 Gopi Krishna, *The Biological Basis of Religion and Genius* (New York: Harper and Row 1972) 88–90.

98 John Ebel, "The Church Has Everything for Modern Youth," *The Register*, Denver Edition, June 3, 1971, 7, https://archives.archden.org/islandora/object/arch-den%3A8465/datastream/OBJ/view.

Chapter Fifteen: Julian Huxley, Edgar Mitchell, and a Challenge Set to Verse

99 George Tompkins, "Gopi Krishna and Human Evolution," *Cosmic Light*, Winter 2000.

100 "Apollo Astronaut Edgar Mitchell Dies at Age 85," NASA History, February 5, 2016, www.nasa.gov/feature/apollo-astronaut-edgarmitchell-dies-at-age-85; and "Our Origins: A Shift in Perspective," IONS, n.d., https://noetic.org/about/origins/.

101 Personal interviews by Teri Degler with John White, April–May 2021. All references to John White unless otherwise stated come from these interviews.

102 Gopi Krishna, "Meditation as a Means to Self-Knowledge," ICR Newsletter, September 21, 2021.

103 A contemporary description of this experimental research project and his proposal for literary research project, which was continued by ICR, can be found at www.icrcanada.org/research/memorandum.

Chapter Sixteen: LSD, False Gurus, and the Real Nature of Mystical Experience

104 It's possible this was a review copy of *The Secret of Yoga* and that the printed books hadn't arrived in Kashmir yet.

105 I.H. Elyonor, *Translingual: The Language of the Dead, the Communication of All Times* (Germany: Books on Demand 2021) 203–223. Note: the entire book contains references to Gopi Krishna, and the author assumes that I.H. Elyonor is a pen name for Eleanore (pronounce Elee-a-nor) Berg but cannot confirm this.

106 In these days of the web and instant communication, it might seem inconceivable that it was not more widely known among Gopi Krishna's associates that a French Sanskrit scholar named Lilian Silburn had been working on a French translation of the *Vijnana Bhairava* and with another Kashmiri yogi, Lakshman Joo, or that, according to Paul Reps, Lakshman Joo had begun working on an English translation as early as the 1950s. Reps, a student of Zen Buddhism, worked on the material with Lakshman Joo and published his version in *Zen Flesh, Zen Bones* in 1957, saying its Tantric centering exercises might have been an early forerunner of Zen meditation practice. Eventually Gopi Krishna was made aware that Lakshman Joo was an authority on the *Vijnana Bhairava*, and he encouraged his helpers on the project to get in touch with him. Although Lakshman Joo lived for some time in Nishat, he spent much of his time in complete seclusion and this might explain to some extent why Gopi Krishna was not in direct contact with him, if indeed he was not.

107 "Elmer E. Green, PhD, Biography," www.elmergreenfoundation.org/elmer-green-biography.

108 William Irwin Thompson, "The Common Ground of Mysticism and Science," Harper's Magazine, November 1972, https://harpers.org/archive/1972/11/the-common-ground-of-mysticism-and-science.

109 Based on the online inflation calculator www.inflationtool.com/us-dollar/1975-to-present-value, accessed 06/02/2022.

110 Elmer E. Green, "Biofeedback and Yoga," *Subtle Energies & Energy Medicine, 10*, 47–52, https://journals.sfu.ca/seemj/index.php/seemj/article/viewFile/265/228.

111 Karan Nagar, the section of Srinagar where Gopi Krishna's house was located, had been given its name in honor of Karan Singh when his father was still Maharaja of Jammu and Kashmir.

112 Personal communication with Teri Degler, June 12, 2021.

113 Gopi Krishna, *Kundalini: Empowering Human Evolution*, ed. *Gene Kieffer* (New York: Paragon House 1996) 195–204. This book was originally published as *Kundalini for the New Age: Selected Writings of Gopi Krishna* in 1988 by Bantam Books.

Chapter Seventeen: Research Begins—The All India Institute for Medical Science

114 Personal interviews, Gay Luce and Eric Peper with Gopi Krishna, June 1972. Luce and Peper's recording was turned off during part of the biofeedback session, quite probably because of Gopi Krishna's general attitude regarding such experiments. However, it seems indisputable that what they were measuring was Gopi Krishna's ability to alter brain waves.

115 Crane Brinton, "Will History Be Repeated?" *New York Times*, June 9, 1957, www.nytimes.com/1957/06/09/archives/will-history-be-repeated.html.

116 Armoury de Riencourt, *The Eye of Shiva* (London: Souvenir Press 1980).

117 Unfortunately, the first names of Mr. Tan and Mr. Fung are not known.

118 This is now the University of Colorado.

119 C. Grof and S. Grof, "Spiritual Emergency: The Understanding and Treatment of Transpersonal Crises," *International Journal of Transpersonal Studies, 36*(2), 2017, https://digitalcommons.ciis.edu/cgi/viewcontent.cgi?article=1524&context=ijts-transpersonalstudies. It was not until 1994 that this category was included in the DSM-IV: "Due to growing recognition of the overlap of spiritual/mystical experiences and mental health problems, in the early 1990s authors Lukoff, Lu, & Turner (Turner et al., 1995, p. 435) made a proposal for a new diagnostic category entitled 'Religious or Spiritual Problems'. The category was approved by the DSM-IV Task Force in 1993 (Turner et al., 1995, p. 436) and is included in the fourth edition of the Diagnostic and Statistical Manual of Mental Disorders (DSM-IV) (American Psychiatric Association, 1994). The inclusion marks increasing professional acceptance of spiritual issues in the assessment of mental health problems. " ("Spiritual Crisis," Wikipedia, accessed February 24, 2023, citing R.P. Turner, D. Lukoff, F.T., Barnhous, and F.G. Lu, "Religious or spiritual problem: A culturally sensitive diagnostic category in the DSM-IV," Journal of Nervous and Mental Disease, 183(7), 1995, 435–444, doi:10.1097/00005053-199507000-00003).

120 Zulfikar Majid, "Women Medicos Opt Psychiatry for a Career in Kashmir," Deccan Herald, June 15, 2014, www.deccanherald.com/content/413697/women-medicos-opt-psychiatry-career.html.

Chapter Eighteen: Yoga, Science, and Man—Gopi Krishna vs the Maharishi

121 Conference proceedings for the Seminar on Yoga, Science, and Man are available. See Worldcat: www.worldcat.org/title/seminar-on-yoga-science-and-man-14th-to-16th-march-1975/oclc/6519477.

122 Personal interview, Teri Degler with Nirmal Shivpuri, February 18, 2017.

123 The Martin Luther King, Jr. Research and Education Institute, King Papers. https://kinginstitute.stanford.edu/king-papers/documents/swami-vishwananda. Editor's note: There is no known relationship between this revered Swami Viswananda and a popular contemporary "guru" using this name.

124 Comment by Bodhipaska, www.wildmind.org/mantras/figures/tm. Author's note: It is not the purpose of this book to debate the merits of either TM or the studies that have been done on it since the 1970s. Extensive information on both sides of this debate can be found on the internet.

125 Jonathan C. Smith, *Pseudoscience and Extraordinary Claims of the Paranormal: A Critical Thinker's Toolkit* (Malden, MA: Wiley-Blackwell, 2009) 1.

126 Gopi Krishna, "On War," unpublished text.

127 George Feuerstein, *Encyclopedic Dictionary of Yoga* (New York: Paragon House 1990) 9, 95.

128 I. Gandhi and K. Singh, *Kashmir and Beyond, 1966–84: Select Correspondence between Indira Gandhi and Karan Singh, ed. J. Alam* (New Delhi: Penguin Books India 2011) 282–283.

129 The nonprofit Canadian Psychic Research Foundation was also formed at this time, but other than Gopi Krishna helping volunteers design a questionnaire to be used in interviewing individuals with paranormal abilities, he had no association with this organization.

Chapter Nineteen: Dr. Karan Singh, the Indian Government, and Project Consciousness

130 Gopi Krishna, *An Interview in Zürich* (Amazon KDP Edition: ICR and KRF2016).

131 John White, "From Sex to Higher Consciousness," unpublished article.

132 Gopi Krishna, *The Kashmir Discourses* (Amazon KDP Edition: ICR and KRF2020).

133 Gopi Krishna, "Kundalini: The Guardian of Human Evolution," *Spiritual India and Kundalini 1(1–3), 1978.*

134 "Nimhans Celebrates Its Silver Jubilee," *India Today*, March 3, 2014, www.indiatoday.in/magazine/science-and-technology/story/19790930-nimhans-celebrates-its-silver-jubilee-822501-2014-03-03.

135 "Nphy NIMHANS Founder Dr. T. Desiraju Remembered at Yoga Appreciation Course Inauguration," *Neurophysiology Times*, June 26, 2011, https://nphy.weebly.com/nphytimes/
nphy-nimhans-founder-dr-t-desiraju-remembered-at-yoga-appreciation-course-in-auguration.

Chapter Twenty: Advice for Spiritual Seekers and Kundalini Experiencers

136 The term tummo, or dumo, fire from Tibetan Buddhism is more properly simply tummo, which refers to inner fire. It is often equated to the Sanskrit caṇḍālī, another name for kundalini. The Taoist term chi is more properly qi. Jing-qi-shen is often referred to collectively as the "Three Treasures."

137 The Sufi Order of the West is now known as Inyatiyya. See https://inayatiyya.org/pir-vilayat-inayat-khan.

138 Personal interviews, Teri Degler with Michael Bradford and Alf Walker, 2017–2021. Bradford spent six years volunteering for the Central Institute for Kundalini Research in India, and Walker spent approximately a year doing the same.

139 Gopi Krishna, *Gopi Krishna: The New York Discourses* (Amazon KDP Edition: ICR and KRF 2019).

140 The Canadian volunteers in Switzerland and India are identified by first names only as one volunteer requested this.

141 Gopi Krishna , *Koundalinî, l'énérgie évolutrice en l'homme, trans. Tara Michaël,* with a long introduction of the book in English by Gopi Krishna, *Kundalini: The Evolutionary Energy in Man* (Paris: Le Courrier du Livre 1978).

142 Personal correspondence, Teri Degler with Edward Kelly, April 2022.

Chapter Twenty-One: Saints and Sinners, Wise Men and Fools

143 It was not possible to confirm with absolute certainty that Gopi Krishna was meeting with Thomas Banyacya as the Hopi Elder he met with is referred to simply as Thomas in correspondence; however, it was established to the best of the author's research abilities.

144 Although Gopi Krishna may have published an article called "The Magic of Mind," no book by this title was ever published. The material in what were the two volumes of his autobiography that were meant to supplement the material in his original autobiography were combined through the efforts of Leslie Shepard and Michael Bradford to create the book *Living with Kundalini*. This material does not cover the years after 1950, and it is assumed that Gopi Krishna would have written more autobiographical material if time had allowed.

Chapter Twenty-Two: Upheaval and Controversy Take a Toll

145 Gopi Krishna , "Life Is Everlasting," in Kundalini: Empowering Human Evolution: Selected Writings of Gopi Krishna, ed. Gene Kieffer (New York: Paragon House 1996) 281–302.

146 "The Nobel Laureates Declaration on the Survival of Mankind," https://unitedearth. us/assets/downloads/Declaration%20on%20the%20Survival%20of%20Mankind.pdf.

147 An MP3 audio recording of "An Interview with Claes Nobel" is available from ICR Canada.

148 Eventually FIND became more formally established as the federally registered nonprofit Canadian corporation the Institute for Consciousness Research.

149 "An Interview with Claes Nobel" contains additional information about the Experimental Project, and a more thorough description can be found in "The Memorandum for Kundalini Research," www.icrcanada.org/research/memorandum.

150 Due to health and the other pressing issues, the deadline for submitting the foreword was not met. Motoyama and the publisher then asked if Gopi Krishna might contribute an afterword for the book. It does not appear that Gopi Krishna was ever able to do so.

Chapter Twenty-Three: International Talks—Sufis, Hopis, and Humanists

151 Gene Kieffer, ed., *Kundalini: Empowering Human Evolution*: *Selected Writings of Gopi Krishna* (New York: Paragon House 1996.) A full recording of the interviews is available in CD format from ICR Canada.

152 Stanislav Grof, "A Brief History of Transpersonal Psychology," The International Journal of Transpersonal Studies 12(1), 2008, https://digitalcommons.ciis.edu/cgi/ viewcont,ent.cgi?article=1182&context=ijts-transpersonalstudies.
Note that Michael Murphy and Richard Price were also involved in the launch of the ITA. For a brief description of the Davos conference, see "History of the International Transpersonal Association," www.grof-legacy-project-usa.org/ history-of-international-transpersonal-association.

153 It was not possible to determine when or where these tests were done.

154 In addition to Da Free John, Franklin Albert Jones took on a number of names, including Da Love-Ananda and ultimately Adi Da.

155 The Davos speech can be found in *Krishna, Kundalini: Empowering Human Evolution. A German version of the Alpbach talk is found in Rainer Kakuska, ed., Andere Wirklichkeiten: Die neue Konvergenz von Naturwissenschaften und spirituellen Traditionen (München: Dianos Trikont München 1984).*

156 Michael Random, *Les arts martiaux ou l'esprit des budo* (Paris: Fernand Nathan 1977).

157 Krishna, Kundalini: Empowering Human Evolution, 30–31.

158 Krishna, Kundalini: Empowering Human Evolution,144–145.

159 Krishna, Kundalini: Empowering Human Evolution, 46.

Chapter Twenty-Four: Dehra Dun—The Experimental Centre for Kundalini Research

160   Rainer Kakuska, ed., *Andere Wirklichkeiten: Die neue Konvergenz von Naturwissen-schaften und vertreter spirituellen Disziplinen(München: Dianos Trikont München 1984).* This book is a compilation of the proceedings from the Alpbach conference. Translation of Kakuska's commentary done by Teri Degler.

161   Gopi Krishna, "The Unifying Principle for Science and Religion," The Last Discourses (Amazon edition: ICR and KRF 2010).

162   The video "Louis Rogers Interviews Pandit Gopi Krishna, 1978" is available online at www.youtube.com/watch?v=A538vXGCisI.

163   The October 23, 1983, seminar was convened by Harry H. Lerner, an active member of PAUN, an aspect of the movement for a United Nations Parliamentary Assembly going back to the 1920s, striving to make the UN more democratic by a greater voice and greater participation to the members of parliament; see https://en.wikipedia.org/wiki/United_Nations_Parliamentary_Assembly.

164   Robert Muller was also a noted author: www.thepositiveencourager.global/robert-mull-ers-work-to-build-a-positive-planet/ and www.robertmuller.org/rm/R1/Biography.html. The sponsors for the evening included the Native American Indigenous Medicine Council, the World Alliance of NGOs for Disarmament, the World Citizens for World Peace, and the World Citizens Assembly.

165   U.A. Asrani, *Yoga Unveiled: Through a Synthesis of Personal Mystic Experiences and Psychological and Psychosomatic Studies* (Delhi: Motilal Banarsidass 1977).

166   Personal interview, Teri Degler with Michael Bradford, October 12, 2022. Michael stated that, although he appreciated Gopi Krishna's comments lauding his contributions, one of his main duties was simply to occupy the property in Dehra Dun so that squatters could not take possession of the land.

167   Personal interview, Teri Degler with Dr. Karan Singh, August 2016.

168   Personal interview, Teri Degler with Michael Bradford, October 13, 2022.

169   Krishna, *The Last Discourses*.

Bibliography

Asrani, U.A. *Yoga Unveiled: Through a Synthesis of Personal Mystic Experiences and Psychological and Psychosomatic Studies.* Delhi: Motilal Banarsidass, 1977.

Bell, Bethen. "Erin Pizzey: The Woman Who Looked beyond the Bruises," BBC News, November 10, 2021.

www.bbc.com/news/uk-england-london-59064064.

Bradford, Michael. Interview by Teri Degler. May 2019.

De Riencourt, Armoury. *The Eye of Siva.* London: Souvenir Press, 1980.

Ebel, John. "The Church Has Everything for Modern Youth." *The Register, Denver archdiocesian edition, June 3, 1971,* https://archives.archden.org/islandora/object/archden%3A8465/datastream/OBJ/view.

Feuerstein, Georg. *Encyclopedic Dictionary of Yoga.* New York: Paragon House, 1990.

Ganjoo, Triloki Nath. "Sri Sheetal Nath: Abode of Sheetleshwar Bhairava," https://kashmirdairy.wordpress.com/me-sheetlesvara-the-sheetalnath.

Gandhi, Indira , and Singh, Karan Singh., Kashmir and Beyond, 1966–84: Select Correspondence between Indira Gandhi and Karan Singh. J. Alam, ed. New Delhi: Penguin Books India, 2011.

Grof, Stanislav. "A Brief History of Transpersonal Psychology," *The International Journal of Transpersonal Studies 1*, 2008.

Grof, Christina, and Grof, Stanislav. "Spiritual Emergency: The Understanding and Treatment of Transpersonal Crises." *International Journal of Transpersonal Studies 36,* 2017. https://doi.org/10.24972/ijts.2017.36.2.30.

James, William. *The Varieties of Religious Experience.* Oxford: Oxford University Press, 2012.

Kakuska, Rainer, ed. *Andere Wirklichkeiten: Die neue Konvergenz von Naturwissenschaften und vertreter spirituellen Disziplinen.* Munich: Goldmann Verlag, Smith, 265–275.

Kaul, Jayalal. *Lal Ded.* New Delhi: Sahita Akadmi, 1973.

Kaul, Jyotima. Interview by Teri Degler. February 2014.

Kaul, Ragya. Interview by Teri Degler. February 2016.

Kaul, Rakesh. Interview by Teri Degler. May 2016.

Kelly, Edward. "Re: Gopi Krishna Biography." Email interview, received by Teri Degler October 4, 2022.

Kehr, Sunita. Interview by Teri Degler. February 2016.

Kieffer, Gene. Interview by Teri Degler. May 2016.

Kluger, Volker. "The 'Peace Angel of Helsinki' Wanted to Save the World." *Journal of Olympic History 25*(1), 2017. International Society of Olympic History. http://isoh.org/wp-content/uploads/2019/02/314.pdf.

Krippner, Stanley, and Powers, Susan. *Broken Images, Broken Selves: Dissociative Narratives in Clinical Practice.* Washington, DC: Brunner/Mazel, 1997.

Krishna, Gopi. *An Interview in Zürich.* Amazon Edition. Institute for Consciousness Research and Kundalini Research Foundation, 2018.

Krishna, Gopi. *The Biological Basis of Religion and Genius.* New York: Harper and Row, 1972.

Krishna, Gopi. *Higher Consciousness: The Evolutionary Thrust of Kundalini.* New York: Julian Press, 1974.

Krishna, Gopi. Gopi Krishna: The Kashmir Discourses. Amazon Edition: Institute for Consciousness Research and Kundalini Research Foundation, 2020.

Krishna, Gopi. *Koundalini, l'énergie évolutrice en l'homme.* Tara Michaël, trans. Paris: Le Courrier du Livre, 1978.

Krishna, Gopi. *Kundalini: Empowering Human Evolution: Selected Writings of Gopi Krishna.* Gene Kieffer, ed. New York: Paragon House, 1996. This book was originally published as *Kundalini for the New Age: Selected Writings of Gopi Krishna* in 1988 by Bantam Books.

Krishna, Gopi. *Living with Kundalini: The Autobiography of Gopi Krishna.* Leslie Shepard, ed. Boulder, CO: Shambhala, 1992.

Krishna, Gopi. "Meditation as a Means to Self-Knowledge." *Institute for Consciousness Research Newsletter*, September 2021, 1.

Krishna, Gopi. *Gopi Krishna: The Kashmir Discourses.* Amazon Edition: Institute for Consciousness Research and Kundalini Research Foundation, 2020.

Krishna, Gopi. *The New York Discourses.* Amazon Edition. Institute for Consciousness Research and Kundalini Research Foundation, 2018.

Krishna, Gopi. *The Shape of Events to Come.* Kashmir: Central Institute for Kundalini Research, 1968.

Krishna, Gopi. *The Shape of Events to Come.* New York: New Concepts, 1979.

Krishna, Gopi. The Toronto Discourses. Amazon Edition. Institute for Consciousness Research and Kundalini Research Foundation, 2020.

Krishna, Gopi, and Hillman, James, commentary. Kundalini: *The Evolutionary Energy in Man.* Boulder, CO: Shambhala, 1967.

Majid, Zulfikar. "Women Medicos Opt Psychiatry for a Career in Kashmir." *Decan Herald*, June 15, 2014. www.deccanherald.com/content/413697/women-medicos-opt-psychiatry-career.html, accessed 04/11/2021.

Marjanovic, Boris. *Abhinavagupta's Commentary on the Bhagavad Gītā*. Varanasi: Indica Books, 2004.

Müller, Max, trans. *The Chandogya Upanishad*. Third Prapathaka, Khanda 13:8. www.hinduwebsite.com/sacredscripts/hinduism/upanishads/chandogya.asp.

Nikhilananda, Swami. *English translation of Chandogya Upanishad*. www.consciouslivingfoundation.org/ebooks/13/CLF-chhandogya_upanishad.pdf , accessed 04/11/2021.

"Nimhans Celebrates Its Silver Jubilee." *India Today*, March 3, 2014. www.indiatoday. in/magazine/science-and-technology/story/19790930-nimhans-celebrates-its-silver-jubilee-822501-2014-03-03, accessed 05/102021.

Nphy Times, "Nphy NIMHANS Founder Dr. T Desiraju Remembered." *Neurophysiology Times*, June 26, 2011 https://nphy.weebly.com/nphytimes/nphy-nimhans-founder-dr-t-desiraju-remembered-at-yoga-appreciation-course-inauguration, accessed 04/10/2021.

Quien Hopman, Rhea. *Tontyn Hopman's Autobiography on Kundalini*. Unpublished manuscript, © Rhea Quien Hopman.

Random, Michael. *Les arts martiaux ou l'esprit des budo*. Paris: Fernand Nathan, 1977.

Russell, Dick. *The Life and Ideas of James Hillman*. New York: Helios Press, 2018.

Schweig, Graham. *Bhagavad Gītā : The Beloved Lord's Secret Song of Love*. New York: Harper One, 2007.

Shivpuri, Nirmal. Interview by Teri Degler. May 2015.

Shivpuri, Jagdish. Interview by Teri Degler. February 2016.

Silburn, Lilian. *Kundalini: The Energy of the Depths*. Jacque Gontier, trans. New York: State University of New York Press, 1988.

Smith, Jonathan C. *Pseudoscience and Extraordinary Claims of the Paranormal: A Critical Thinker's Toolkit*. Oxford: John Wiley & Sons, 2009.

Subramanian, V.K., trans. *Saundaryalaharī of Śaṅkarācārya*. Delhi: Motilal Banarsidass, 2006.

Sunil Raina Rajanak, "The Goddess of Kashmir," *Speaking Tree,* May 2017 www. speakingtree.in/article/goddess-of-kashmir, accessed 07/10/2020.

Van Löben Sels, Robin. "Re: Gopi Krishna Biography." Email interview received by Teri Degler 06/12/2019.

White, John. "From Sex to Higher Consciousness." Unpublished article.

White, John. "Re: Gopi Krishna Biography." Email interview received by Teri Degler , October 5, 2019.

White, John. *What Is Enlightenment? Exploring the Goal of the Spiritual Path*. New York: Paragon House, 1998.

Winkler, Willie. "Barbara Rotraut Pleyer: Der gekaufte Engel des BND." *Süddeutsche Zeitung*, February 9, 2018. www.sueddeutsche.de/politik/barbara-rotraut-pleyer-der-gekaufte-engel-des-bnd-1.380365.

Index

G

I

J

K

U

unio mystica 65
United Nations Organization for Disarmament 289

V

vānaprastha 66
verse. *See* poetry
Vijnana Bhairava 167, 183, 193, 197, 236
viveka 9
Vivekananda 136
Vyasa, Gopi Krishna likened to 8

W

Wald, George 271
Weizsäcker, Carl Friedrich von 132, 159, 160, 163, 225, 253, 278, 279
White, John 173, 174, 186, 188, 213, 225-226, 229
Wolfram, Gerhard 145
women
    biologically adapted to kundalini awakening 44
    dowry system and wedding costs 42
    mother-in-law abuse 43
    and Pathan invasion 51
    prostitutes 78
    widows 43, 79

Y

yamas and niyamas 23
yoga
    Bihar School of Yoga 224, 228
    discussed in the *Bhagavad Gītā* 71
    eightfold path 23, 283
    hatha yoga 71
    karma yoga 239, 283
    Kripalu yoga 162, 243
    misconception of the West 199
    ode to Lalleshwari illustrates teachings 107
    Sahaja yoga 176
    teachers who misunderstand kundalini 69
    true purpose of 115, 274, 283, 284
    yogis' spiritual experiences similar to mystics 115, 289
Yoga Sutras 116
Yorke, Gerald Joseph 104

About the Author

Award-winning author Teri Degler has eleven books to her credit, including *The Fiery Muse: Creativity and the Spiritual Quest* and *The Divine Feminine Fire: Creativity and Your Yearning to Express Your Self*. For years, Teri has researched and written on Tantra, yoga philosophy, and the lives of highly creative mystics. Much of her work has centered on the divine feminine known as kundalini-shakti in Hinduism and the parallels that can be found in Sophia in Old Testament Christianity and Shekinah in Jewish mysticism. Teri's books have been translated into French, German, and Italian. Her freelance writing on topics ranging from spirituality to environmental activism have appeared in many publications in the US and Canada. She teaches workshops on creativity and has made many media appearances.

Made in United States
Orlando, FL
26 June 2023

34547521R00205